ALSO BY DAVID GRAEBER

Debt: The First 5,000 Years

THE DEMOCRACY PROJECT

THE
DEMOCRACY
PROJECT

A HISTORY, A CRISIS,
A MOVEMENT

David Graeber

SPIEGEL & GRAU

NEW YORK

The Democracy Project is a work of nonfiction.
Some names and identifying details have been changed.

Published in the United States by Spiegel & Grau, an imprint of The Random
House Publishing Group, a division of Random House, Inc., New York.

SPIEGEL & GRAU and Design is a registered trademark of Random House, Inc.

Grateful acknowledgment is made to
The Weekly Standard for permission to reprint an excerpt from "Anarchy in
the U.S.A.: The Roots of American Disorder" by Matthew Continetti,
The Weekly Standard, November 28, 2011. Reprinted by permission.

LIBRARY OF CONGRESS CATALOGING-IN-PUBLICATION DATA
Graeber, David.
The Democracy Project : a history, a crisis,
a movement / David Graeber.
p. cm.
Includes bibliographical references and index.
ISBN 978-0-8129-9356-1 — ISBN 978-0-679-64600-6 (ebk.)
1. Democracy—History. I. Title
JC421.G677 2013
321.8—dc23   2012031998

Printed in the United States of America on acid-free paper

www.spiegelandgrau.com

2 4 6 8 9 7 5 3 1

FIRST EDITION

Book design by Casey Hampton

to my father

CONTENTS

INTRODUCTION

On April 26, 2012, about thirty activists from Occupy Wall Street gathered on the steps of New York's Federal Hall, across the street from the Stock Exchange.

For more than a month, we had been trying to reestablish a foothold in lower Manhattan to replace the camp we'd been evicted from six months earlier at Zuccotti Park. Even if we weren't able to establish a new camp, we were hoping to at least find some place we could hold regular assemblies, and set up our library and kitchens. The great advantage of Zuccotti Park was that it was a place where anyone interested in what we were doing knew they could always come to find us, to learn about upcoming actions or just talk politics; now the lack of such a place was causing endless problems. The city authorities, however, had decided that we would never have another Zuccotti. Wherever we found a spot we could legally set up shop, they simply changed the laws and drove us off. When we tried to establish ourselves in Union Square, city authorities changed park regulations. When a band of occupiers started sleeping on the sidewalk on Wall Street itself, relying on a judicial decision that explicitly said citizens had a right to sleep on the street in New York as a form of political protest, the city deemed that part of lower Manhattan a "special security zone" in which the law did not apply.

Finally, we settled on the Federal Hall steps, a broad marble staircase leading up to a statue of George Washington, guarding the door to the building in which the Bill of Rights had been signed 223 years before. The steps were not under city jurisdiction; they were federal land, under the administration of the National Park Service, and representatives of the U.S. Park Police—cognizant, perhaps, that the entire space was considered a monument to civil liberties—had told us they had no objections to our occupying the steps, as long as no one actually slept there. The steps were wide enough that they could easily accommodate a couple of hundred people, and at first, about that many occupiers showed up. But before long, the city had moved in and convinced the parks people to let them effectively take over: they'd erected steel barriers around the perimeter, and others that divided the steps themselves into two compartments. We quickly came to refer to them as the "freedom cages." A SWAT team was positioned by the entrance, and a white-shirted police commander carefully monitored everyone who tried to enter, informing them that for safety reasons no more than twenty people were allowed in either cage at any time. Nonetheless, a determined handful persevered. They kept up a twenty-four-hour presence, taking shifts, organizing teach-ins during the day, engaging in impromptu debates with bored Wall Street traders who wandered over during breaks, and keeping vigil on the marble stairs at night. Soon large signs were banned. Then anything made of cardboard. Then came the random arrests. The police commander wanted to make clear to us that, even if he couldn't arrest all of us, he could certainly arrest any one of us, for pretty much any reason, at any time. That day alone I had seen one activist shackled and led off for a "noise violation" while chanting slogans, and another, an Iraq war veteran, booked on public obscenity charges for using four-letter words while making a speech. Perhaps it was because we'd advertised the event as a "speak-out." The officer in charge seemed to be making a point: even at the very birthplace of the First Amendment, he still had the power to arrest us just for engaging in political speech.

A friend of mine named Lopi, famous for attending marches on a giant tricycle emblazoned with a colorful placard that read "Jubilee!" had organized the event, billing it as "Speak Out of Grievances against Wall Street: A Peaceable Assembly on the steps of the Federal Hall Memorial Building, the birthplace of the Bill of Rights which is currently under lock down from the army of the 1%." Myself, I've never been much of a rabble-rouser. During the entire time I'd been involved in Occupy, I'd never once made a speech. So I was hoping to be there mainly as a witness, to provide moral and organizational support. For much of the first half hour of the event, as one occupier after another moved to the front of the cage, before an impromptu collection of video cameras on the sidewalk, to talk about war, ecological devastation, the corruption of government, I lingered on the margins, trying to chat up the police.

"So you're part of a SWAT team," I said to one grim-faced young man guarding the entrance to the cages, a large assault rifle at his side. "Now, what does that stand for, SWAT? 'Special Weapons . . .'"

". . . and Tactics," he said—quickly, before I would have any chance to get out the original name for the unit, which was Special Weapons Assault Team.

"I see. So I'm curious: what sort of special weapons do your commanders think might be required to deal with thirty unarmed citizens engaging in peaceable assembly on the federal steps?"

"It's just a precaution," he replied uncomfortably.

I'd already passed up two invitations to speak, but Lopi was persistent, so eventually, I figured I'd better say something, however brief. So I took my place in front of the cameras, glanced up at George Washington gazing at the sky over the New York Stock Exchange, and started improvising.

"It strikes me that it's very appropriate that we are meeting here, today, on the steps of the very building where the Bill of Rights was signed. It's funny. Most Americans think of themselves as living in a free country, the world's greatest democracy. They feel it's our constitutional rights and freedoms, placed there by our Founding Fathers, that define us as a nation, that make us who we really are—even, if you listen to politicians, that give us the right to invade other countries more or less at will. But actually, you know, the men who wrote the Constitution didn't want it to include a Bill of Rights. That's why they're amendments. They weren't in the original document. The only reason that all those ringing phrases about freedom of speech and freedom of assembly ended up in the Constitution is because anti-Federalists like George Mason and Patrick Henry were so outraged when they saw the final draft that they began to mobilize against ratification unless the text was changed—changed to include, among other things, the right to engage in that very kind of popular mobilization. That terrified the Federalists since one of the reasons they convened the Constitutional Convention to begin with was to head off the danger they saw of even more radical popular movements that had been calling for a democratization of finance, even debt cancellation. Mass public assemblies and an outbreak of popular debate like they'd seen during the revolution was the very last thing they wanted. So eventually, James Madison gathered up a list of more than two hundred proposals, and used them to write the actual text of what we now call the Bill of Rights.

"Power never gives up anything voluntarily. Insofar as we have freedoms, it's not because some great wise Founding Fathers granted them to us. It's because people like us insisted on exercising those freedoms—by doing exactly what we're doing here—before anyone was willing to acknowledge that they had them.

"Nowhere in the Declaration of Independence or the Constitution does it say anything about America being a democracy. There's a reason for that. Men like George Washington were openly opposed to democracy. Which makes it a bit odd we're standing here under his statue today. But the same was true of all of them: Madison, Hamilton, Adams . . . They wrote explicitly that they were trying to set up a system that could head off and control the dangers of democracy, even though it was people who did want democracy that had made the revolution that put them in power to begin with. And of course, most of us are here because we still don't think we're living under a democratic system in any meaningful sense of the term. I mean, look around you. That SWAT team over there tells you everything you really need to know. Our government has be-

witnessed two candidates—one a sitting president imposed as a fait accompli on a Democratic Party base that felt he had often betrayed them; the other foisted by sheer power of money on a Republican base that made it clear it would have preferred almost anybody else—spending the main part of their energy on courting billionaires, as the public occasionally checks in via television, in the full knowledge that, unless they happen to be among that roughly 25 percent of Americans who live in swing states, their votes won't make the slightest difference anyway. Even for those whose votes do matter, it's simply assumed that the choice is between which of the two parties will play the dominant role in making a deal to cut their pensions, Medicare, and Social Security—since sacrifices will have to be made, and the realities of power are such that no one even considers the possibility those sacrifices could be borne by the rich.

In a recent piece in *Esquire*, Charles Pierce points out that the performances of TV pundits this election cycle often seem little more than sado-masochistic celebrations of popular powerlessness, akin to reality TV shows where we like to watch aggressive bosses pushing their acolytes around:

We have allowed ourselves to become mired in the habits of oligarchy, as though no other politics are possible, even in a putatively self-governing republic, and resignation is one of the most obvious of those habits. We acclimate ourselves to the habit of having our politics acted upon us, rather than insisting that they are ours to command. TV stars tell us that political stars are going to cut their Grand Bargain and that "we" will then applaud them for making the "tough choices" on our behalf. That is how you inculcate the habits of oligarchy in a political commonwealth. First, you disabuse people of the notion that government is the ultimate expression of that commonwealth, and then you eliminate or emasculate any centers of power that might exist independent of your smothering influence— like, say, organized labor—and then you make it quite clear who's in charge. I'm the boss. Get used to it.[1]

This is the kind of politics one is left with when any notion of the very possibility of democracy goes by the boards. But it's also a momentary phenomenon. We might do well to remember that the same conversations were happening in the summer of 2011, when all the political class could talk about was an artificially concocted crisis over the "debt ceiling" and the "grand bargain" (to cut Medicare and Social Security again) that would inevitably ensue. Then in September of that year, Occupy happened, and with it hundreds of genuine political forums where ordinary Americans could talk about their actual concerns and problems—and the conventional pundit conversation stopped in its tracks. It wasn't because occupiers brought the politicians specific demands and proposals; instead, they'd created a crisis of legitimacy within the entire system by providing a glimpse of what real democracy might be like.

Of course, these same pundits have been declaring Occupy dead since the evictions of November 2011. What they don't understand is that once people's political horizons have been broadened, the change is permanent. Hundreds of thousands of Americans (and not only Americans, of course, but Greeks, Spaniards, and Tunisians) now have direct experience of self-organization, collective action, and human solidarity. This makes it almost impossible to go back to one's previous life and see things the same way. While the world's financial and political elites skate blindly toward the next 2008-scale crisis, we're continuing to carry out occupations of buildings, farms, foreclosed homes, and workplaces—temporary or permanent—organizing rent strikes, seminars, and debtors' assemblies, and in doing so, laying the groundwork for a genuinely democratic culture, and introducing the skills, habits, and experience that would make an entirely new conception of politics come to life. With it has come a revival of the revolutionary imagination that conventional wisdom has long since declared dead.

Everyone involved recognizes that creating a democratic culture will have to be a long-term process. We are talking about a profound moral transformation, after all. But we're also aware that such things have happened before. There have been social movements in the United States that have effected profound moral transformations—the abolitionists and feminism come most immediately to mind—but doing so took a good deal of time. Like Occupy, such movements also operated largely outside the formal political system, employed civil disobedience and direct action, and never imagined they could achieve their goals in a single year. Obviously, there were plenty of others that tried to bring about equally profound moral transformations but failed. Still, there are very good reasons to believe that fundamental changes are taking place in the nature of American society—the same ones that made it possible for Occupy to take off so rapidly in the first place—that afford a real opportunity for such a long-term revival of the democratic project to succeed.

The social argument I'll be making is fairly simple. What's being called the Great Recession merely accelerated a profound transformation of the American class system that had already been under way for decades. Consider the following two statistics: at the time of this writing, one out of every seven Americans is being pursued by a debt collection agency; at the same time, one recent poll revealed that for the first time, only a minority of Americans (45 percent) describe themselves as "middle class." It's hard to imagine these two facts are unrelated. There has been a good deal of discussion of late of the erosion of the American middle class, but most of it misses out on the fact that "middle class" in the United States has never primarily been an economic category. It has always had everything to do with that feeling of stability and security that comes from being able to simply assume that—whatever one might think of politicians—everyday institutions like the police, education system, health clinics, and even credit providers are basically on your side. If so, it's hard to imagine how someone living through the experience of seeing their family home foreclosed on by an illegal robo-signer would be feeling particularly middle class. And this is true regardless of their income bracket or degree of educational attainment.

The growing sense, on the part of Americans, that the institutional structures that surround them are not really there to help them—even, that they are dark and inimical forces—is a direct consequence of the financialization of capitalism. Now, this might seem an odd statement to make, because we are used to thinking of finance as something very distant from such everyday concerns. Most people are aware that the vast majority of Wall Street profits are no longer from the fruits of industry or commerce but from sheer speculation and the creation of complex financial instruments, but the usual criticism is that this is just a matter of speculation, or the equivalent of elaborate magic tricks, whisking wealth into existence by simply saying it exists. In fact, what financialization has really meant is collusion between government and financial institutions to ensure that a larger and larger proportion of citizens fall deeper and deeper in debt. This occurs on every level. New demands for academic qualifications are introduced to jobs like pharmacy and nursing, forcing anyone who wants to work in such industries to take out government-backed student loans, ensuring that a significant portion of their subsequent wages will go directly to the banks. Collusion between Wall Street financial advisors and local politicians forces municipalities into bankruptcy, or near-bankruptcy, whereupon local police are ordered to massively increase enforcement of lawn, trash, and maintenance regulations against homeowners so that the resulting flow of fines will increase revenues to pay the banks. In every case a share of the resulting profits is funneled back to politicians through lobbyists and PACs. As almost every function of local government becomes a mechanism for financial extraction, and the federal government makes clear that it considers its primary business to keep stock prices up and money flowing to the holders of financial instruments (not to mention guaranteeing that no major financial institution, whatever its behavior, ever be allowed to fail), it becomes increasingly unclear what the difference between financial power and state power really is.

This is of course precisely what we were getting at when we first decided to call ourselves the 99 percent. In doing so, we did something almost unprecedented. We managed to get the issues not only of class, but of class power, back into the center of American political debate. It was only possible, I suspect, because of gradual changes in the nature of the economic system—at OWS we are increasingly beginning to refer to it as "mafia capitalism"—that make it impossible to imagine the American government as having anything to do with the popular will, or even popular consent. At times like these, any awakening of the democratic impulse can only be a revolutionary urge.

THE DEMOCRACY PROJECT

ONE

THE BEGINNING IS NEAR

n March 2011, Micah White, editor of the Canadian magazine *Adbusters*, asked me to write a column on the possibility of a revolutionary movement springing up in Europe or America. At the time, the best I could think to say is that when a true revolutionary movement does arise, everyone, the organizers included, is taken by surprise. I had recently had a long conversation with an Egyptian anarchist named Dina Makram-Ebeid to that effect, at the height of the uprising at Tahrir Square, which I used to open the column.

"The funny thing is," my Egyptian friend told me, "you've been doing this so long, you kind of forget that you can win. All these years, we've been organizing marches, rallies. . . . And if only 45 people show up, you're depressed. If you get 300, you're happy. Then one day, you get 500,000. And you're incredulous: on some level, you'd given up thinking that could even happen."

Hosni Mubarak's Egypt was one of the most repressive societies on earth—the entire apparatus of the state was organized around ensuring that what ended up happening could never happen. And yet it did.

So why not here?

To be honest, most activists I know go around feeling much like my Egyptian friend used to feel—we organize much of our lives around the possibility of something that we're not sure we believe could ever really happen.

And then it did.

Of course in our case, it wasn't the fall of a military dictatorship, but the outbreak of a mass movement based on direct democracy—an outcome, in its own way, just as long dreamed of by its organizers, just as long dreaded by those who held ultimate power in the country, and just as uncertain in its outcome as the overthrow of Mubarak had been.

The story of this movement has been told in countless outlets already, from the *Occupy Wall Street Journal* to the actual *Wall Street Journal,* with varying motives, points of view, casts of characters, and degrees of accuracy. In most, my own importance has been vastly overstated. My role was that of a bridge between camps. But my aim in this chapter is not so much to set the historical record straight; or, even, to write a history at all, but rather to give a sense of what living at the fulcrum of such a historical convergence can be like. Much of our political culture, even daily existence, makes us feel that such events are simply impossible (indeed, there is reason to believe that our political culture is designed to make us feel that way). The result has a chilling effect on the imagination. Even those who, like Dina or myself, organized much of our lives, and most of our fantasies and aspirations, around the possibility of such outbreaks of the imagination were startled when such an outbreak actually began to happen. Which is why it's crucial to begin by underlining that transformative outbreaks of imagination have happened, they are happening, they surely will continue to happen again. The experience of those who live through such events is to find our horizons thrown open; to find ourselves wondering what else we assume cannot really happen actually can. Such events cause us to reconsider everything we thought we knew about the past. This is why those in power do their best to bottle them up, to treat these outbreaks of imagination as peculiar anomalies, rather than the kind of moments from which everything, including their own power, originally emerged. So telling the story of Occupy—even if from just one actor's point of view—is important; it's only in the light of the sense of possibility Occupy opened up that everything else I have to say makes sense.

———

When I wrote the piece for *Adbusters*—the editors gave it the title "Awaiting the Magic Spark"—I was living in London, teaching anthropology at Goldsmiths, University of London, in my fourth year of exile from U.S. academia. I had been fairly deeply involved with the U.K. student movement that year, visiting many of the dozens of university occupations across the country that had formed to protest the Conservative government's broadside assault on the British public education system, taking part in organizing and street actions. *Adbusters* specifically commissioned me to write a piece speculating on the possibility that the student movement might mark the beginning of a broad, Europe-wide, or even worldwide, rebellion.

I had long been a fan of *Adbusters*, but had only fairly recently become a contributor. I was more a street action person when I wasn't being a social theorist. *Adbusters*, on the other hand, was a magazine for "culture jammers": it was originally created by rebellious advertising workers who loathed their industry and so decided to join the other side, using their professional skills to subvert the corporate world they had been trained to promote. They were most famous for creating "subvertisments," anti-ads—for instance, "fashion" ads featuring bulimic models vomiting into toilets—with professional production values, and then trying to place them in mainstream publications or on network television—attempts that were inevitably refused. Of all radical magazines, *Adbusters* was easily the most beautiful, but many anarchists considered their stylish, ironic approach distinctly less than hard-core. I'd first started writing for them when Micah White contacted me back in 2008 to contribute a column. Over the summer of 2011, he had become interested in making me into something like a regular British correspondent.

Such plans were thrown askew when a year's leave took me back to America. I arrived that July, the summer of 2011, in my native New York, expecting to spend most of the summer touring and doing interviews for a recently released book on the history of debt. I also wanted to plug back into the New York activist scene, but with some hesitation, since I had the distinct impression that the scene was in something of a shambles. I'd first gotten heavily involved in activism in New York between 2000 and 2003, the heyday of the Global Justice Movement. That movement, which began with the Zapatista revolt in Mexico's Chiapas in 1994 and reached the United States with the mass actions that shut down the World Trade Organization meetings in Seattle in 1999, was the last time any of my friends had a sense that some sort of global revolutionary movement might be taking shape. Those were heady days. In the wake of

Seattle, it seemed every day there was something going on, a protest, an action, a Reclaim the Streets or activist subway party, and a thousand different planning meetings. But the ramifications of 9/11 hit us very hard, even if they took a few years to have their full effect. The level of arbitrary violence police were willing to employ against activists ratcheted up unimaginably; when a handful of unarmed students occupied the roof of the New School in a protest in 2009, for instance, the NYPD is said to have responded with four different anti-terrorist squads, including commandos rappelling off helicopters armed with all sorts of peculiar sci-fi weaponry.* And the scale of the antiwar and anti–Republican National Convention protests in New York ironically sapped some of the life out of the protest scene: anarchist-style "horizontal" groups, based on principles of direct democracy, had come to be largely displaced by vast top-down antiwar coalitions for whom political action was largely a matter of marching around with signs. Meanwhile the New York anarchist scene, which had been at the very core of the Global Justice Movement, wracked by endless personal squabbles, had been reduced largely to organizing an annual book fair.

THE APRIL 6 MOVEMENT

Even before I returned full-time for the summer, I began reengaging with the New York activist scene when I'd visited the

---

* I am referring here to the second New School occupation, in 2009—an earlier occupation of the cafeteria in 2008 led to a minor student victory, with relatively little police violence. The second was met by instant and overwhelming force.

ous forms of nonviolent resistance that had overthrown the regime of Slobodan Milosevic in late 2000. The Serbian group, he explained, had been one of the primary inspirations for April 6. The Egyptian group's founders had not only corresponded with Otpor! veterans, many had even flown to Belgrade, in the organization's early days, to attend seminars on techniques of nonviolent resistance. April 6 even adopted a version of Otpor!'s raised-fist logo.

"You do realize," I said to him, "that Otpor! was originally set up by the CIA?"

He shrugged. Apparently the origin of the Serbian group was a matter of complete indifference to him.

But Otpor!'s origins were even more complicated than that. In fact, several of us hastened to explain, the tactics that Otpor! and many other of the groups in the vanguard of the "colored" revolutions of the aughts—from the old Soviet empire down to the Balkans—implemented, with help from the CIA, were the ones the CIA originally learned from studying the Global Justice Movement, including tactics executed by some of the people who were gathered on the Hudson River that very night.

It's impossible for activists to really know what the other side is thinking. We can't even really know exactly who the other side is: who's monitoring us, who if anyone was coordinating international security efforts against us. But you can't help but speculate. And it was difficult not to notice that back around 1999, right around the time that a loose global network of antiauthoritarian collectives began mobilizing to shut down trade summits from Prague to Cancun using surprisingly effective techniques of decentralized direct democracy and nonviolent civil disobedience, certain elements in the U.S. security apparatus began not only studying the phenomenon, but trying to see if they could foster such movements themselves. This kind of turnabout was not unprecedented: in the 1980s the CIA had done something similar, using the fruits of 1960s and 1970s counterinsurgency research into how guerrilla armies worked to try to manufacture insurgencies like the Contras in Nicaragua. Something like that seemed to be happening again. Government money began pouring into international foundations promoting nonviolent tactics, and American trainers—some veterans of the antinuclear movement of the 1970s—were helping organize groups like Otpor! It's important not to overstate the effectiveness of such efforts. The CIA can't produce a movement out of nothing. Their efforts proved effective in Serbia and Georgia, but failed completely in Venezuela. But the real historical irony is that it was these techniques, pioneered by the Global Justice Movement, and successfully spread across the world by the CIA to American-aided groups, that in turn inspired movements that overthrew American client states. It's a sign of the power of democratic direct action tactics that once they were let loose into the world, they became uncontrollable.

US UNCUT

For me, the most concrete thing that came out of that evening with the Egyptians was that I met Marisa. Five years before, she had been one of the student activists who'd made a brilliant—if ultimately short-lived—attempt to re-create the 1960s activist group Students for a Democratic Society (SDS). Most New York activists still referred to the key organizers as "those SDS kids"—but, while most of them were at this point trapped working fifty to sixty hours a week paying off their student loan debts, Marisa, who had been in an Ohio branch of SDS and only later moved to the city, was still very much active—indeed, she seemed to have a finger in almost everything worthwhile that was still happening in the New York activist scene. Marisa is one of those people one is almost guaranteed to underestimate: small, unassuming, with a tendency to fold herself into a ball and all but disappear in public events. But she is one of the most gifted activists I've ever met. As I was later to discover, she had an almost uncanny ability to instantly assess a situation and figure out what's happening, what's important, and what needs to be done.

As the little meeting along the Hudson broke up, Marisa told me about a meeting the next day at EarthMatters in the East Village for a new group she was working with called US Uncut—inspired, she explained, by the British coalition UK Uncut, which had been created to organize mass civil disobedience against the Tory government's austerity plans in 2010. They were mostly pretty liberal, she hastened to warn me, not many anarchists, but in a way that was what was so charming about the group: the New York chapter was made up of people of all sorts of different backgrounds—"real people, not activist types"—middle-aged housewives, postal workers. "But they're all really enthusiastic about the idea of doing direct action."

The idea had a certain appeal. I'd never had a chance to work with UK Uncut when I was in London, but I had certainly run across them.

The tactical strategy of UK Uncut was simple and brilliant. One of the great scandals of the Conservative government's 2010 austerity package was that at the same time as they were trumpeting the need to triple student fees, close youth centers, and slash benefits to pensioners and people with disabilities to make up for what they described as a crippling budget short-fall, they exhibited absolutely no interest in collecting untold billions of pounds sterling of back taxes owed by some of their largest corporate campaign contributors—revenue that, if collected, would make most of those cuts completely unnecessary. UK Uncut's way of dramatizing the issue was to say: fine, if you're going to close our schools and clinics because you don't want to take the money from banks like HSBC or companies like Vodafone, we're just going to conduct classes and give medical treatment in their lobbies. UK Uncut's most dramatic action had taken place on the 26th of March, only a few weeks before my return to New York, when, in the wake of a half-million-strong labor march in London to protest the cuts, about 250 activists had occupied the ultra-swanky department store Fortnum & Mason. Fortnum & Mason was mainly famous for selling the world's most expensive tea and biscuits; their business was booming despite the recession, but their owners had also somehow managed to avoid paying £40 million in taxes.

At the time, I was working with a different group, Arts Against Cuts, mainly made up of women artists, whose primary contribution on the day of the march was to provide hundreds of paint bombs to student activists geared up in black hoodies, balaclavas, and bandanas (in activist language, in "Black Bloc").* I had never actually seen a paint bomb before,

---

* There is a widespread impression that "the Black Bloc" is some kind of murky organization, given to ultra-militant anarchist ideologies and tactics. Actually, it's a tactic that activists—usually anarchists—can employ at any demo; it involves covering one's face, wearing fairly uniform black clothing, and forming a mass willing and able to engage in mili-

and when some of my friends started opening up their back-packs I remember being impressed by how small they were. The paint bombs weren't actual bombs, just tiny water balloons of the same shape as and just slightly larger than an egg, half full of water, half of different colors of water-soluble paint. The nice thing was that one could throw them like baseballs at almost any target—an offending storefront, a passing Rolls or Lamborghini, a riot cop—and they would make an immediate and dramatic impression, splashing primary colors all over the place, but in such a way that we never ran the remotest danger of doing anyone any physical harm.

The plan that day was for the students and their allies to break off from the labor march at three o'clock in small groups and fan out through London's central shopping area, blockading intersections and decorating the marquees of notable tax evaders with paint bombs. After about an hour, we heard about the UK Uncut occupation of Fortnum & Mason and we trickled down to see if we could do anything to help. I arrived just as riot cops were sealing off the entryways and the last occupiers who didn't want to risk arrest were preparing to jump off the department store's vast marquee into the arms of surrounding protesters. The Black Bloc assembled, and after unleashing our few remaining balloons, we linked arms to hold off an advancing line of riot cops trying to clear the street so they

---

tant tactics if required, which in the Anglophone world could mean anything from linking arms to form a wall against police, to targeted damage to corporate storefronts. It's not regularly employed: there hadn't been a significant Black Bloc in London for years before members of the student movement decided to experiment with the approach that April and to my knowledge hasn't been one since.

could begin mass arrests. A few weeks later, in New York, my legs were still etched with welts and scrapes from being kicked in the shins on that occasion. (I remember thinking at the time that I now understood why ancient warriors wore greaves—if there are two opposing lines of shield-bearing warriors facing each other, the most obvious thing to do is to kick your opponent in the shins.)

As it turned out, US Uncut wasn't up to anything nearly that dramatic. The meeting, as I've mentioned, was held on the back porch of the famous vegetarian deli EarthMatters on the Lower East Side, where they sell herbal teas almost as expensive as Fortnum & Mason's, and, indeed, was populated by just as diverse and offbeat a crowd as Marisa had predicted. Their plan was to create an action similar to the one that UK Uncut had devised at Fortnum & Mason: to protest the closing of classrooms all over the city because of budget shortfalls, they were going to hold classes in the lobby of Bank of America, a financial behemoth that pays no taxes at all. Someone would play the role of a professor and give a lecture on corporate tax evasion in the lobby; Marisa would film the whole thing for a video they'd release on the Internet. The problem, they explained, was they were having some trouble finding someone to take on the part of the professor.

I had tickets to fly back to London that Sunday, so I wasn't exactly thrilled about the prospect of arrest, but this seemed a lot like fate. After a moment's hesitation, I volunteered.

As it turned out there wasn't much to worry about—US Uncut's idea of an "occupation" was to set up shop in the bank lobby, take advantage of the initial confusion to begin the "teach-in," and then leave as soon as the police began to threaten to start making arrests. I managed to scare up something that looked vaguely like a tweed jacket in the back of my closet, studied up on Bank of America's tax history (one tidbit I put in the "cheat sheet" to be distributed at the event: "In 2009, Bank of America earned $4.4 billion, paid no federal taxes whatsoever, but nonetheless got a tax credit of $1.9 billion. It did, however, spend roughly $4 million on lobbying, money that went directly to the politicians who wrote the tax codes that made this possible"),[1] and showed up for the action—which Marisa filmed for immediate streaming on the Internet. Our occupation lasted about fifteen minutes.

When I came back to New York in July, one of the first people I called was Marisa, and she plugged me back into another Uncut action, in Brooklyn. This time we ran away even quicker.

16 BEAVER STREET

Later that month, my friend Colleen Asper talked me into attending an event on July 31, hosted by the 16 Beaver Group.

16 Beaver is an art space named after their address just a block from the New York Stock Exchange. At the time, I knew it as the kind of place where artists who are also fans of Italian Autonomist theory hold seminars on CyberMarx, or radical Indian cinema, or the ongoing significance of Valerie Solanas's SCUM Manifesto. Colleen had urged me to come down that Sunday if I wanted to get a sense of what was happening in New York. I'd agreed, then kind of half forgotten, since I was spending that morning with a British archaeologist friend passing through town for a conference, and we'd both become en-

grossed exploring midtown comic book emporia, trying to find appropriate presents for his kids. Around 12:30 I received a text message from Colleen:

> C: You coming to this 16 Beaver thing?
> D: Where is it again? I'll go.
> C: Now ☺ Till 5 though, so if you come later, there will still be talking
> D: I'll head down
> C: Sweet!
> D: Remind me what they're even talking about
> C: A little bit of everything.

The purpose of the meeting was to have presentations about various anti-austerity movements growing around the world—in Greece, Spain, and elsewhere—and to end with an open discussion about how to bring a similar movement here.

I arrived late. By the time I got there I'd already missed the discussion of Greece and Spain, but was surprised to see so many familiar faces in the room. The Greek talk had been given by an old friend, an artist named Georgia Sagri, and as I walked in an even older friend, Sabu Kohso, was in the middle of talk about antinuclear mobilizations in the wake of the Fukushima meltdown in Japan. The only discussion I caught all the way through was the very last talk, about New York, and it was very much an anticlimax. The presenter was Doug Singsen, a soft-spoken art historian from Brooklyn College, who told the story of the New Yorkers Against Budget Cuts Coalition, which had sponsored a small sidewalk camp they called Bloombergville, named after Mayor Michael Bloomberg, opposite City Hall in lower Manhattan. In some ways it was a tale of frustration. The coalition had started out as a broad alliance of New York unions and community groups, with the express purpose of sponsoring civil disobedience against Bloomberg's draconian austerity budgets. This was unusual in itself: normally, union officials balk at the very mention of civil disobedience—or, at least, any civil disobedience that is not of the most completely scripted, prearranged sort (for instance, arranging with the police in advance when and how activists are to be arrested). This time unions like the United Federation of Teachers played an active role in planning the camp, inspired, in part, by the success of similar protest encampments in Cairo, Athens, and Barcelona—but then got cold feet and pulled out the moment the camp was actually set up. Nonetheless, forty or fifty dedicated activists, mostly socialists and anarchists, stuck it out for roughly four weeks, from mid-June to early July. With numbers that small, and no real media attention or political allies, acting in defiance of the law was out of the question, since everyone would just be arrested immediately and no one would ever know. But they had the advantage of an obscure regulation in New York law whereby it was not illegal to sleep on the sidewalk as a form of political protest, provided one left a lane open to traffic and didn't raise anything that could be described as a "structure" (such as a lean-to or tent). Of course, without tents, or any sort of structure, it was hard to describe the result as really being a "camp." The organizers had done their best to liaison with the police but they weren't in a particularly strong position to negotiate. They ended up being pushed farther and farther from City Hall before dispersing altogether.

The real reason the coalition fragmented so quickly, Singsen explained, was politics. The unions and most of the community groups were working with allies on the City Council, who were busy negotiating a compromise budget with the mayor. "It soon became apparent," he said, "that there were two positions. The moderates, who were willing to accept the need for some cuts, thinking it would place them in a better negotiating position to limit the damage, and the radicals—the Bloombergville camp—who rejected the need for any cuts at all." Once a deal seemed in sight, all support for civil disobedience, even in its mildest form, disappeared.

Three hours later, Sabu, Georgia, Colleen, a couple of the student organizers from Bloombergville, and I were nursing our beers a few blocks away and trying to hash out what we thought of all of this. It was a particular pleasure to see Georgia again. The last time we'd met it had been in Exarchia, a neighborhood in Athens full of squatted social centers, occupied parks, and anarchist cafés, where we'd spent a long night downing glasses of ouzo at street corner cafés while arguing about the radical implications of Plato's theory of agape, or universal love—conversations periodically interrupted by battalions of riot police who would march through the area all night long to make sure no one ever felt comfortable. Colleen explained this was typical of Exarchia. Occasionally, she told us, especially if a policeman had recently been injured in a clash with protesters, the police would choose one café, thrash everyone in sight, and destroy the cappuccino machines.

Back in New York, it wasn't long before the conversation turned to what it would take to startle the New York activist scene out of its doldrums.

"The main thing that stuck in my head about the talk about

Bloombergville," I volunteered, "was when the speaker was saying that the moderates were willing to accept some cuts, and the radicals rejected cuts entirely. I was just following along nodding my head, and suddenly I realized: wait a minute! What is this guy saying here? How did we get to a point where the *radical* position is to keep things exactly the way they are?"

The Uncut protests and the twenty-odd student occupations in England that year had fallen into the same trap. They were militant enough, sure: students had trashed Tory headquarters and ambushed members of the royal family. But they weren't *radical*. If anything the message was reactionary: *stop the cuts!* What, and go back to the lost paradise of 2009? Or even 1959, or 1979?

"And to be perfectly honest," I added. "It feels a bit unsettling watching a bunch of anarchists in masks outside Topshop, lobbing paint bombs over a line of riot cops, shouting, 'Pay your taxes!'" (Of course, I had been one of those radicals with paint bombs.)

Was there some way to break out of the trap? Georgia was excited by a campaign she'd seen advertised in *Adbusters* called "Occupy Wall Street." When Georgia described the ad to me, I was skeptical. It wouldn't be the first time someone had tried to shut down the Stock Exchange. There might have been one time they actually pulled it off back in the 1980s or 1990s. And in 2001, there were plans to put together a Wall Street action right after the IMF actions in Washington that fall. But then 9/11 happened, three blocks away from the proposed site of the action, and we had to drop our plans. My assumption was that doing anything anywhere near Ground Zero was going to be off-limits for decades—both practically and symbolically.

And more than anything, I was unclear about what this call to occupy Wall Street hoped to accomplish.

No one was really sure. But what also caught Georgia's eye was another ad she'd seen online for what was being called a "General Assembly," an organizing meeting to plan the Wall Street occupation, whatever it would turn out to be.

In Greece, she explained, that's how they had begun: by occupying Syntagma Square, a public plaza near parliament, and creating a genuine popular assembly, a new agora, based on direct democracy principles.* *Adbusters,* she said, was pushing for some kind of symbolic action. They wanted tens of thousands of people to descend on Wall Street, pitch tents, and refuse to leave until the government agreed to one key demand. If there was going to be an assembly, it was going to be beforehand, to determine what exactly that demand was: that Obama establish a committee to reinstate Glass-Steagall (the Depression-era law that had once prevented commercial banks from engaging in market speculation) or a constitutional amendment abolishing corporate personhood, or something else.

Colleen pointed out that *Adbusters* was basically founded by marketing people and their strategy made perfect sense from a marketing perspective: get a catchy slogan, make sure it expresses precisely what you want, then keep hammering away at it. But, she added, is that kind of legibility always a virtue for a social movement? Often the power of a work of art is precisely

---

* There was apparently a major struggle between the Marxists and the anarchists over that particular phrase: the Marxists wanted the slogan to be "real democracy"; following the Indignados in Spain, the anarchists had insisted on "direct democracy." They held a vote and the anarchists won.

the fact that you're not quite sure what it's trying to say. What's wrong with keeping the other side guessing? Especially if keeping things open-ended lets you provide a forum for a discontent that everyone feels, but haven't found a way to express yet.

Georgia agreed. Why not make the assembly the message in itself, as an open forum for people to talk about problems and propose solutions outside the framework of the existing system. Or to talk about how to create a completely new system altogether. The assembly could be a model that would spread until there was an assembly in every neighborhood in New York, on every block, in every workplace.

This had been the ultimate dream during the Global Justice Movement, too. At the time we called it "contaminationism." Insofar as we were a revolutionary movement, as opposed to a mere solidarity movement supporting revolutionary movements overseas, our entire vision was based on a kind of faith that democracy was contagious. Or at least, the kind of leaderless direct democracy we had spent so much care and effort on developing. The moment people were exposed to it, to watch a group of people actually listen to each other, and come to an intelligent decision, collectively, without having it in any sense imposed on them—let alone to watch a thousand people do it at one of the great Spokescouncils we held before major actions—it tended to change their perception over what was politically possible. Certainly it had had that effect on me.

Our expectation was that democratic practices would spread, and, inevitably, adapt themselves to the needs of local organizations: it never occurred to us that, say, a Puerto Rican nationalist group in New York and a vegan bicycle collective in San Francisco were going to do direct democracy in anything like the same way. To a large degree, that's what happened.

We'd had enormous success transforming activist culture itself. After the Global Justice Movement, the old days of steering committees and the like were basically over. Pretty much everyone in the activist community had come around to the idea of prefigurative politics: the idea that the organizational form that an activist group takes should embody the kind of society we wish to create. The problem was breaking these ideas out of the activist ghetto and getting them in front of the wider public, people who weren't already involved in some sort of grassroots political campaign. The media were no help at all: you could go through a year's worth of media coverage and still not have the slightest idea that the movement was about promulgating direct democracy. So for contaminationism to work, we had to actually get people in the room. And that proved extraordinarily difficult.

Maybe, we concluded, this time it would be different. After all, this time it wasn't the Third World being hit by financial crises and devastating austerity plans. This time the crisis had come home.

We all promised to meet at the General Assembly.

AUGUST 2

Bowling Green is a tiny park two blocks away from the Stock Exchange at the very southern end of Manhattan. It got its name because in the seventeenth century, Dutch settlers used it for playing nine-pins. Now it's a fenced green, with a fairly wide cobbled space to the north of it, and, directly to the north of that, a peninsular traffic island dominated by a large bronze statue of a bull stomping the earth, an image of barely contained and potentially deadly enthusiasm that denizens of Wall

Street seem to have adopted as a symbol of the animal spirits (in John Maynard Keynes's coinage) driving the capitalist system. Ordinarily, it's a quiet park, sprinkled with foreign tourists, and streetside vendors selling six-inch replicas of the bull.

It was around 4:30 on the day of the General Assembly and I was already slightly late for the four o'clock meeting, but this time, intentionally. I had taken a circuitous route that passed directly down Wall Street just to get a sense of the police presence. It was worse than I'd imagined. There were cops everywhere: two different platoons of uniformed officers lounging around looking for something to do, two different squads of horse cops standing sentinel on approach streets, scooter cops zipping up and down past the iron barricades built after 9/11 to foil suicide bombers. And this was just an ordinary Tuesday afternoon!

When I got to Bowling Green what I found was if anything even more disheartening. At first I wasn't sure I had shown up for the right meeting at all. There was already a rally well under way. There were two TV cameras pointing at an impromptu stage defined by giant banners, megaphones, and piles of pre-printed signs. A tall man with flowing dreadlocks was making an impassioned speech about resisting budget cuts to a crowd of perhaps eighty people, arranged in a half circle around him. Most of them seemed vaguely bored and uncomfortable including, I noticed, the TV news crews, since, on inspection, the cameramen appear to have left their cameras unattended. I found Georgia on the sidelines, brow furled, as she looked out at the people assembled on stage.*

---

* Colleen was there, too, but escorting her mother, who was passing through town. I later learned her mom became so uncomfortable with

"Wait a minute," I asked. "Are those guys WWP?"

"Yeah, they're WWP."

I'd been out of town for a few years so it took a few moments to recognize them. For most anarchists, the Workers World Party (WWP) was our ultimate activist nemesis. Apparently led by a small cadre of mostly white party leaders who at public events were invariably found lingering discreetly behind a collection of African American and Latino front men, they were famous for pursuing a political strategy straight out of the 1930s: creating great "popular front" coalitions like the International Action Center (IAC) or ANSWER (an acronym for Act Now to Stop War and End Racism), composed of dozens of groups who turned out by the thousands to march around with preprinted signs. Most of the rank-and-file members of these coalition groups were attracted by the militant rhetoric and apparently endless supply of cash, but remained blissfully unaware of what the central committee's positions on world issues really were. These positions were almost a caricature of unreconstructed Marxism-Leninism, so much so that many of us had from time to time speculated that the whole thing actually was some kind of elaborate, FBI-funded joke: the WWP still supported, for instance, the 1968 Soviet invasion of Czechoslovakia and Chinese suppression of democracy protests at Tiananmen Square, and they took such a strict "anti-imperialist" line that they not only opposed any overseas U.S. intervention, but also actively supported anyone the U.S. government claimed to disapprove of, from the government of North Korea, to Rwandan Hutu militias. Anarchists tended to

---

the Stalinist-style presence that Colleen felt obliged to take her to an art gallery instead.

refer to them as "the Stalinists." Trying to work with them was out of the question; they had no interest in working with any coalition they did not completely control.

This was a disaster.

So how did the WWP end up in control of the meeting? Georgia wasn't sure. But we both knew as long as they were in control, there was no possibility of a real assembly taking place. And indeed, when I asked a couple of bystanders what was going on, they confirmed the plan was for a rally, to be followed by a brief open mic, and then a march on Wall Street itself, where the leaders would present a long list of pre-established demands.

For activists dedicated to building directly democratic politics—horizontals, as we like to call ourselves—the usual reaction to this sort of thing is despair. It was certainly my first reaction. Walking into such a rally feels like walking into a trap. The agenda is already set, but it's unclear who set it. In fact it's often difficult even to find out what the agenda is until moments before the event begins, when some man announces it on a megaphone. The very sight of the stage and stacks of preprinted signs and hearing the word "march" evoked memories of a thousand desultory afternoons spent marching along in platoons like some kind of impotent army, along a prearranged route, with protest marshals liaising with police to herd us all into steel-barrier "protest pens." Events in which there was no space for spontaneity, creativity, improvisation—where, in fact, everything seemed designed to make self-organization or real expression impossible. Even the chants and slogans were to be provided from above.

I spotted a cluster of what seemed to be the core WWP leadership group—you can tell because they tend to be middle-aged and white, and always hovering just slightly offstage (those who appear on the actual stage are invariably people of color).

One, a surprisingly large individual broke off periodically to pass through the audience. "Hey," I said to him when he passed my way, "you know, maybe you shouldn't advertise a General Assembly if you're not actually going to hold one."

I may have put it in a less polite way. He looked down at me. "Oh, yeah, that's solidarity, isn't it? Insult the organizers. Look, I'll tell you what. If you don't like it, why don't you leave?"

We stared at one another unpleasantly for a moment and then he went away.

I considered leaving but noticed that no one else seemed particularly happy with what was happening, either. To adopt activist parlance, this wasn't really a crowd of verticals—that is, the sort of people who actually like marching around with pre-issued signs and listening to spokesmen from somebody's central committee. Most seemed to be horizontals: people more sympathetic with anarchist principles of organization, nonhierarchical forms of direct democracy. I spotted at least one Wobbly, a young man with dark glasses and a black Industrial Workers of the World (IWW) T-shirt, several college students wearing Zapatista paraphernalia, and a few other obvious anarchist types. I also noticed several old friends, including Sabu, there with another Japanese activist, who I'd known from street actions in Quebec City back in 2001. Finally, Georgia and I looked at each other and both realized we were thinking the same thing: "Why are we so complacent? Why is it that every time we see something like this happening, we just mutter and go home?"—though I think the way we actually put it at the time was more like, "You know something? Fuck this shit. They advertised a General Assembly. Let's hold one."

So I walked up to a likely-seeming stranger, a young Korean-American man looking with irritation at the stage—his name, I later learned, was Chris, and he was an anarchist who worked with Food Not Bombs. But I didn't know that then. All I knew was that he looked pissed off.

"Say," I asked, "I was wondering. If some of us decided to break off and start a real General Assembly, would you be interested?"

"Why, are there people talking about doing that?"

"Well, we are now."

"Shit, yeah. Just tell me when."

"To be honest," volunteered the young man standing next to him, whose name, I later learned, was Matt Presto, and who like Chris would later become a key OWS organizer, "I was about ready to take off anyway. But that might be worth staying for."

So with the help of Chris and Matt, Georgia and I gathered up some of the more obvious horizontals and formed a little circle of twenty-odd people at the foot of the park, as far as we could get from the microphones. Almost immediately, delegates from the main rally appeared to call us back again.

The delegates were not WWP folk—they tend to stay aloof from this sort of thing—but fresh-faced young students in button-down shirts.

"Great," I muttered to Georgia. "It's the ISO."

The ISO is the International Socialist Organization. In the spectrum of activists, the WWP is probably on the opposite pole from anarchists, but ISO is annoyingly in the middle: as close as you can get to a horizontal group while still not actually being one. They're Trotskyists, and in principle in favor of direct action, direct democracy, and bottom-up structures of every kind—though their main role in any meeting seemed to be to discourage more radical elements from actually practicing any of these things. The frustrating thing about the ISO is that, as individuals, they tended to be such obviously good people. Most were likable kids, students mostly, incredibly well-meaning, and unlike the WWP, their higher-ups (and despite the theoretical support for direct democracy, the group itself had a very tightly organized, top-down command structure) did allow them to work in broad coalitions they didn't control—if only with an eye to possibly taking them over. They were the obvious people to step in and try to mediate.

"I think this is all some kind of misunderstanding," one of the young men told our breakaway circle. "This event isn't organized by any one group. It's a broad-based coalition of grassroots groups and individuals dedicated to fighting the Bloomberg austerity package. We've talked to the organizers. They say there's definitely going to be a General Assembly after the speakers are finished." There were three of them, all young and clean-cut, and, I noticed, each of them, at one point or another, used exactly the same phrase, "a broad-based coalition of grassroots groups and individuals."

There wasn't much we could do. If the organizers were promising a General Assembly, we had to at least give them a chance. So we reluctantly complied, and went back to the meeting. Needless to say, no general assembly materialized. The organizers' idea of an "assembly" seemed to be an open mic, where anyone in the audience had a few minutes to express their general political position or thoughts about some particular issue, before we set off on the preordained march.

After twenty minutes of this, Georgia took her turn to speak. I should note here that Georgia was, by profession, a performance artist. As such she has always made a point of cultivating a certain finely fashioned public persona—basically, that of a madwoman. Such personas are always based on some elements of one's real personality, and in Georgia's case there was much speculation among her close friends about just how much of it was put on. Certainly she is one of the more impulsive people I've ever met. But she had a knack, at certain times and places, for hitting exactly the right note, usually by scrambling all assumptions about what was actually supposed to be going on. Georgia started her three minutes by declaring, "This is not a General Assembly! This is a rally put on by a political party! It has absolutely nothing to do with the global General Assembly movement"—replete with references to Greek and Spanish assemblies and their systematic exclusion of representatives of organized political groups. To be honest I didn't catch the whole thing because I was trying to locate other potential holdouts and convince them to join us once we again decided to defect. But like everyone who was there that day, I remember the climax, when Georgia's time was up and she ended up in some sort of heated back-and-forth exchange with an African-American woman who'd been one of the WWP's earlier speakers and who began an impromptu response.

"Well, I find the previous speaker's intervention to be profoundly disrespectful. It's little more than a conscious attempt to disrupt the meeting—"

"This isn't a meeting! It's a rally."

"Ahem. I find the previous speaker's intervention to be profoundly disrespectful. You can disagree with someone if you like, but at the very least, I would expect us all to treat each other with two things: with respect, and with solidarity. What the last speaker did—"

"Wait a minute, you're saying hijacking a meeting isn't a violation of respect and solidarity?"

At which point another WWP speaker broke in, in indignant mock-astonishment, "I can't believe you just *interrupted* a black person!"

"Why shouldn't I?" said Georgia. "I'm black, too."

I should point out here that Georgia is blond.

The reaction might be described as a universal "hunh?"

"You're *what*?"

"Just like I said. I'm black. Do you think you're the only black person here?"*

The resulting befuddlement bought her just enough time to announce that we were reassembling the real GA, and to meet back by the gate to the green in fifteen minutes. At which point she was shooed off the stage.

There were insults and vituperations. After about a half hour of drama, we formed the circle again, on the other side of Bowling Green, and this time almost everyone still remaining abandoned the rally to come over to our side. We realized we had an almost entirely horizontal crowd: not only Wobblies and Zapatista solidarity folk, but several Spaniards who had been active with the Indignados in Madrid, a couple of insur-

---

* Needless to say Georgia's claims were the topic of much comment among her friends for weeks afterward. There was speculation. Georgia is from Greece, one of the few countries in the world where being blond can actually mean discrimination, since Greeks often assume it means one is an impoverished immigrant Albanian. When questioned later, Georgia just insisted that there was nothing to be discussed. "Yes, I'm black," she said, as if the matter was self-evident.

rectionist anarchists who'd been involved in the occupations at Berkeley a few years before, a smattering of bemused on-lookers who had just come to see the rally, maybe four or five, and an equal number of WWP (not including anyone from the central committee) who reluctantly came over to monitor our activities. A young man named Willie Osterwail, who'd spent some time as a squatter in Barcelona, volunteered to facilitate.

We quickly determined we had no idea what we were actually going to do.

One problem was that *Adbusters* had already advertised a date for the action: September 17. This was a problem for two reasons. One was that it was only six weeks away. It had taken over a year to organize the blockades and direct actions that shut down the WTO meetings in Seattle in November 1999. *Adbusters* seemed to think we could somehow assemble twenty thousand people to camp out with tents in the middle of Wall Street, but even assuming the police would let that happen, which they wouldn't, anyone with experience in practical organizing knew that you couldn't assemble numbers like that in a matter of weeks. Gathering a big crowd like that would usually involve drawing people from around the country, which would require support groups in different cities and, especially, buses, which would in turn require organizing all sorts of fund-raisers, since as far as we knew we had no money of any kind. (Or did we? *Adbusters* was rumored to have money. But none of us even knew if *Adbusters* was directly involved. They didn't have any representatives at the meeting.) Then there was the second problem. There was no way to shut down Wall Street on September 17 because September 17 was a Saturday. If we were going to do anything that would have a direct impact on—or even be noticed by—actual Wall Street executives, we'd have to somehow figure out a way to still be around Monday at 9 A.M. And we weren't even sure the Stock Exchange was the ideal target. Just logistically, and perhaps symbolically, we'd probably have better luck with the Federal Reserve, or the Standard & Poor's offices, each just a few blocks away.

————

We decided to table that problem for the time being. We also decided to table the whole question of demands, and instead form breakout groups. This is standard horizontal practice: everyone calls out ideas for working groups until we have a list (in this case they were just four: Outreach, Communications/Internet, Action, and Process/Facilitation), then the group breaks out into smaller circles to brainstorm, having agreed to reassemble, say, an hour later, whereupon a spokesman for each breakout group presents report-backs on the discussion and any decisions collectively made. I joined the Process group, which, predictably, was primarily composed of anarchists, determined to ensure the group become a model. We quickly decided that the group would operate by consensus, with an option to fall back on a two-thirds vote if there was a deadlock, and that there would always be at least two facilitators, one male, one female, one to keep the meeting running, the other to "take stack" (that is, the list of people who've asked to speak). We discussed hand signals and nonbinding straw polls, or "temperature checks." *

By the time we'd reassembled it was already dark. Most of the working groups had only come to provisional decisions. The Action group had tossed around possible scenarios but

* Specifics of how these consensus tools work will be covered in Chapter 4.

their main decision was to meet again later in the week to take a walking tour of the area. The Communications group had agreed to set up a listserv and meet to discuss a web page—their first order of business was to try to figure out what already existed (for instance, who it was who already had created a Twitter account called #OccupyWallStreet, since they didn't seem to be at the meeting), and what, if anything, *Adbusters* had to do with it or what they had already done. Outreach had decided to meet on Thursday to design flyers, and to try to figure out how we should describe ourselves, especially in relation to the existing anti-cuts coalition. Several of the Outreach group—including my friend Justin, the one I knew from Quebec City—were working as labor organizers and were pretty sure they could get union people interested. All of us decided we'd hold another General Assembly, hopefully a much larger one, at the Irish Hunger Memorial nearby that Tuesday at 7:30 P.M.

Despite the provisional nature of all of our decisions—since none of us was quite sure if we were building on top of existing efforts or creating something new—the mood of the group was one of near complete exhilaration. We felt we had just witnessed a genuine victory for the forces of democracy, one where exhausted modes of organizing had been definitively brushed aside. In New York, a victory like that was almost completely unprecedented. No one was sure exactly what would come of it, but at least for that moment almost all of us were delighted at the prospect of finding out.

By the time we all headed home it was already about eleven. The first thing I did was call Marisa. "You can't believe what just happened," I told her. "You've *got* to get involved."

THE 99 PERCENT

FROM: David Graeber <david@anarchisms.org>
SUBJECT: **hello! quick question**
DATE: August 3, 2011 12:46:29 AM CDT
TO: Micah White <micah@adbusters.org>

Hello Micah,

So I just had the strangest day. About 80 people came down to assemble near the big bull sculpture near Bowling Green at 4:30 because we'd heard there was going to be a "General Assembly" to plan the September 17 action called by . . . well, you guys. We show up and discover, no, actually, no assembly, it was the Workers World Party with speakers and a microphone and signs, doing a rally, then they were going to have a brief speak-out and a march. Normally this is greeted with cynical resignation, but this time, a few of us . . . decided to hell with it, assembled the horizontals, who turned out to be 85% of the crowd, defected, held a general meeting, created a structure and process, working groups, and got going on an actual organization. It was sort of a little miracle and we all left feeling extremely happy for a change.

One question that came up however was: "what does Adbusters really have to do with any of this? Are they extending resources of any sorts? Or was it just a call?" I said I'd check . . .

David

I sent that off before going to bed that night. The next morning I got this reply:

Hey David,

Thank you for this report on what happened, I'm glad that you were there to pull things around.

Here's the situation . . .

At Adbusters, we've been kicking around the idea of a wall street occupation for a couple of months. On June 7, we sent out a listserv to our 90,000 email list of jammers with a short note floating the idea. The response was overwhelmingly positive, so we decided to run with it. The current issue of our magazine, the one that is just now coming onto newsstands (Adbusters #97—The Politics of Post-Anarchism), contains a double page poster calling for the occupation on September 17. The front cover of the American edition also has an #OCCUPYWALLSTREET mini-picture. This will be like a slow fuse getting the word about the occupation out there to the English speaking world for next month or more . . .

At this point, we decided that given our limited resources and staff, our role at Adbusters could only be to get the meme out there and hope that local activists would empower themselves to make the event a reality. Following the same model of Spain where the people, not political parties and organizations, decided on everything.

The "General Assembly" which you attended was put together by an unaffiliated group—the same group that was behind the No Cuts NYC and Bloombergville (an anti-cuts protest camp that lasted about two weeks). My contact has been with "Doug Singsen" of No Cuts NYC. I don't know anything about Doug nor why the Assembly

was hijacked by the Workers World Party, or if that was
intended from the start . . .

Micah

Adbusters had just thrown out an idea. They'd done this many
times before, and in the past, nothing had ever really come of
it; but this time all sorts of different, and apparently unrelated,
groups seemed to be trying to grab hold of it. But we were
the ones who actually ended up doing the organizing on the
ground. By the next day the listserv for our little group was
up and all the people who had been at the original meeting
started trying to figure out who we were, what we should call
ourselves, what we were actually trying to do. Once again, it
all started with the question of the one single demand. After
throwing out a few initial ideas—Debt cancellation? Abolishing permit laws to legalize freedom of assembly? Abolish corporate personhood?—Matt Presto, who had been with Chris
among the first to rally to us at Bowling Green, pretty much
put the matter to rest when he pointed out there were really
two different sorts of demands. Some were actually achievable,
like *Adbusters'* suggestion—which had appeared in one of their
initial publicity calls—of demanding a commission to consider
restoring Glass-Steagall. Maybe a good idea, but was anyone
really going to risk brutalization and arrest to get someone to
appoint a committee? Appointing a committee is what politicians usually do when they *don't* want to take any real action.
Then there's the kind of demand you make because you know
that even though overwhelming majorities of Americans think
it would be a good idea, the demand is likely never going to

happen under the existing political order—say, abolish corporate lobbying. But was it our job to come up with a vision for a new political order, or to help create a way for everyone to do so? Who were we anyway to come up with a vision for a new political order? So far, basically just a bunch of people who had come to a meeting. If we were all attracted to the idea of creating General Assemblies, it's because we saw them as a forum for the overwhelming majority of Americans locked out of the political debate to develop their own ideas and visions.

That seemed to settle matters for most of us. But it led to another question: How exactly were we to describe that overwhelming majority of Americans who had been locked out of the political debate? Who were we calling to join us? The oppressed? The excluded? The people? All the old phrases seemed hackneyed and inappropriate. How to frame it in a way that made it self-evident why the obvious way to reclaim a voice was to occupy Wall Street?

That summer I'd been giving almost constant interviews about debt, since I had just written a book about debt, and had even been asked to weigh in, now and then, on venues like CNN, *The Wall Street Journal,* and even the New York *Daily News* (or, at least, on their blogs—I rarely got to be on the actual shows or in print editions). So I'd been trying to keep up with the U.S. economic debate. At least since May, when the economist Joseph Stiglitz had published a column in *Vanity Fair* called "Of the 1%, By the 1%, and For the 1%," there was a great deal of talk in newspaper columns and economic blogs about the fact that 1 or 2 percent of the population had come to grab an ever-increasing share of the national wealth, while everyone else's income was either stagnating, or in real terms actually shrinking.

What particularly struck me in Stiglitz's argument was the connection between wealth and power: the 1 percent were the ones creating the rules for how the political system works, and had turned it into one based on legalized bribery:

> Wealth begets power, which begets more wealth. During the savings-and-loan scandal of the 1980s—a scandal whose dimensions, by today's standards, seem almost quaint—the banker Charles Keating was asked by a congressional committee whether the $1.5 million he had spread among a few key elected officials could actually buy influence. "I certainly hope so," he replied. . . . The personal and the political are today in perfect alignment. Virtually all U.S. senators, and most of the representatives in the House, are members of the top 1 percent when they arrive, are kept in office by money from the top 1 percent, and know that if they serve the top 1 percent well they will be rewarded by the top 1 percent when they leave office.[2]

The 1 percent held the overwhelming majority of securities and other financial instruments; and they also made the overwhelming majority of campaign contributions. In other words, they were exactly that proportion of the population that was able to turn their wealth into political power—and use that political power to accumulate even more wealth. It also struck me that since that 1 percent effectively was what we referred to as "Wall Street," this was the perfect solution to our problem: Who were the excluded voices frozen out of the political system, and why were we summoning them to the financial district in Manhattan—and not, say, Washington, D.C.? If Wall Street represented the 1 percent, then we're everybody else.

> FROM: David Graeber <david@anarchisms.org>
> SUBJECT: **Re: [september17discuss] Re: [september17] Re: a SINGLE DEMAND for the occupation?**
> DATE: August 4, 2011 4:25:38 PM CDT
> TO: september17@googlegroups.com
>
> What about the "99% movement"?
>
> Both parties govern in the name of the 1% of Americans who have received pretty much all the proceeds of economic growth, who are the only people completely recovered from the 2008 recession, who control the political system, who control almost all financial wealth.
>
> So if both parties represent the 1%, we represent the 99% whose lives are essentially left out of the equation.
>
> David

The next day, Friday, August 5, was the day we'd set for the Outreach meeting, at the Writers Guild offices downtown, where my old friend Justin Molino worked. Everyone seemed to like the 99 percent idea. There were some tentative concerns: someone remarked that someone had already tried an "Other 98 percent" campaign. Obviously, the idea was not completely original. Probably any number of different people thought of something around the same lines around the same time. But as it turned out, we happened to put it together in exactly the right time and place. Before long, Georgia, along with Luis and Begonia, two of the Spanish Indignados, were preparing a flyer—our first—to advertise the Tuesday General Assembly, which we were already starting to call the "GA."*

MEETINGS

Marisa came to that next GA, and during breakout we got the idea of initiating a Trainings working group. Our group was composed mainly of young activists who had cut their teeth at Bloombergville. They were enthusiastic about the idea of consensus process and direct action, but few had any real experience with either. Process at first was a shambles—many participants didn't seem to understand that a block (that is, a veto—normally to be appealed to only as a last resort) was different than a "no" vote, and even facilitators, who were supposed to be running the meetings, tended to start each discussion of proposals not by asking if anyone had clarifying questions or concerns, but by simply saying, "Okay, that's the proposal. Any blocks?" Apart from trainings on democratic process, there was a shortage of basic street skills: we needed to find people to provide legal training, if nothing else so everyone would know what to do if they were arrested, as some of us were definitely going to be, whether or not we decided to do anything illegal. We needed more, still: medical training, to know what to do if someone next to them was injured, and

* As a matter of historical record, since there is so much discussion of the origin of the slogan "We Are the 99 Percent," the answer is that—appropriately enough—it was a collective creation. I threw in the 99 percent part, Begonia and Luis added the "we," and the verb was ultimately by added by Chris, of Food Not Bombs, when he created the "We Are the 99 Percent" tumblr page a month later.

civil disobedience training, to teach when and how to lock arms, go limp, and comply or not comply with orders. I spent a lot of the next few weeks tracking down old friends from the Direct Action Network who had gone into hiding, retired, burnt out, given up, got jobs, or gone off to live on some organic farm, convincing them this wasn't another false start, it was real this time, and getting them to join us and share their experience. It took a while, but gradually many did filter back.

At that first GA at the Irish Hunger Memorial, we decided all subsequent GAs would be held in Tompkins Square Park in the East Village—that is, not in the relatively desolate environs of Wall Street itself, but in the heart of a real New York community, the kind of place we hoped to see local assemblies eventually emerge. Marisa and I agreed to facilitate the first of them, on August 13, since Marisa had a good deal of experience with consensus process. In fact, she was so good—and everyone else at first so uncertain—she ended up having to help facilitate the next four. She became the woman holding everything together: at practically every working group meeting, coordinating, hatching plans. Without her, I'd be surprised if anything would have happened at all.

———

Over the next few weeks a plan began to take shape. We decided that what we really wanted to achieve was something like what had already been accomplished in Athens, Barcelona, and Madrid, where thousands of ordinary citizens, most of them completely new to political mobilization of any kind, had been willing to occupy public squares in protest against the entire class of their respective countries. The idea would be to occupy a similar public space to create a New York General

Assembly, which could, like its European cousins, act as a model of genuine direct democracy to counterpoise to the corrupt charade presented to us as "democracy" by the U.S. government. The Wall Street action would be a stepping-stone toward the creation of a whole network of such assemblies.

Those were our aims, but it was impossible to predict what would really happen on the 17th. *Adbusters* had assured us there were ninety thousand people following us on their web page. They had also called for twenty thousand to fill the streets. That obviously wasn't going to happen. But how many would really show up? What's more, what would we do with the people once they did? We were all keenly aware of what we were up against. The NYPD numbered close to forty thousand—Mayor Bloomberg likes to claim that if New York City had been an independent country, its police force would be the seventh largest army in the world.* Wall Street in turn was probably the single most heavily policed public space on the planet. Would it be possible to have any sort of action next to the Stock Exchange at all? Certainly shutting it down, even for a moment, was pretty much out of the question—probably under any circumstances, under the new security environment after 9/11, certainly, not with only six weeks to prepare.

Crazy ideas were being tossed about at working group meetings and on the listserv. We were likely to be wildly outnumbered by the cops. Perhaps we could somehow use the overwhelming police presence against itself, to make them look ridiculous? One idea was to announce a cocaine blockade: we

---

* Though it's worthwhile to point out this is untrue. The number would be more like 37th: New York City would come in just ahead of Tunisia, and just behind Portugal.

could form a human chain around the area of the Stock Ex-change, and then declare that we were allowing no cocaine to enter until Wall Street would agree to our demands ("And after three days, no hookers either!"). Another, more practical, idea was to have the working group that was already coordinating with people occupying squares in Greece, Spain, Germany, and the Middle East to create some sort of Internet hookup, and then somehow project their images onto the wall of the Stock Exchange, allowing speakers from each occupation to express their opinions of Wall Street financiers directly. Something like that, we felt, would help with long-term movement building: it would actually accomplish something on the first day, render-ing it a minor historical event of a sort—even if there never was a second. Minor victories of that sort are always crucial; you always want to be able to go home saying you've done some-thing that no one has ever done before. But technically, given our constraints of time and money, it proved impossible to pull off.*

To be perfectly honest, for many of us veterans the greatest concern during those hectic weeks was how to ensure the ini-tial event wouldn't turn out a total fiasco. We wanted to make sure that all the enthusiastic young people going into a major action for the first time wouldn't end up immediately beaten, arrested, and psychologically traumatized as the media, as usual, looked the other way. Before the action launched, some internal conflicts had to be worked out.

---

* Later, various occupations did acquire the technical means to beam powerful images on the sides of buildings, but the NYPD has held that doing so without permission is a form of trespassing and has forbidden the practice.

Most of New York's grumpier hard-core anarchists refused to join in, and in fact mocked us from the sidelines as "reformist." More open, "small-a" anarchists such as myself spent much of our time trying to make sure the remaining verticals didn't institute anything that could become a formal leadership structure, which, based on past experience, would have guaranteed failure. The WWP pulled out of the organizing early on, but a handful of ISO students and their supporters, usually consisting of about a dozen in all, continually pushed for greater centralization. One of the greatest battles was over the question of police liaisons and marshals. The verticals—taking their experience from Bloombergville—took the position that it was a simple practical necessity to have two or three trained negotiators to interface with the police, and marshals to convey information to occupiers. The horizontals insisted that any such arrangement would instantly turn into a leadership structure, conveying orders, since police will always try to identify leaders, and, if they can't find any, create a leadership structure by making arrangements directly with the negotiators and then insisting that the negotiators (and marshals) enforce them. That one actually went to a vote—or, more precisely, a straw poll, when the facilitator asks people to put their fingers up (for approval), down (for disapproval), or sideways (for abstention or to express uncertainty), just to get a sense of how everyone felt, to see if there was any point in trying to push on. In this case there wasn't. More than two thirds strongly opposed creating either liaisons or marshals. At that moment commitment to horizontality was definitively confirmed.

There were controversies over the participation of various fringe groups, ranging from followers of Lyndon LaRouche to one woman from a shadowy (and possibly nonexistent) group that called itself US Day of Rage, who systematically blocked any attempt to reach out to unions because she felt we should be able to attract dissident Tea Partiers. At one point, debates at the GA had become so contentious that we ended up changing our hand signals: we had been using a signal for "direct response," two hands waving up and down, each with fingers pointing, to be used when someone had some kind of crucial information ("no the action isn't on Tuesday, it's on Wednesday!") and was asking the facilitator to break through the stack of speakers to clarify. Before long, people were using the signal to mean "the group needs to know just how much I disagree with that last statement" and we were reduced to the spectacle of certain diehards sitting on the ground waving their index fingers at each other continuously as they went on some back-and-forth argument until everyone else forced them to shut up. I ended up suggesting we get rid of "direct response" entirely and substitute one raised finger for "point of information"—which I'm pretty sure I didn't make up, I must have seen it somewhere—and which, strangely, once adopted, put an instant end to back-and-forths and improved the quality of our debate.

THE DAY

I'm not sure when and how the Tactical working group came to their decision, but pretty early on the emerging consensus was that we were going to occupy a park. It was really the only practical option.

　　Here, as in Egypt, we all knew that anything we said in a public meeting, or wrote on a public listserv, was certain to be known to the police. So when, a few weeks before the date, the

Tactical group chose a public location—Chase Plaza, a spacious area in front of the Chase Manhattan Bank building two blocks from the Stock Exchange, replete with a lovely Picasso sculpture, and theoretically open at all hours to the general public—and announced in our outreach literature that we'd be holding our General Assembly there on September 17, they assumed the city would just shut the place down. I'd spent most of the evening of the 16th at a civil disobedience training in Brooklyn conducted by Lisa Fithian, another Global Justice veteran and inveterate organizer who now specialized in teaching labor groups more creative tactics. That evening around midnight a few of us—me, Marisa, Lisa, and Mike McGuire, a scruffy, bearded anarchist veteran who'd just arrived from Baltimore—stopped off at Wall Street to reconnoiter, only to discover, sure enough, the plaza fenced off and closed to the public for an unspecified period of time with no reason given.

"It's all right," said Marisa. "I'm pretty sure the Tactical group has a whole series of backup plans." She didn't know what those backup plans were—at that point she'd been working mainly with Trainings, and the Video Live-Streaming group—but was sure they existed. We poked around a bit, speculating about the viability of various open spaces, and eventually took the subway home.

The next day the plan was for everyone to start assembling around noon by the bull statue at Bowling Green, but the four of us met an hour or two early, and I spent some time wandering about, snapping pictures on my iPhone of police setting up barricades around the Stock Exchange, and sending the images out on Twitter. This had an unexpected effect. The official #OccupyWallStreet Twitter account (which turned out to have been created and maintained by a small transgender collective from Montreal) immediately sent word that I was on the scene and seemed to have some idea what was going on. Within a couple of hours, my account had about two thousand new followers. About an hour later, I noticed that every time I'd send out an update, ten minutes later someone in Barcelona had translated it and sent it out again in Spanish. I began to get a sense of just how much global interest there was in what was going on that day.

Still, the great mystery was how many people would actually show up. Since we hadn't had time to make any serious efforts to organize transportation, it was really anyone's guess—what's more, we were well aware that if any large number of people did show up, we'd pretty much have no choice but to camp out somewhere, even if that hadn't been the plan, since we hadn't organized housing and didn't have any place to put them.

At first, though, it didn't seem like that was going to be much of a problem, since our numbers seemed disappointingly small. What's more, many who showed up seemed decidedly offbeat—I remember a collection of about a dozen "Protest Chaplains" dressed in white robes and singing radical hymns, and perhaps a dozen yards away a rival chorus, also made up of about a dozen more singers, followers of Lyndon LaRouche, performing elaborate classical harmonies. Small knots of homeless traveling kids, or maybe they were just crusty-looking activists, would occasionally appear and take a few turns marching around the barricades the police had constructed around the bull statue, which was assiduously protected at all times by a squadron of uniformed officers.

Gradually I noticed our numbers were starting to build. By the time the Reverend Billy, a famous radical performance artist, had begun to preach from the steps of the Museum of the American Indian, on the south end of Bowling Green Park, it seemed like there were at least a thousand of us. At some point someone pressed a map into my hand. It had five different numbers on it: each corresponded to a park within walking distance that might serve as a fit place for the GA. Around 2:30, word went out that we were all to proceed to location #5.

That was Zuccotti Park.

———

By the time we got to Zuccotti Park it was clear we had so many people—two thousand at the very least—that we weren't quite sure how it was going to be possible to hold a General Assembly at all. Someone—some said it was one of the student organizers from out of town—stood on one of the big stone benches festooned around the park to announce that we were all going to break into groups of thirty for an hour and start brainstorming ideas for a genuinely democratic society, or anything else that struck participants as their most vital political concern. This turned out to be a very good idea. Before long the entire park was a maze of little circles, which gave the Process working group—hastily reassembled—a chance to scramble up a plan.

This was, clearly, going to be the facilitation job of the century. Luckily, by this time we did have a number of experienced volunteers—Marina Sitrin, another Direct Action Network activist I'd originally called in to help with legal training, Marisa, a talented young lawyer named Amin Husain, Matt, and Lisa Fithian. We quickly settled on two primary facilitators, two backup facilitators (I was one of the backups), two stack takers, one scribe to write down decisions, one vibes watcher to

pass through the crowd monitoring if everyone could hear, or
if there were obvious signs of dissatisfaction, frustration, or
boredom that needed to be addressed. We also decided that we
would form a giant circle. As a young Spanish woman who had
flown in to help out explained to us, and Georgia later confirmed, this was an extremely stupid mistake. There is actually
no way that a team of facilitators standing in the middle of a
circle of people that large, even if shouting at the top of their
lungs, could possibly make themselves heard to more than half
the assembled multitude at once. The proper thing to do would
have been to form a semicircle, and then make aisles, so that
speakers could walk to the front and address the assembly. By
the time we'd figured that out, it was too late.

So once we'd reconvened the group into a circle, we spent
the first several minutes trying to figure out how to communi-
cate to everyone simultaneously. We managed to scare up several different megaphones, and at one point stitched three
together into a single jury-rigged contraption, pointing in three
different directions. But that didn't really work. Finally, we realized we'd have to fall back on the People's Microphone—
another trick familiar to most of us from the days of the Global
Justice Movement.

No one was quite sure where the People's Mic had originally come from. It was already a familiar tool to many California activists by the time of the WTO actions in Seattle in
November 1999. In a way, it's kind of remarkable that it hasn't
been attested long before—it's a perfect solution to an obvious
problem that people in large assemblies must have faced time
and time again for thousands of years. Perhaps it was widely
used in earlier periods of human history but was simply never
remarked on because its use was considered self-evident. The

trick is very simple. One person speaks loudly, pausing every ten or twenty words or so. When they pause, everyone within earshot repeats what they said, and their words carry twice as far as they would have otherwise. It's not only practical, but, we found, it has a curious, and profoundly democratic, effect. First of all, it strongly discourages speechifying. Almost anyone will know better than to ramble on unnecessarily if they know that a thousand people are waiting to repeat every word. Second, since anyone can speak, and everyone must repeat, it forces participants to genuinely listen to everybody else.

At that point though we were not thinking so much about the philosophical implications as immediate practical concerns. We were two thousand people in a park, surrounded by at least a thousand police. Scouts had confirmed that horses, scooters, paddy wagons, and riot gear were all assembled ostentatiously in the vicinity. Police white-shirts—that is, commanders—were asking anyone they thought might look like a leader what our plans were. It very much helped at this point that even if anyone had been inclined to act as liaison, they wouldn't have been able to tell them.

The meeting went on till very late. We had made a point of announcing no specific plan for what to do after the assembly— partly because we didn't want to make decisions for others, partly to ensure that rather than falling into abstract theoretical arguments, the first order of business of the GA would be the very practical question of deciding what we all wanted to do next. This worked very well in setting the tone. Any number of scenarios were broached, considered, mostly abandoned. Police kept sending out word that they were preparing to evict us—first saying they would clear the park at 10 P.M., then 10:30, then 11. People studiously ignored them, or told them we were still meeting. Before long it became apparent there were two schools of thought: a larger group, which wanted to take the park and hold it as a permanent base of operations, much like Tahrir Square in Egypt, Syntagma Square in Athens, or the Plaça de Catalunya in Barcelona, and a smaller, but equally determined, group that felt we needed to march directly to Wall Street, and if possible, take the street directly opposite the Stock Exchange. Some argued that technically it was not even illegal for us to camp there. As Bloombergville had established, it was legal to sleep on the sidewalk as a form of political expression provided one left a corridor for passersby. A few intrepid souls had even tried to test the waters several weeks before, and put down sleeping bags opposite the Stock Exchange. They were immediately arrested, but after insisting on being brought before a judge had managed to secure a clear statement from that judge that their action was legal, and their arrest was not. Some insisted that with such a precedent the police would not dare arrest us for the very same act, in the very same place, a second time. Others pointed out that with the city already likely shelling out close to a million dollars for police overtime alone during an action of this sort, they were not likely to worry about spending twenty or thirty thousand more in false arrest settlements. They'd surely arrest us anyway.

When operating by consensus, a group does not vote, it works to create a compromise, or even better, a creative synthesis, that everyone can accept. So here. The pivotal point was when Mike, the anarchist veteran from Baltimore, made the following proposal.

"There seem to be two positions," he said.

"There seem to be two positions," the crowd answered.

"Either we stay in the park, or march on Wall Street."

"Either we stay in the park, or march on Wall Street."

"We don't know if they'll let us stay here overnight."

"We don't know if they'll let us stay here overnight."

"Clearly the thing the police want least is for us to march on Wall Street."

"Clearly the thing the police want least is for us to march on Wall Street."

"So I propose the following . . ."

"So I propose the following . . ."

"We make it known that we are going to occupy the square . . ."

"We make it known that we are going to occupy the square . . ."

"And if the police try to drive us out, that we will immediately march on Wall Street."

"And if the police try to drive us out, that we will immediately march on Wall Street."

After about a half an hour of swirling discussion, clarifications, and suggestions, we called for consensus around a proposal based on Mike's suggestion, and the group decided to do exactly that.

———

The real credit for what happened after that—within a matter of weeks, a movement that had spread to eight hundred different cities, with outpourings of support from radical opposition groups as far away as China—belongs mainly to the young people who so steadfastly dug themselves in and refused to leave, despite the endless (and in many cases, obviously illegal) acts of police repression designed to intimidate, and to make life so miserable in the park that its inhabitants would become demoralized and abandon the project—for example refusing to allow activists to cover their computers with tarps during rainstorms—and, eventually, calculated acts of terrorism involving batons and pepper spray. But dogged activists have held out heroically under such conditions before, from 1990s forest defense camps to as recently as Bloombergville, and the world simply ignored them.

I couldn't help but ask myself the same question my Egyptian friend Dina pondered after the overthrow of Mubarak's government:

Why didn't it happen this time? What did we finally do right?

TWO

WHY DID IT WORK?

Nevertheless one of us was prepared for what happened next. It was surprising enough that the police did not immediately evict the occupiers. We expected the most likely scenario was for hundreds of riot cops, backed up by horses and copters, to be unleashed against us that very night. This would certainly be in keeping with the style of the NYPD, whose usual strategy is to overwhelm protesters with sheer force of numbers. Yet in this case, someone made the decision to hold back.

One reason was the ambiguity of the legal situation: while public parks close by 12 P.M., Zuccotti Park was a public-private hybrid, owned by an investment firm, Brookfield Office Properties. Technically such "privately owned public properties" are accessible to the public twenty-four hours a day. Still, by our experience, the mere existence of such a law would have been of little relevance if the authorities decided they wanted to evict us anyway, but it allowed something of a fig leaf. But why did they even want a fig leaf?

At first, the police strategy was, instead, one of constant petty harassment, to make conditions so unpleasant we would eventually leave. "No tents" became "no tarps"; power was cut off; generators were appropriated; all forms of amplification were declared illegal, but mysterious construction projects involving jackhammers began all around us. While no one was arrested for sleeping in the park, protesters were made aware they could be arrested for almost anything else: on the very first day, when a small group marched to a nearby branch of Bank of America to chant slogans outside, two were arrested for having bandanas around their necks—on the basis of an obscure eighteenth-century masking law originally created to control Irish highwaymen in colonial New York. The fact that none of the protesters were actually wearing their bandanas as masks and the arrest was clearly illegal was irrelevant—or, depending on how you look at it, the entire point. The next day, police upped the ante by arresting two occupiers for writing slogans with chalk on the sidewalk. When onlookers pointed out that in New York it is not illegal to write with chalk on the sidewalk, the arresting officer remarked, "Yeah, I know."

The park continued to host thousands during the day, and hundreds remained at night. A community began to emerge, with a library and kitchen and free medical clinic, livestream video teams, arts and entertainment committees, sanitation squads, and so on. Before long there were thirty-two different working groups, ranging from an Alternative Currency group to a Spanish-language caucus. General Assemblies were held at 3 P.M. every day. Even more remarkably, other camps began springing up across America. They, too, created General Assemblies and tried to implement the hand signals and other means of operating by consensus-based direct democracy. Within a week or two there were at least a hundred, and within a month, purportedly, six hundred different occupations: Occupy Portland, Occupy Tuscaloosa, Occupy Phoenix, Occupy Cincinnati, Occupy Montreal.*

The occupiers were not only studiously nonviolent, at first their tactics, other than the encampment itself, consisted of little more than marching—though they began to expand to nonviolent civil disobedience with the famous blockade of the Brooklyn Bridge on October 2. Here is where the NYPD unleashed their traditional ferocity. This wasn't surprising: nonviolent protesters, in New York, as in most U.S. cities, even at legal but unpermitted events, can regularly expect to be physically attacked: anyone who strayed off the sidewalk, for example, could not only expect to be arrested, but, typically, slammed against the nearest vehicle, or have their heads repeatedly smacked against the concrete. Batons were used freely on unresisting marchers. All of this is standard fare and most of us protest veterans saw nothing particularly remarkable about it. What was unprecedented in this case was that some in the mainstream media, at first largely the cable media like MSNBC, but before long, even network news, began to notice and make an issue of it. This was in part because some of the camera phone videos of the police violence went viral on the Internet; before long, Tony Bologna, a police officer caught on

---

* It's hard to know how much to credit the six hundred figure—I think it's accurate, technically, but a number of the smaller "occupations" probably consisted of just one or two people.

video arbitrarily pepper-spraying two young women trapped behind a barricade, then casually sauntering away, became very close to a household name. But in the past, even such a viral video would never have made it onto the evening news.

As a result, our numbers grew dramatically. What's more, union support materialized* and rallies became larger and larger—instead of a couple thousand people coming to Zuccotti to rally or assemble for marches during the day, the crowds swelled to the tens of thousands. Thousands across America began trying to figure out how to send in contributions, and calling in an almost unimaginable wave of free pizzas. The social range of the occupiers also expanded: the crowd, which in the first few days was extremely white, soon diversified, so that within a matter of weeks we were seeing African-American retirees and Latino combat veterans marching and serving food alongside dreadlocked teenagers. There was a satellite General Assembly conducted entirely in Spanish. What's more, ordinary New Yorkers, thousands of whom eventually came to visit, if only out of curiosity, were astonishingly supportive: according to one poll, not only did majorities agree with the protests, 86 percent supported the protesters' right to maintain the encampment. Across the country, in just about every city in America, unlikely assortments of citizens began pitching tents, middle-aged office workers listened attentively to punk rockers or pagan priestesses lecturing on the subtleties of consensus and facilitation, or argued about

---

* Union support was only partly due to the media attention—there had been a long courtship with an emerging alliance of more radical union activists over the course of the summer, but the union leadership had decided to sit out September 17 itself.

the technical differences between civil disobedience and direct action or the truly horizontal way to organize sanitation.

In other words, for the first time in most of our living memories, a genuine grassroots movement for economic justice had emerged in America. What's more, the dream of contaminationism, of democratic contagion, was, shockingly, starting to work. Why?

Enough time has passed, I think, that we can begin to piece together some of the answers.

QUESTION 1

Why was the U.S. media coverage of OWS so different from virtually all previous coverage of left-wing protest movements since the 1960s?

There has been a lot of discussion about why the national media treated Occupy so differently from protest movements of the past—really, almost any since the 1960s. Much attention has been paid to social media, or perhaps a felt need for balance to compensate for the inordinate attention paid to relatively small numbers of Tea Partiers in the immediate years before. No doubt all these were factors, but then again, the media's initial portrayal of the Occupy protests was as airily dismissive as their portrait of what they dubbed the "Anti-Globalization Movement" in 1999: a collection of confused kids with no clear conception of what they were fighting for. *The New York Times,* the self-proclaimed paper of historical record, wrote absolutely nothing about the occupation for the first five days. On the sixth, they published an editorial disguised as a news story in the Metropolitan section, titled "Gunning for Wall Street, with Faulty Aim,"[1] by staff writer Ginia Bellafante, mocking the movement as a mere pantomime of progressivism with no discernible purpose.

Still, the media's eventual decision to take the protests seriously was pivotal. The rise of Occupy Wall Street marked, for perhaps the first time since the civil rights movement in the 1950s, a success for Gandhian tactics in America, a model that depends on a certain degree of sympathy from the media. Gandhian nonviolence is meant to create a stark moral contrast: it strips bare the inherent violence of a political order by showing that, even when faced by a band of nonviolent idealists, the "forces of order" will not hesitate to resort to pure physical brutality to defend the status quo. Obviously, this contrast can only be drawn if word gets out about what's happening, which has in the past rendered Gandhian tactics almost completely ineffective in the United States. Since the 1960s, the American mainstream media has refused to tell the story of *any* protest in a way that might imply that American police, acting under orders, engaged in "violence"—no matter what they do.*

One flagrant example was the treatment of tree sitters and their allies protecting old-growth forests in the 1990s in the Pacific Northwest. Activists attempted a campaign of classic Gandhian nonviolence by sitting in trees and daring developers to cut them down and "locking down"—that is, chaining

---

* Indeed, as I have noted elsewhere, it would be almost impossible for them to do so, since American journalists define the word "violence" as "the unauthorized use of force." Gandhi, I might add, succeeded in part because he had an old school friend who had become a prominent British journalist.

themselves together, or to bulldozers or other equipment, in ways that made them extremely difficult to remove, but at the same time left arms and legs incapacitated. When one tree sitter was killed and local police refused to order a murder investigation, activists locked down to blockade the scene to prevent evidence being destroyed. Police reacted by taking cotton swabs and rubbing cayenne pepper concentrate—otherwise known as pepper spray—directly in their eyeballs in amounts calculated to cause maximum physical pain. Apparently, however, the torture and murder of pacifists was not enough to convince most of the American media that police behavior was *necessarily* inappropriate, and local courts declared the application of pepper spray to eyeballs an acceptable tactic. Without coverage or legal recourse, the contradictions that Gandhian tactics are meant to bring out in the open were simply lost. The activists were tortured and killed without furthering Gandhi's aim of "quickening the conscience of the public" in any meaningful sense. In Gandhian terms, then, the protest failed. The next year other activists planned a campaign of lockdowns to blockade the WTO meetings in Seattle and veterans of forest defense campaigns warned them, correctly as it turned out, that police would simply attack and torture those in lockdown, all with an approving media looking on. And indeed this was precisely what happened. Many of the forest activists, in turn, played a key role in creating the famous Black Bloc that, after the predicted attacks had begun, struck back by a calculated campaign of smashing corporate windows—an act the media then used to justify the police attacks on nonviolent activists with batons, tear gas, plastic bullets, and pepper spray that had begun the day before. Yet as Black Bloc participants were quick to point out: they would have justified it anyway. Breaking some windows didn't hurt anyone, but it did succeed in putting the issue on the map.

This was the kind of history we were facing even before the wake of 9/11, when police assaults on nonviolent protesters became far more systematic and intense, as in the case of the New School occupation and other events. Nonetheless, in our planning assemblies for Occupy we decided to take a Gandhian approach. And somehow, this time it worked.

The conventional story is that the rise of social media made the difference: while activists at Seattle had made extensive use of web-based guerrilla reporting, by 2011 the omnipresence of phone cameras, Twitter accounts, Facebook, and YouTube ensured such images could spread instantly to millions. The image of Tony Bologna casually blasting two young women behind a barricade with a chemical weapon appeared almost instantly on screens across the nation (the most popular of the many camera phone uploads you can find on the Internet has well over a million views). I would hardly deny social media was important here, but it still doesn't explain why the mainstream media did not play its usual role of presenting only the official police point of view.

Here I think the international context is crucial. Another effect of the Internet is that in media terms, the United States is not nearly as much of an island as it once was. From the very beginning, international coverage of the protests was very different from American coverage. In the international press, there were no attempts to ignore, dismiss, or demonize the protesters. In the English-speaking world, *The Guardian* in England, for example, began producing detailed stories on the background and aspirations of the Occupiers almost from day one. Reporters from Al Jazeera, the satellite TV news network based in Qatar that played an instrumental role in the Arab Spring by airing videos and other testimony of state violence provided by grassroots activists through social media, quickly appeared on-site to play the same role in New York as it had in Cairo and Damascus. This led to wire stories in newspapers almost everywhere except America. These in turn not only helped inspire a wave of similar occupations as far away as Bahia and KwaZulu Natal, but sympathy protests in such unlikely places as China, organized by left-wing populist groups opposed to the Chinese Communist Party's embrace of Wall Street–friendly policies at home, who had learned of the events by monitoring foreign news services on the web.

On the very same day as the blockade of the Brooklyn Bridge on October 2, OWS received a message signed by fifty Chinese intellectuals and activists:

> The eruption of the "Wall Street Revolution" in the heart of the world's financial empire shows that 99% of the world's people remain exploited and oppressed—regardless of whether they are from developed or developing countries. People throughout the world see their wealth being plundered, and their rights being taken away. Economic polarization is now a common threat to all of us. The conflict between popular and elite rule is also found in all countries. Now, however, the popular democratic revolution meets repression not just from its own ruling class, but also from the world elite that has formed through globalization. The "Wall Street Revolution" has met with repression from U.S. police, but also suffers from a media blackout organized by the Chinese elite. . . .
>
> The embers of revolt are scattered amongst us all, wait-

ing to burn with the slightest breeze. The great era of popular democracy, set to change history, has arrived again![2]

The only plausible explanation for this kind of enthusiasm is
that dissident Chinese intellectuals, like most people in the
world, saw what happened in Zuccotti Park as part of a wave
of resistance sweeping the planet. Clearly, the global financial
apparatus, and the whole system of power on which it was
built, had been tottering since its near collapse in 2007. Everyone had been waiting for the popular backlash. Were the uprisings in Tunisia and Egypt the beginning? Or were those strictly
local or regional affairs? Then they began to spread. When the
wave hit the very "heart of the world's financial empire" no
one could deny that something epochal was happening.*

Now, this convergence between social media and international excitement explains why the U.S. media bubble could be
momentarily popped, but it isn't sufficient in itself to explain
why it actually was popped: why, CNN, for instance, eventually began treating the occupation as a major news story. The
U.S. media after all has a notorious history of concluding that
North American phenomena that nearly everyone else in the
world considers significant are of no interest to American audi-
ences. This is particularly true of figures on the left. Mumia
Abu-Jamal is a household name in France, but relatively un-
known in the United States. Or even more strikingly, Noam

---

* I remember a Taiwanese woman around 2000 who recalled her reaction
to watching the protests against the WTO in Seattle the year before. "I
had always assumed there must be decent people in America who tried
to fight what their country was doing to the rest of the world. I knew
they had to exist. But I'd never actually *seen* them."

Chomsky's political works are reviewed in mainstream news-papers and magazines in almost every country in the world except America.

Twenty years ago, one suspects that is exactly what the media would have concluded—that no one in America would care. I think when the future history of OWS is told, the media attention it garnered will be shown to owe much to the almost unprecedented attention so recently given to the right-wing populists of the Tea Party. The media's massive coverage of the Tea Party probably created some feeling that there should be a minimal gesture in the way of balance. Another factor in the media coverage was the existence of a few pockets of genuinely left-of-center media like MSNBC that were willing to latch on to OWS insofar as they thought the movement might morph into something along the lines of a left-wing Tea Party, that is, a political group that accepted funding, ran candidates, and pursued a legislative agenda. This at least would explain why, the moment it became fully clear that the movement was not about to go that route, media attention halted almost as abruptly as it had begun.

Still, none of this explains why, even before the mainstream media picked up the story, the movement spread so quickly inside America—including to places where Al Jazeera isn't even available.

QUESTION 2

Why did the movement spread so quickly across America?

When she wasn't helping with logistics and organizing facilita-tion trainings, Marisa Holmes spent much of her time during the early days of the occupation video-recording one-on-one interviews with fellow campers. Over and over, she heard the same story: "I did everything I was supposed to! I worked hard, studied hard, got into college. Now I'm unemployed, with no prospects, and $20,000 to $50,000 in debt." Some of these campers were from solidly middle-class families. More seemed children of relatively modest backgrounds who had worked their way into college by talent and determination, but whose lives were now in hock to the very financial industries that had trashed the world economy and found themselves entering a job market almost entirely bereft of jobs. Stories like this struck a chord with me, since I had been spending much of that summer giving lectures on the history of debt. I tried to keep my life as an author apart from my life as an activist, but I found it increasingly difficult, since every time I'd give a talk with an appreciable number of young people in attendance, at least one or two would approach me afterward to ask about the prospects of creating a movement over the issue of student loans. One of the themes of my work on debt was that its power lies in intense moral feelings it invokes, against the lenders and, more to the point, against the indebted themselves: the feelings of shame, disgrace, and violent indignation from being told, effectively, that one is the loser in a game no one forced one to play. Of course anyone who does not wish to spend the rest of their life as a dishwasher or sales clerk—in other words, in a job with no sorts of benefits, knowing one's life could be destroyed by a single unforeseen illness—has been led to believe that they have no choice but to pursue higher education in America, which means one effectively begins one's life as a debtor. And to begin one's life as a debtor is to be treated as if one already lost.

Some of the stories I heard during my tour were extraordinary. I particularly remember a grave young woman who approached me after a reading at a radical bookstore to tell me that though of modest origins, she had managed to work her way into a Ph.D. in Renaissance literature at an Ivy League college. The result? She was $80,000 in debt, with no immediate prospects of anything but adjunct work, which couldn't possibly cover her rent, let alone her monthly loan payments. "So you know what I ended up doing?" she asked me. "I'm an escort! It's pretty much the only way to get enough cash to be able to have any hope of getting out of this. And don't get me wrong, I don't regret the years I spent in graduate school for a moment, but you have to admit it's a little bit ironic."

"Yes," I said, "not to mention a remarkable waste of human resources."

Perhaps the image stuck to me because of my personal history—I often think I represent the last generation of working-class Americans who had any sort of realistic shot at joining the academic elite through sheer hard work and intellectual attainment (and even in my case it turns out to have been temporary). Partly because the woman's story brought home the degree to which debt is not only hardship, but degradation. After all, we all know what sort of people frequent expensive escorts in New York City. There was, right after 2008, a moment where it looked like Wall Street spending on cocaine and sexual services was going to have to be retrenched somewhat; but after the bailouts, like spending on expensive cars and jewelry, it appears to have rapidly shot up again. This woman was basically reduced to a situation where the only way she could pay her loans was to work fulfilling the sexual fantasies of the very people who had loaned her the money, and whose banks her family's tax dollars had just bailed out. What's more, her case was just an unusually dramatic example of a nationwide trend. For debt-strapped women in college (and remember, a growing majority of those seeking higher education in America today are women), selling one's body has become a growing—last, desperate—expedient to those who see no other way to finish their degree. The manager of one website that specializes in matching sugar daddies with those seeking help with student loans or school fees estimates he already has 280,000 college students registered. And very few of these are aspiring professors. Most aspire to little more than a modest career in health, education, or social services.[3]

It was stories like that I had in the back of my mind when I wrote a piece for *The Guardian* about why the Occupy movement had spread so quickly. The piece was meant to be part descriptive, part predictive:

> We are watching the beginnings of the defiant self-assertion of a new generation of Americans, a generation who are looking forward to finishing their education with no jobs, no future, but still saddled with enormous and unforgiveable debt. Most, I found, were of working class or otherwise modest backgrounds, kids who did exactly what they were told they should, studied, got into college, and are now not just being punished for it, but humiliated—faced with a life of being treated as deadbeats, moral reprobates. Is it really surprising they would like to have a word with the financial magnates who stole their future?
>
> Just as in Europe, we are seeing the results of colossal social failure. The occupiers are the very sort of people, brimming with ideas, whose energies a healthy society

would be marshalling to improve life for everyone. Instead
they are using it to envision ways to bring the whole system
down.[4]

The movement has diversified far beyond students and recent
graduates, but I think for many in the movement the concern
with debt and a stolen future remains a core motivation for
their involvement. It's telling to contrast the Occupy movement
in this way with the Tea Party, with which it is so often compared. Demographically, the Tea Party is at its core a movement of the middle-aged and well-established. According to
one poll in 2010, 78 percent of the Tea Partiers were over the
age of thirty-five, and about half of those, over fifty-five.[5] This
helps explain why Tea Partiers and occupiers generally take
a diametrically opposite view of debt. True, both groups objected in principle to government bailouts of the big banks, but
in the case of the Tea Partiers, this is largely rhetoric. The Tea
Party's real origins go back to a viral video of CNBC reporter
Rick Santelli speaking from the floor of the Chicago Mercan-
tile Exchange on February 19, 2009, decrying rumors that
the government might soon provide assistance to indebted
homeowners: "Do we really want to subsidize the losers' mortgages?" Santelli asked, adding, "This is America! How many
of you people want to pay for your neighbor's mortgage that
has an extra bathroom and can't pay their bills?" In other
words, the Tea Party originated as a group of people who at
least imagined themselves as creditors.

Occupy, in contrast, was and remains at its core a forward-
looking youth movement—a group of forward-looking people
who have been stopped dead in their tracks. They played according to the rules and watched the financial class completely

fail to play by the rules, destroy the world economy through fraudulent speculation, get rescued by prompt and massive government intervention, and, as a result, wield even greater power and be treated with even greater honor than before, while they are relegated to a life of apparently permanent humiliation. As a result, they were willing to embrace positions more radical than anything seen, on a mass scale, in America for generations: an explicit appeal to class politics, a complete reconstruction of the existing political system, a call (for many at least) not just to reform capitalism but to begin dismantling it entirely.

———

That a revolutionary movement emerged from such a situation is hardly new. For centuries now, revolutionary coalitions have always tended to consist of a kind of alliance between children of the professional classes who reject their parents' values, and talented children of the popular classes who managed to win themselves a bourgeois education, only to discover that acquiring a bourgeois education does not actually mean one gets to become a member of the bourgeoisie. You see the pattern repeated over and over, in country after country: Chou En-lai meets Mao Zedong, or Che Guevara meets Fidel Castro. U.S. counterinsurgency experts have long known the surest harbinger of revolutionary ferment in any country is the growth of a population of unemployed and impoverished college graduates: that is, young people bursting with energy, with plenty of time on their hands, every reason to be angry, and access to the entire history of radical thought. In the United States, you can add to these volatile elements the depredations of the student loan system, which ensures such budding revolutionaries can-

not fail to identify banks as their primary enemy, or to understand the role of the federal government—which maintains the
student loan program, and ensures that their loans will be held
over their heads forever, even in the event of bankruptcy—in
maintaining the banking system's ultimate control over every
aspect of their future lives. As *n+1*'s Malcolm Harris, who
writes frequently on generational politics in America, puts it:

> Today, student debt is an exceptionally punishing kind to
> have. Not only is it inescapable through bankruptcy, but
> student loans have no expiration date and collectors can
> garnish wages, social security payments, and even unem-
> ployment benefits. When a borrower defaults and the guar-
> anty agency collects from the federal government, the
> agency gets a cut of whatever it's able to recover from then
> on (even though they have already been compensated for
> the losses), giving agencies a financial incentive to dog for-
> mer students to the grave.[6]

It's also not surprising that, when the Great Recession that
we're still struggling through struck in 2008, young people
were its most dramatic victims. In fact, this generation's prospects were, in historical terms, uniquely bleak even before the
economy collapsed. The generation of Americans born in the late
1970s is the first in U.S. history to face the prospect of living
standards lower than their parents'. By 2006, this generation
was worse off than their parents at a similar age in almost
every register: they received lower wages and less benefits, were
more indebted, and are far more likely to be either unemployed
or in jail. Those who entered the workforce on finishing high
school could expect to find themselves lower-paying jobs than

their parents found, and ones that are far less likely to provide benefits (in 1989, almost 63.4 percent of high school graduates got jobs that provided health care; now, twenty years later, the number is 33.7 percent). Those that entered the workforce after finishing college or university found themselves with better jobs, back when there were jobs, but since the cost of higher education has been growing at a rate that outstrips any other commodity in U.S. history, larger and larger portions of this generation have been graduating with crippling levels of debt. In 1993, less than half of those who left college, left indebted. Now the proportion is over two thirds; basically, all but the very most financially elite.

The immediate effect of this was to destroy much of what was most valuable in the college experience itself, which had once been the only four years of genuine freedom in an American's life: a time to not only pursue truth, beauty, and understanding as values in themselves, but to experiment with different possibilities of life and existence. Now all of this was relentlessly subordinated to the logic of the market. Where once universities held themselves out as embodiments of the ancient ideal that the true purpose of wealth is to afford one the means and leisure to pursue knowledge and understanding of the world, now the only justification for knowledge was held to be to facilitate the pursuit of wealth. Those who insisted on treating college as anything but a calculated investment—those who, like my friend at the radical bookstore, had the temerity to wish to contribute to our understanding of the sensibilities of English Renaissance poetry despite an uncertain job market— were likely to do so at a terrible personal cost.

So the initial explanation for the spread of the movement is straightforward enough: a population of young people with a good deal of time, and every reason to be angry—and among whom the most creative, idealistic, and energetic tended to have reason to be angriest of all. Yet this was just the initial core. To become a movement it had to appeal to a much larger section of the population. And again, very quickly, this began to happen.

Here, too, we witnessed something extraordinary. Beyond students, the constituencies that rallied the most quickly were, above all, working class. This might not seem that surprising considering the movement's own emphasis on economic inequality; but in fact it is. Historically, those who have successfully appealed to class populism in the United States have done so largely from the right, and have focused on professors more than plutocrats. In the weeks just before the occupation, the blogosphere had been full of contemptuous dismissals of appeals for educational debt relief as the whining of pampered elitists.[7] And it's certainly true that historically the plight of the indebted college graduate would hardly be the sort of issue that would speak directly to the hearts of, say, members of New York City's Transit Workers Union. But this time it clearly did. Not only were the TWU's leaders some of the earliest and most enthusiastic endorsers of the occupation, with avid support from rank and file, they actually ended up suing the New York Police Department for commandeering their buses to conduct the mass arrest of OWS activists blocking the Brooklyn Bridge.* This leads to the third key question:

---

* I should note that there are other factors at play here. The TWU is historically an African-American union, and anti-intellectual populism is, in the United States, an almost exclusively white phenomenon, in no way shared by people of color or organizations representing them. But many unions with a largely white membership supported OWS, too.

QUESTION 3

Why would a protest by educated but indebted youth strike such a chord across working-class America—in a way that it almost certainly would not have in 1967, or even 1990?

Some of it, perhaps, lies in the fact that the lines between students and workers have somewhat blurred. Most students turn to paid employment at least at some point in their college careers. Furthermore, while the number of Americans entering college has grown considerably over the last twenty years, the number of graduates remains about the same; as a result, the ranks of the working poor are now increasingly filled with dropouts who couldn't afford to finish their degrees, still paying for those years they did attend, usually still dreaming of someday returning. Or who still carry on as best they can, juggling part-time jobs and part-time classes.[8]

When I wrote the story in *The Guardian*, the discussion section was full of the usual dismissive comments: these were a bunch of pampered children living off someone else's dime. One commentator was obsessed by the fact that several of the women protesters immortalized in press photos had pink hair. This was held out as proof that they existed in a bubble of privilege, apart from "real" Americans. One thing clear about such commentators was that they had never spent very much time in New York. Just as styles that were in the 1960s identified with hippies— long hair, hash pipes, ripped T-shirts—became, by the 1980s, a kind of uniform for casually employed working-class youth in much of small-town America, so has much of the style of the 1980s punk movement, pink hair, tattoos, piercings—come to play the same role today for the precarious, unsteadily employed, working class in America's great metropolises. One need only look around at the people preparing one's coffee, delivering one's packages, or moving one's furniture.

One reason the old 1960s antipathy between "hippies and hard hats" has dissolved into an uneasy alliance, then, is partly because cultural barriers have been overcome, and partly because of the changing composition of the working class itself, the younger elements of which are far more likely to be entangled in an increasingly exploitive and dysfunctional higher education system. But there is another, I suspect, even more critical element. This is the changing nature of capitalism itself.

There has been much talk in recent years about the financialization of capitalism, or even in some versions the "financialization of everyday life." In the United States and much of Europe, this has been accompanied by deindustrialization; the U.S. economy is no longer driven by exports, but by the consumption of products largely manufactured overseas, paid for by various forms of financial manipulation. This is usually spoken of in terms of the dominance of what's called the FIRE sector (Finance, Insurance, Real Estate) in the economy. For instance, the share of total U.S. corporate profits derived from finance alone has tripled since the 1960s:

1965	1970	1975	1980	1985	1990	1995	2000	2005
13%	15%	18%	17%	16%	26%	28%	30%	38%

Even this breakdown underestimates the numbers considerably, since it only counts nominally financial firms. In recent decades almost all manufacturers have gone into the finance business, and this accounts for much of their profits as well. The reason the auto industry collapsed during the financial meltdown of 2008, for example, was that companies like Ford and GM had by then for years been earning almost all of their profits not from making cars, but from financing them. Even GE earned about half its profits from its financial division. So while by 2005, 38 percent of total corporate profits derived from finance companies, the real number was probably more like half when you count the finance-related profits of companies whose ostensible business was nonfinancial. Meanwhile, only about 7 or 8 percent of all profits came from industry.*

When in 1953, GM chairman Charles Erwin Wilson coined the famous phrase "What's good for General Motors is good for America," it was taken in many quarters as the ultimate statement of corporate arrogance. In retrospect, it has become easier to see what he really meant. At that time, the auto industry generated enormous profits; the lion's share of the money that flowed into companies like GM and their executives was delivered directly to government coffers as taxes (the regular corporate tax rate under President Dwight Eisenhower was 52 percent, and the top personal tax rate, that applied for instance to corporate executives, 91 percent). At the time, the bulk of government revenue was derived from corporate taxes. High corporate taxes encouraged executives to pay higher wages (why not distribute the profits to one's workers, and at least gain the competitive advantage of grateful and loyal employees, if the government would otherwise take it anyway?); government used the tax revenue to build bridges, tunnels, and highways. These construction projects, in turn, not only bene-

---

* Technically the number is 12.5 percent, but again, this counts the financial divisions of manufacturing firms as "manufacturing" profits and not financial profit.

fited the auto industry, they created even more jobs, and gave government contractors the opportunity to enrich the politicians who distributed the booty with hefty bribes and kickbacks. The results might have been ecologically catastrophic, especially in the long term, but at the time, the relationship between corporate success, taxes, and wages seemed like a surefire engine for permanent prosperity and growth.

Half a century later we are clearly living in a different economic universe. The profits to be won from industry have shriveled. Wages and benefits have stagnated or declined; infrastructure is crumbling. However, in the 1980s when Congress eliminated the usury laws (opening the way to a world where U.S. courts and police served as enforcers to loans that can go as high as 300 percent annual interest, the sort of arrangements one could previously only make with organized crime), they also allowed almost any corporation to go into the finance business. The word "allowed" in the last sentence may strike you as strange, but it's important to understand that the language we typically use to describe this period is profoundly deceptive. For instance, we usually speak of changes in legislation surrounding finance as a matter of "deregulation," of the government stepping out of the way and letting corporations play the market however they like. Nothing can be further than the truth. By allowing any corporation to become part of the financial services industry, government was granting them the right to *create money*. This is because banks, and other lenders, do not, generally speaking, lend money they already have. They create the money by making loans. (This is the phenomenon Henry Ford was referring to when he made his famous comment that if the American people were ever to figure out how banking really works, "there would be a revolution before tomorrow morning." The Federal Reserve creates money and loans it to banks that are allowed to lend ten dollars for every one they hold as reserves; thus, effectively, allowing them to create money.) True, the financial divisions of car companies were limited to creating money that would be returned to them to buy their own cars, but the arrangement allowed them to derive hefty profits from interest, fees, and penalties, and eventually those finance-related profits dwarfed profits from the cars themselves.* At the same time, corporations like GM, GE, and the rest were, like the largest banks, in many cases paying no federal taxes at all. Insofar as their profits went to the government, it was given directly to politicians in the form of bribes—bribery having been renamed "corporate lobbying"—to convince them to enact further legislation, often written by the companies themselves, facilitating further extractions from citizens caught in their web of credit. And since the IRS was no longer receiving any appreciable amount of revenue from corporate taxes, the government, too, was increasingly in the business of extracting its money directly from citizens' personal incomes, or, in the case of now cash-strapped local governments, from a remarkably similar campaign of multiplying fees and penalties.[9]

If the relation between corporations and government in the 1950s bears little resemblance to the mythical "free market capitalism" on which America is supposed to be founded, in the case of current arrangements it's hard to see why we are still using the word "capitalism" at all.

Back when I was in college, I learned that capitalism was a

---

* Unless, that is, one prefers to see these charges, as many do, as a form of hidden inflation, again, authorized by government policy.

system where private firms earned profits by hiring others to produce and sell things; on the other hand, systems in which the big players simply extracted other people's wealth directly, by threat of force, were referred to as "feudalism."* By this definition, what we call "Wall Street" has come to look, increasingly, like a mere clearinghouse for the trading and disposal of feudal rents, or, to put it more crudely, scams and extortion, while genuine 1950s-style industrial capitalists are increasingly limited to places like India, Brazil, or Communist China. The United States does, of course, continue to have a manufacturing base, especially in armaments, medical technology, and farm equipment. Yet except for military production, these play an increasingly minor role in the generation of corporate profits.

With the crisis of 2008, the government made clear that not only was it willing to grant "too big to fail" institutions the right to print money, but to itself create almost infinite amounts of money to bail them out if they managed to get themselves into trouble by making corrupt or idiotic loans. This allowed institutions like Bank of America to distribute that newfound cash to the very politicians who voted to bail them out and, thus, secure the right to have their lobbyists write the very leg-

---

* Similarly, social theorist Max Weber argued that the "irrational political capitalism" of "military adventurers . . . tax farmers, speculators, money dealers, and others" of, say, the Roman world was a historical dead end, since it was ultimately parasitical off the state, and had nothing in common with the rational investment of production of modern industrial capitalism. By Weber's logic, contemporary global capitalism, which is dominated by speculators, currency traders, and government contractors, has long since reverted to the dead-end irrational variety.

islation that was supposed to "regulate them." This, despite having just nearly destroyed the world economy. It's not entirely clear why such firms should not, at this point, be considered *part* of the federal government, other than that they keep their profits for themselves.

Huge proportions of ordinary people's incomes end up going to feed this predatory system through hidden fees and, especially, penalties. I remember I once allowed a Macy's clerk to talk me into acquiring a Macy's charge card, in order to buy a $120 pair of Ray-Ban sunglasses. I sent in a check to pay the charge before leaving the country for an extended trip, but apparently miscalculated by some $2.75 when figuring the tax; when I returned a few months later, I discovered I had accrued something like $500 in late fees. We're not in the habit of calculating such numbers because they are, even more than debts, seen as the wages of sin: you only pay them because you did something wrong (in my case, miscalculate a math sum and neglect to have the bills forwarded to my overseas address). In fact, the entire system is now geared toward ensuring we make such mistakes, since the entire system of corporate profits depends on them.

How much of the average American's life income ends up getting passed to the financial services industry in the form of interest payments, fines, fees, service charges, insurance overhead, real estate finder's fees, and so on? No doubt a defender of the industry would insist some of these are payment for legitimate services—e.g., real estate finder's fees—but in many cases, these finder's fees are imposed even on renters who have found apartments themselves. The real estate sector has imposed laws making it effectively impossible to acquire an apartment without paying such a fee. If nothing else, it is clear that there has been a massive increase in such fees in recent decades without any notable increase or improvement in the services provided.

How much of a proportion of the average American family's income ends up funneled off to the financial services industry? Figures are simply not available. (This in itself tells you something, since figures are available on just about everything else.) Still, one can get a sense. The Federal Reserve's "financial obligations ratio" reports that the average American household shelled out roughly 18 percent of its income on servicing loans and similar obligations over the course of the last decade—it's an inadequate figure in many ways (it includes principal payments and real estate taxes, but excludes penalties and fees) but it gives something like a ballpark sense.

This already suggests most Americans are delivering as much as one dollar out of five they make directly to Wall Street in one form or another—that is, if you take "Wall Street" in its popular sense, as a code word for the financial sector as a whole. But of course "average Americans" don't really exist. The depredations of the financial industry fall very unevenly. First of all, while much of this money is simply pocketed by executives at financial companies (all those bankers' bonuses and so on), some gets redistributed in the form of dividends. Not to everyone, however. Before the crash there was a perception that everyone was in on the deal; that capitalism was becoming a popular enterprise where all Americans, through their investments and retirement accounts, got to own a piece of the action. This was always wildly overstated, and after the crash, when 401(k)s took an enormous hit, but large investors recovered quickly, you don't hear much of that anymore. No one can really deny that the profit system is still what it always was: a way of redistributing money to those already on the top of the chain. Wealthy Americans, even if they are not employed in the financial sector themselves, end up net winners. Pretty much everyone else has a certain proportion of their income siphoned off.

Those on the bottom of the financial food chain, on the other hand—and this is true any way you measure it, by race, gender, age, employment—invariably end up paying disproportionately more. In 2004, for example, those eighteen to twenty-four ended up paying 22 percent of their income on debt payments (this includes principal, but doesn't include service charges, fees, and penalties)—with about a fifth paying more than 40 percent—and for twenty-five- to thirty-four-year-olds, the cohort most impacted by student loans, things were even worse: they spent an average of a quarter of their income on debts. And these figures are true of younger Americans as a whole, regardless of education. We need hardly speak of the fate of that roughly 22 percent of American households so poor they have no access to conventional credit at all, who have to resort to pawn shops, auto title, or payday loan offices that charge as much as 800 percent annual interest.

And all this was true before the crash!

In the immediate wake of 2008 everyone in America who had any means to reduce their debt, and hence, the amount of their income siphoned off to Wall Street, immediately began to do so—whether by frenetically paying off credit card debt, or walking away from underwater mortgages. This might give a sense of how dramatic was the change:

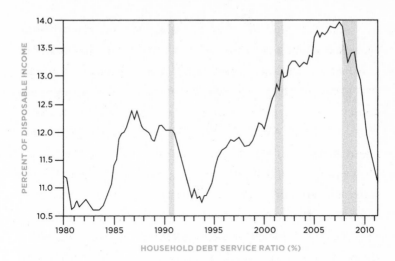

HOUSEHOLD DEBT SERVICE RATIO (%)

Yet at the same time, certain types of loans had been set up in such a way that this really wasn't possible. For example, while it's possible, if not easy, to renegotiate a mortgage,* student loans cannot be; in fact, if you so much as miss a few payments, you are likely to have thousands of dollars in penalties slapped onto the principal. As a result student loan debt continues to balloon at a giddy rate, the total amount owed having long since overtaken total credit card debt and other forms of debt as well:

TOTAL DEBT BALANCE AND ITS COMPOSITION

Mortgage	HE Revolving	Auto Loan	Credit Card	Student Loan	Other
72%	5%	6%	6%	8%	3%

* 2011Q3 Total: $11.656 Trillion

* Though in fact shockingly low percentages of mortgages actually were renegotiated, despite government programs purportedly put in place to facilitate this.

Aside from students, the other group stuck in the debt trap is the working poor—above all working women and people of color—who continue to see huge chunks of their already stagnating earnings culled directly by the financial services industry. They are often called the "subprimers," since they are those most likely to have signed up for (or been tricked into) subprime mortgages. Having fallen victim to subprime mortgages with exploding adjustable rates, they are now faced with being harassed by collectors, having their cars repossessed, and, most pernicious of all, having to resort to payday loans for emergency expenses, such as those related to health care, since these are the Americans least likely to have meaningful health benefits. Those paydays operate with annual interest rates of roughly 300 percent a year.

Americans in either of those overlapping categories—the working class and underemployed graduates with crippling student loans—are actually paying more of their income to Wall Street than they pay to the government in taxes.

Back in September, even before the occupation began, Chris—the Food Not Bombs activist who helped us create the first democratic circle in Bowling Green in August—set up a web page on tumblr called "We Are the 99 Percent," where supporters could post pictures of themselves, holding up a brief account of their life situations. At the time of this writing there are more than 125 pages of these, their authors varying enormously in race, age, gender, and just about everything else.

Recently there was an Internet discussion about the "ideology of the 99 percent" as revealed by these testimonies. It all began when Mike Konczal, of the blog Rortybomb, carried out a statistical analysis to determine the twenty-five most frequently used words in the html texts, and discovered that the most frequent was "job," the second, "debt," but that almost all the rest referred to necessities of life, homes, food, health care, education, children (after "job" and "debt," the next most popular words were: work, college, pay, student, loan, afford, school, and insurance). Glaringly absent was any reference to consumer goods. In trying to understand the implications, Konczal appealed to my own book on debt:

> Anthropologist David Graeber cites historian Moses Finley, who identified "the perennial revolutionary programme of antiquity, cancel debts and redistribute the land, the slogan of a peasantry, not of a working class." And think through these cases. The overwhelming majority of these statements are actionable demands in the form of (i) free us from the bondage of these debts and (ii) give us a bare minimum to survive on in order to lead decent lives (or, in pre-Industrial terms, give us some land). In Finley's terms, these are the demands of a peasantry, not a working class.[10]

Konczal saw this as a profound diminution of horizons: no longer are we hearing demands for workplace democracy, or dignity in labor, or even economic justice. Under this newly feudalized form of capitalism, the downtrodden are reduced to the situation of medieval peasants, asking for nothing more than the means to make their own lives. But as others soon pointed out, there was a certain paradox here, because ultimately the effect is not to diminish horizons, but to broaden them. Defenders of capitalism have always made the argument that while as an economic system it surely creates vast inequalities, its overall effect is a broad movement toward greater security and prosperity for everyone, even the humblest. We have reached the point where even in the richest capitalist nation on earth, the system cannot provide minimal life security, or even basic life necessities for increasing proportions of the population. It was hard to escape the conclusion that the only way to restore us to lives of minimal decency was to come up with a different system entirely.[11]

For my own part, the whole discussion might serve as a case study in the limits of statistical analysis. Not that such analysis isn't revealing in its own way, but it all depends on what you set out to count in the first place. When I read through the tumblr page for the first time, what really struck me was the predominance of women's voices, and the emphasis not just on acquiring the means for a decent life, but the means to be able to care for others. The latter was evident in two different aspects, actually. First was the fact that so many of those who chose to tell their stories worked in, or aspired to work in, a line of work that involved providing care for others: health care, education, community work, the provision of social services, and so on. Much of the terrible poignancy of so many of these accounts revolves around an unstated irony: that in America today, to seek a career that allows one to care for others usually means to end up in such straitened circumstances that one cannot properly care for one's own family. This is, of course, the second aspect. Poverty and debt have a very different meaning for those who build their lives around relationships with others: it is much more likely to mean being unable to provide birthday presents for one's daughter, or watching her develop symptoms of diabetes without being able to take her to a doctor, or watching one's mother die without ever having been able to take her off for a week or two of vacation, not even once in her life.

There was a time when the paradigmatic politically self-conscious working-class American was a male breadwinner working in an auto factory or steel mill. Now it is more likely to be a single mother working as a teacher or a nurse. Compared to men, women are more likely to enter college, more likely to finish college, *and* more likely to be poor, the three elements that often lead to greater political consciousness. Labor union participation still lags slightly: only 45 percent of union members are women, but if current trends continue, a majority will be women in eight years. Labor economist John Schmitt observes: "We've seen a big increase over the last quarter century of women in unions, particularly as the unionization of the service sector expands," he states. "The perception that unions are great for white guys in their 50s is false."[12]

Moreover, this convergence is beginning to change our very conceptions of work. Here I think Konczal got it wrong. It's not that the 99 percenters are not thinking about the dignity of labor. Quite the contrary. They are broadening our conception of meaningful work to include everything we do that isn't for ourselves.

QUESTION 4

Why did the movement refuse to make demands of or engage with the existing political system? And why did that refusal make the movement more compelling rather than less?

One would imagine that people in such a state of desperation would wish for some immediate, pragmatic solution to their dilemmas. Which makes it all the more striking that they were drawn to a movement that refused to appeal directly to existing political institutions at all.

Certainly this came as a great surprise to members of the corporate media, so much so that most refused to acknowledge what was happening right before their eyes. From the original, execrable, Ginia Bellafante piece in the *Times*, there has been an endless drumbeat coming from media of all sorts accusing the movement of a lack of seriousness, owing to its refusal to issue a concrete set of demands. Almost every time I'm interviewed by a mainstream journalist about Occupy Wall Street I get some variation of the same lecture:

> How are you going to get anywhere if you refuse to create a leadership structure or make a practical list of demands? And what's with all this anarchist nonsense—the consensus, the sparkly fingers? Don't you realize all this radical language is going to alienate people? You're never going to be able to reach regular, mainstream Americans with this sort of thing!

Asking why OWS refuses to create a leadership structure, and asking why we don't come up with concrete policy statements, is of course two ways of asking the same thing: Why don't we engage with the existing political structure so as to ultimately become a part of it?

If one were compiling a scrapbook of worst advice ever given, this sort of thing might well merit an honorable place. Since the financial crash of 2008, there have been endless attempts to kick off a national movement against the depredations of America's financial elites taking the approach such journalists recommended. All failed. Most failed miserably.* It

---

* One notorious example is an earlier call for an occupation of Zuccotti Park called by a group called Empire State Rebellion, to demand the

was only when a movement appeared that resolutely refused to take the traditional path, that rejected the existing political order entirely as inherently corrupt, that called for the complete reinvention of American democracy, that occupations immediately began to blossom across the country. Clearly, the movement did not succeed despite the anarchist element. It succeeded *because* of it.

For "small-a" anarchists such as myself—that is, the sort willing to work in broad coalitions as long as they work on horizontal principles—this is what we'd always dreamed of. For decades, the anarchist movement had been putting much of our creative energy into developing forms of egalitarian political process that actually work; forms of direct democracy that actually could operate within self-governing communities outside of any state. The whole project was based in a kind of faith that freedom is contagious. We all knew it was practically impossible to convince the average American that a truly democratic society was possible through rhetoric. But it was possible to show them. The experience of watching a group of a thousand, or two thousand, people making collective decisions without a leadership structure, motivated only by principle and solidarity, can change one's most fundamental assumptions about what politics, or for that matter, human life, could actually be like. Back in the days of the Global Justice Movement we thought that if we exposed enough people, around the world, to these new forms of direct democracy, and traditions of direct action, that a new, global, democratic culture would begin to emerge. But as noted above, we never really broke out

resignation of Federal Reserve chairman Ben Bernanke, on June 14, 2011. Four people showed up.

of the activist ghetto; most Americans never even knew that direct democracy was so central to our identity, distracted as they were by media images of young men in balaclavas breaking plate glass windows, and the endless insistence of reporters that the whole argument was about the merits of something they insisted on calling "free trade."* By the time of the antiwar movements after 2003, which mobilized hundreds of thousands, activism in America had fallen back on the old-fashioned vertical politics of top-down coalitions, charismatic leaders, and marching around with signs. Many of us diehards kept the faith. After all, we had dedicated our lives to the principle that something like this would eventually happen. But we had also, in a certain way, failed to notice that we'd stop really believing that we could actually win.

And then it happened. The last time I went to Zuccotti Park, before the eviction, and watched a sprawling, diverse group that ranged from middle-aged construction workers to young artists using all our old hand signals in mass meetings, my old friend Priya, the tree sitter and eco-anarchist now established in the park as a video documentarian, admitted to me, "Every few hours I do have to pinch myself to make sure it isn't all a dream."

* The term "free trade" is, like "free market" and "free enterprise," an obvious propaganda term. What the movement was in fact opposed to was the creation of the world's first effective planetary administrative bureaucracy—ranging from the IMF, World Bank, WTO, and similar bodies to those created by treaties like the European Union or NAFTA—ostensibly to regulate and facilitate global trade. Or even more specifically, the fact that such bodies were, effectively, democratically unaccountable and covers for financial imperialism and global plunder. My own take on the movement can be found in *Direct Action: An Ethnography* (Oakland: AK Press, 2009).

So this is the ultimate question: not just why an anti–Wall Street movement finally took off—to be honest, for the first few years after the 2008 collapse, many had been scratching their heads over why one hadn't—but why it took the form it did? Again, there are obvious answers. Once thing that unites almost everyone in America who is not part of the political class, whether right or left, is a revulsion of politicians. "Washington" in particular is perceived to be an alien bubble of power and influence, fundamentally corrupt. Since 2008, the fact that Washington exists to serve the purposes of Wall Street has become almost impossible to ignore. Still, this does not explain why so many were drawn to a movement that comprehensively rejected existing political institutions of any sort.

————

I think the answer is once again generational. The refrain of the earliest occupiers at Zuccotti Park when it came to their financial, educational, and work lives was: "I played by the rules. I did exactly what everyone told me I was supposed to do. And look where that got me!" Exactly the same could be said of these young people's experience of politics.

For most Americans in their early twenties, their first experience of political engagement came in the elections of 2006 and 2008, when young people turned out in roughly twice the numbers they usually did, and voted overwhelmingly for the Democrats. As a candidate, Barack Obama ran a campaign carefully designed to appeal to progressive youth, with spectacular results. It's hard to remember that Obama not only ran as a candidate of "Change," but used language that drew liberally from that of radical social movements ("Yes we can!" was adapted from César Chávez's United Farm Workers movement,

"Be the change!" is a phrase often attributed to Gandhi), and that as a former community organizer, and member of the left-wing New Party, he was one of the few candidates in recent memory who could be said to have emerged from a social movement background rather than from the usual smoke-filled rooms. What's more, he organized his grassroots campaign much like a social movement; young volunteers were encouraged not just to phone-bank and go door-to-door but to create enduring organizations that would continue to work for progressive causes—support strikes, create food banks, organize local environmental campaigns—long after the election. All this, combined with the fact that Obama was to be the first African-American president, gave young people a sense that they were participating in a genuinely transformative moment in American politics.

No doubt most of the young people who worked for, or supported, the Obama campaign were uncertain just how transformative all this would be. But most were ready for genuinely profound changes in the very structure of American democracy. Remember that all this was happening in a country where there is such a straitjacket on acceptable political discourse—what a politician or media pundit can say without being written off as a member of the lunatic fringe—that the views of very large segments of the American public simply are never voiced at all. To give a sense of how radical is the disconnect between acceptable opinion, and the actual feelings of American voters, consider a pair of polls conducted by Rasmussen, the first in December 2008, right after Obama was elected, the second in April 2011. A broad sampling of Americans was asked which economic system they preferred: capitalism or socialism? In 2008, 15 percent felt the United States would be better off adopting a socialist system; three years later, the number had gone up, to one in five. Even more striking was the breakdown by age: the younger the respondent, the more likely they were to object to the idea of spending the rest of their lives under a capitalist system. Among Americans between fifteen and twenty-five, a plurality did still prefer capitalism: 37 percent, as opposed to 33 percent in favor of socialism. (The remaining 30 percent remained unsure.) But think about what this means here. It means that almost two thirds of America's youth are willing to at least consider the idea of jettisoning the capitalist system entirely! In a country where most have never seen a single politician, TV pundit, or talking head willing to reject capitalism in principle, or to use the term "socialism" as anything but a term of condescension and abuse, this is genuinely extraordinary. Granted, for that very reason, it's hard to know exactly what young people who say they prefer "socialism" actually think they're embracing. One has to assume: not an economic system modeled on that of North Korea. What then? Sweden? Canada? It's impossible to say. But in a way it's also beside the point. Most Americans might not be sure what socialism is supposed to be, but they do know a great deal about capitalism, and if "socialism" means anything to them, it means "the other thing," or perhaps better, "*something*, pretty much anything, really, as long as it isn't that!" To get a sense of just how extreme matters have become, another poll asked Americans to choose between capitalism and communism—and one out of ten Americans actually stated they would prefer a Soviet-style system to the economic system existing today.

In 2008, young Americans preferred Obama to John McCain by a rate of 68 percent to 30 percent—again, an approximately two-thirds margin.

It seems at the very least reasonable to assume that most young Americans who cast their votes for Obama expected a little more than what they got. They felt they were voting for a transformative figure. Many did clearly expect some kind of fundamental change in the system, even if they weren't sure what. How, then, might one expect such a young American voter to feel on discovering that they had in fact elected a moderate conservative?

This might seem an extreme statement by the standards of mainstream political discourse but I'm really just using the word "conservative" in the literal sense of the term. That literal sense is now rarely used. Nowadays, in the United States at least, "conservative" has mainly come to be used for "right-wing radical," whereas its long-standing literal meaning was "someone whose main political imperative is to conserve existing institutions, to protect the status quo." This is precisely what Obama has turned out to be. Almost all his greatest political efforts have been aimed at preserving some institutional structure under threat: the banking system, the auto industry, even the health insurance industry. Obama's main argument in calling for health care reform was that the existing system, based on for-profit private insurers, was not economically viable over the long term, and that some kind of change was going to be necessary. What was his solution? Instead of pushing a genuinely radical—or even liberal—restructuring of the system toward fairness and sustainability, he instead revived a Republican model first proposed in the 1990s as the conservative alternative to the Clintons' universal health plan. That model's details were hammered out in right-wing think tanks like the Heritage Foundation and initially put into practice by a Republican governor of Massachusetts. Its appeal was essentially conservative: it didn't solve the problem of how to create a fair and sensible health care system; it solved the problem of how to preserve the existing unfair and unsustainable for-profit system in a form that might allow it to endure for at least another generation.

Considering the state of crisis the U.S. economy was in when Obama took over in 2008, it required perversely heroic efforts to respond to a historic catastrophe by keeping everything more or less exactly as it was. Yet Obama did expend those heroic efforts, and the result was that, in every dimension, the status quo did indeed remain intact. No part of the system was shaken up. There were no bank nationalizations, no breakups of "too big to fail" institutions, no major changes in finance laws, no change in the structure of the auto industry, or of any other industry, no change in labor laws, drug laws, surveillance laws, monetary policy, education policy, transportation policy, energy policy, military policy, or—most crucially of all, despite campaign pledges—the role of money in the political system. In exchange for massive infusions of money from the country's Treasury to rescue them from ruin, industries from finance to manufacturing to health care were required to make only marginal changes to their practices.

The "progressive community" in the United States is defined by left-leaning voters and activists who believe that working through the Democratic Party is the best way to achieve political change in America. The best way to get a sense of their current state of mind, I find, is to read discussions on the liberal blog Daily Kos. By the third year of Obama's first term, the level of rage—even hatred—directed against the president on this blog was simply extraordinary.* He was regularly accused of being a fraud, a liar, a secret Republican who had intentionally flubbed every opportunity for progressive change presented to him in the name of "bipartisan compromise." The intensity of the hatred many of these debates revealed might seem surprising, but it makes perfect sense if you consider that these were people passionately committed to the idea it *should* be possible for progressive policies to be enacted in the United States through electoral means. Obama's failure to do so would seem to leave one with little choice but to conclude that any such project is impossible. After all, how could there have been a more perfect alignment of the political stars than there was in 2008? That year saw a wave election that left Democrats in control of both houses of Congress, a Democratic president elected on a platform of "Change" coming to power at a moment of economic crisis so profound that radical measures of some sort were unavoidable, and at a time when Republican economic policies were utterly discredited and popular rage against the nation's financial elites was so intense that most Americans would have supported almost any policy directed against them. Polls at the time indicated that Americans were overwhelmingly in favor of bailing out mortgage holders, but not bailing out "too big to fail" banks, whatever the negative impact on the economy. Obama's position here was not only the opposite, but actually more conservative than George W.

---

* This began to change somewhat when the presidential election campaign began to kick into gear, because of the lack of specific legislative issues and the specter of a Republican victory, but also, I suspect, because so many progressives stopped following electoral politics entirely.

Bush's: the outgoing Bush administration did agree, under pressure from Democratic representative Barney Frank, to include mortgage write-downs in the TARP program, but only if Obama approved. He chose not to. It's important to remember this because a mythology has since developed that Obama opened himself up to criticism that he was a radical socialist because he went too far; in fact, the Republican Party was a spent and humiliated force, and only managed to revive itself because the Obama administration refused to provide an ideological alternative and instead adopted most of the Republicans' economic positions.

Yet no radical change was enacted; Wall Street gained even greater control over the political process, the "progressive" brand was tainted in most voters' minds by becoming identified with what were inherently conservative, corporate-friendly positions, and since Republicans proved the only party willing to take radical positions of any kind, the political center swung even further to the right. Clearly, if progressive change was not possible through electoral means in 2008, it simply isn't going to be possible at all. And that is exactly what very large numbers of young Americans appear to have concluded.

The numbers speak for themselves. Where youth turnout in 2008 was three times what it had been four years before, two years after Obama's election, it had already dropped by 60 percent. It's not so much that young voters switched sides—those who showed up continued to vote for the Democrats at about the same rate as before—as that they gave up on the process altogether,* allowing the largely middle-aged Tea Partiers to

---

* In Illinois, to cite a typical example, 54 percent of voters over thirty turned out in 2010, but only 23 percent of those under thirty.

dominate the election, and the Obama administration, in reaction, to compliantly swing even further to the right.

So in civic affairs as in economic ones, a generation of young people had every reason to feel they'd done exactly what they were supposed to do according to the rulebook—and got worse than nothing. What Obama had robbed them of was precisely the thing he so famously promised: hope—hope of any meaningful change via institutional means in their lifetimes. If they wanted to see their actual problems addressed, if they wanted to see any sort of democratic transformation in America, it was going to have to be through other means.

QUESTION 5

But why an explicitly revolutionary movement?

Here we come to the most challenging question of all. It's clear that one of the main reasons OWS worked was its very radicalism. In fact, one of the most remarkable things about it is that it was not just a popular movement, not even just a radical movement, but a revolutionary movement. It was kicked off by anarchists and revolutionary socialists—and in the earliest meetings, when its basic themes and principles were first being hammered down, the revolutionary socialists were actually the more conservative faction. Mainstream allies regularly try to soft-pedal this background; right-wing commentators often inveigh that "if only" ordinary Americans understood who the originators of OWS were, they would scatter in revulsion. In fact, there is every reason to believe that not only are Americans far more willing to entertain radical solutions, on either side of the political spectrum, than its media and official opinion makers are ever willing to admit, but that it's precisely OWS's most revolutionary aspects—its refusal to recognize the legitimacy of the existing political institutions, its willingness to challenge the fundamental premises of our economic system— that is at the heart of its appeal.

Obviously, this raises profound questions of who the "mainstream opinion makers really are" and what the mainstream media is for. In the United States, what is put forth as respectable opinion is largely produced by journalists, particularly TV journalists, newspaper columnists, and popular bloggers working for large platforms like *The Atlantic* or *The Daily Beast*, who usually present themselves as amateur sociologists, commenting on the attitudes and feelings of the American public. These pronouncements are often so bizarrely off base that one has to ask oneself what's really going on. One example that has stuck in my head: after the 2000 George W. Bush–Al Gore election was taken to the courts there was immediate and overwhelming consensus among the punditocracy that "the American people" did not want to see a long drawn-out process, but wanted the matter resolved, one way or another, as quickly as possible. But polls soon appeared revealing that in fact the American people wanted the exact opposite: overwhelming majorities, rather sensibly, wished to know who had really won the election, however long it took to find out. This had virtually no effect on the pundits, who simply switched gears to saying that though what they had declared might not be true yet, it definitely would be soon (especially, of course, if opinion makers like themselves kept incessantly flogging away at it).

These are the same purveyors of conventional wisdom who contorted themselves to misread the elections of 2008 and

2010. In 2008, in the midst of a profound economic crisis, we saw first a collapse of a disillusioned Republican base and the emergence of a wave of young voters expecting radical change from the left. When no such change materialized and the financial crisis continued, the youth and progressive vote collapsed and a movement of angry middle-aged voters demanding even more radical change on the right emerged. The conventional wisdom somehow figured out a way to interpret these serial calls for radical change in the face of a clear crisis as evidence that Americans are vacillating centrists. It is becoming increasingly obvious, in fact, that the role of the media is no longer to tell Americans what they should think, but to convince an increasingly angry and alienated public that their neighbors have not come to the same conclusions. The logic is much like that used to dissuade voters from considering third parties: even if the third-party challenger states opinions shared by the majority of Americans, Americans are constantly warned not to "waste their vote" for the candidate that actually reflects their views because no one else will vote for that candidate.* It's hard to imagine a more obvious case of a self-fulfilling prophecy. The result is a mainstream ideology—a kind of conservative centrism that assumes what's important is always moderation and the maintenance of the status quo—which almost no one actually holds (except of course the pundits them-

---

* I heard this trick done endlessly with Ralph Nader: during campaigns, there is almost no discussion or even description of his positions, but merely warnings that a vote for Nader is a vote for the Republican candidate. Afterward, his positions are treated as if they represented the opinions of 2.7 percent of the American public (the percentage of the popular vote he received in 2000).

selves), but which everyone, nonetheless, suspects that everyone else does.

It seems reasonable to ask, How did we get here? How did there come to be such an enormous gap between the way so many Americans actually viewed the world—including a population of young people, most of whom were prepared to contemplate jettisoning the capitalist system entirely—and the opinions that could be expressed in its public forums? Why do the human stories revealed on the We Are the 99% tumblr never seem to make it to the TV, even in (or especially in) "reality" television? How, in a country that claims to be a democracy, did we arrive at a situation where—as the occupiers stressed—the political classes seem unwilling to even talk about the kind of issues and positions ordinary Americans actually held?

To answer the question we need to take a broader historical perspective.

Let's step back and revisit the question of financialization discussed earlier. The conventional story is that we have moved from a manufacturing-based economy to one whose center of gravity is the provision of financial services. As I've already observed, most of these are hardly "services." Former Fed chairman (under Carter and Reagan) Paul Volcker put the reality of the matter succinctly when he noted that the only "financial innovation" that actually benefited the public in the last twenty-five years was the ATM machine. We are talking little more than an elaborate system of extraction, ultimately backed up by the power of courts, prisons, and police and the government's willingness to grant to corporations the power to create money.

How does a financialized economy operate on an international level? The conventional story has it that the United

States has evolved from being a manufacturing-based economy, as in the 1950s, 1960s, and 1970s when the country exported consumer goods like cars, blue jeans, and televisions to the rest of the world, to being a net importer of consumer goods and exporter of financial services. But if these "services" are not really "services" at all, but government-sponsored credit arrangements enforced by the power of courts and police—then why would anyone not under the jurisdiction of U.S. law agree to go along with it?

The answer is that in many ways, they *are* under the jurisdiction of U.S. law. This is where we enter into territory that is, effectively, taboo for public discussion. The easiest way to illustrate might be to make note of the following facts:

- The United States spends more on its military than all other countries on earth combined. It maintains at least two and a half million troops in 737 overseas military bases, from Paraguay to Tajikistan, and, unlike any other military power in history, retains the power to direct deadly force anywhere on earth.
- The U.S. dollar is the currency of global trade, and since the 1970s has replaced gold as the reserve currency of the global banking system.
- Also since the 1970s, the United States has come to run an ever-increasing trade deficit whereby the value of products flowing into America from abroad far outweighs the value of those America sends out again.

Set these facts out by themselves, and it's hard to imagine they could be entirely unrelated. And indeed, if one looks at the matter in historical perspective, one finds that for centuries the world trade currency has always been the money of the dominant military power, and that such military powers always have more wealth flowing into them from abroad than they send out again.* Still, the moment one begins to speculate on the actual connections between U.S. military power, the banking system, and global trade, one is likely to be dismissed— in respectable circles, at least—as a paranoid lunatic.

That is, in America. In my own experience, the moment one steps outside the U.S. (or perhaps certain circles in the U.K.), even in staunch U.S. allies like Germany, the fact that the world's financial architecture was created by, and is sustained by, U.S. military power is simply assumed as a matter of course. This is partly because people outside the United States have some knowledge of the relevant history: they tend to be aware, for instance, that the current world financial architecture, in which U.S. Treasury bonds serve as the principal reserve currency, did not somehow emerge spontaneously from the workings of the market but was designed during negotiations between the Allied powers at the Bretton Woods conference of 1944. In the end, the U.S. plan prevailed, despite the strenuous objections of the British delegation, led by John Maynard Keynes.† Like the "Bretton Woods institutions" (the IMF, World Bank) that were created at that same conference to back

---

* I am simplifying. Imperial states, like the British empire or U.S. postwar system, tend to shift over time from being industrial powers to financial powers. What I say here becomes especially true in the latter phases. I discuss this below.

† Keynes's model for an international currency named the "bancor" would have led to a very different system where instead of the monetization of war debt, the international monetary system would be based on the recycling of trade surpluses. There have been occasional sugges-

up the system, these were political decisions, established by military powers, which created the institutional framework in which what we call the "global market" has taken shape.

So how does it work?

The system is endlessly complicated. It has also changed over time. For most of the Cold War, for instance, the effect (aside from getting U.S. allies to largely underwrite the Pentagon) was to keep cheap raw materials flowing into the United States to maintain America's manufacturing base. But as economist Giovanni Arrighi, following the great French historian Fernand Braudel, has pointed out, that's how empires have tended to work for the last five hundred years or so: they start as industrial powers, but gradually shift to "financial" powers, with the economic vitality in the banking sector.[13] What this means in practice is that the empires come to be based more and more on sheer extortion—that is, unless one really wishes to believe (as so many mainstream economists seem to want us to) that the nations of the world are sending the United States their wealth, as they did to Great Britain in the 1890s, because they are dazzled by its ingenious financial instruments. Really, the United States manages to keep cheap consumer goods flowing into the country, despite the decline of its export sector, by dint of what economists like to call "seigniorage"—which is economic jargon for "the economic advantage that accrues from being the one who gets to decide what money is."

There is a reason, I think, why most economists like to ensure such matters are shrouded in jargon that most people don't understand. The real workings of the system are almost

---

tions of reviving the idea, most recently right around 2008–2009, by then IMF chief Dominique Strauss-Kahn.

the exact opposite of the way they are normally presented to the public. Most public discourse on the deficit treats money as if it were some kind of preexisting, finite substance: like, say, petroleum. It's assumed there's only so much of it, and that government must acquire it either through taxes or by borrowing it from someone else. In reality the government—through the medium of the Federal Reserve—creates money *by* borrowing it. Far from being a drag on the U.S. economy, the U.S. deficit—which largely consists of U.S. war debt—is actually what drives the system. This is why (aside from one brief and ultimately disastrous period of a few years under Andrew Jackson in the 1820s) there has always been a U.S. debt. The American dollar is essentially circulating government debt. Or to be even more specific, war debt. This again has always been true of central banking systems at least back to the foundation of the Bank of England in 1694. The original U.S. national debt was the Revolutionary War debt, and there were great debates at first over whether to monetize it, that is, to eliminate the debt by increasing the money supply. My conclusion that U.S. deficits are almost exclusively due to military spending is derived from a calculation of real military spending as roughly half of federal spending (one has to include not only Pentagon spending but the cost of wars, the nuclear arsenal, military benefits, intelligence, and that portion of debt servicing that is derived from military borrowing), which is, of course, contestable.*

The Bretton Woods decision was, essentially, to interna-

---

* I tell the story in somewhat greater detail in *Debt: The First 5,000 Years*, where among other things, I note that the curve of growth in military spending, and growth in overseas debt, almost perfectly correspond.

tionalize this system: to make U.S. Treasury bonds (again, basically U.S. war debt) the basis of the international financial system. During the Cold War, U.S. military protectorates like West Germany would buy up enormous numbers of such T-bonds and hold them at a loss so as to effectively fund the U.S. bases that sat on German soil (the economist Michael Hudson notes that, for instance, in the late 1960s, the United States actually threatened to pull its forces out of West Germany if its central bank tried to cash in its Treasury bonds for gold[14]); similar arrangements seem to exist with Japan, South Korea, and the Gulf States today. In such cases we are talking about something very much like an imperial tribute system— it's just that, since the United States prefers not to be referred to as an "empire," its tribute arrangements are dressed up as "debt." Just outside the boundaries of U.S. military control, the arrangements are more subtle: for instance, in the relationship between the United States and China, where China's massive purchase of T-bonds since the 1990s seems to be part of a tacit agreement whereby China floods the United States with vast quantities of underpriced consumer goods, on a tab they're aware the United States will never repay, while the United States, for its part, agrees to turn a blind eye to China systematically ignoring intellectual property law.

Obviously the relationship between China and the United States is more complex and, as I've argued in other work, probably draws on a very ancient Chinese political tradition of flooding dangerously militaristic foreigners with wealth as a way of creating dependency. But I suspect the simplest explanation of why China is willing to accept existing arrangements is just that its leadership were trained as Marxists, that is, as historical materialists who prioritize the realities of material infrastructure over superstructure. For them, the niceties of financial instruments are clearly superstructure. That is, they observe that, whatever else might be happening, they are acquiring more and more highways, high-speed train systems, and high-tech factories, and the United States is acquiring less and less of them, or even losing the ones they already have. It's hard to deny that the Chinese may be onto something.

I should emphasize it's not as if the United States no longer has a manufacturing base: it remains preeminent in agricultural machinery, medical and information technology, and above all, the production of high-tech weapons. What I am pointing out, rather, is that this manufacturing sector is no longer generating much in the way of profits; rather, the wealth and power of the 1 percent has come to rely increasingly on a financial system that is ultimately dependent on U.S. military might abroad, just as at home it's ultimately dependent on the power of the courts (and hence, by extension, of repossession agencies, sheriffs, and the police). Within Occupy, we have begun to refer to it simply as "mafia capitalism": with its emphasis on casino gambling (in which the games are fixed), loan-sharking, extortion, and systematic corruption of the political class.

Is this system viable over the long term? Surely not. No empire lasts forever, and the U.S. empire has lately been—as even its own apologists have come to admit of late—coming under considerable strain.

One telling sign is the end of the "Third World debt crisis." For about a quarter century, the United States and its European allies, acting through international agencies such as the IMF, took advantage of endless financial crises among the poorer countries of Asia, Africa, and Latin America to impose a mar-

ket fundamentalist orthodoxy—which invariably meant slash-
ing social services, reallocating most wealth to 1 percent of the
population, and opening the economy to the "financial services" industry. These days are over. The Third World fought
back: a global popular uprising (dubbed by the media the
"anti-globalization movement") made such an issue out of
such policies that by 2002 or 2003, the IMF had been effectively kicked out of East Asia and Latin America, and by 2005
was itself on the brink of bankruptcy. The financial crisis of
2007 and 2008, which struck as U.S. military forces remained
embarrassingly quagmired in Iraq and Afghanistan, has led,
for the first time, to a serious international discussion of
whether the dollar should remain the international reserve currency. At the same time, the formula the major powers once
applied to the Third World—declare a financial crisis, appoint
a supposedly neutral board of economists to slash social services, reallocate even more wealth to the richest 1 percent, and
open the economy to even more pillaging by the financial services industry—is now being applied at home, from Ireland
and Greece to Wisconsin and Baltimore. The response to the
crisis coming home, in turn, has been a wave of democratic
insurrections, beginning in U.S. client states in the Middle East,
and rapidly spreading north across the Mediterranean and on
to North America.

The remarkable thing is that the closer the insurrectionary
wave spread to the center of power, to the "heart of the world's
financial empire" as our Chinese friends put it, the more radical the claims became. The Arab revolts included every sort of
people, from Marxist trade unionists to conservative theologians, but at their core was a classically liberal demand for a
secular, constitutional republic that allowed for free elections

and respected human rights. The occupiers in Greece, Spain, Israel were more often than not studiously anti-ideological— though some were more radical than others (anarchists played a particularly central role in Athens, for example). They insisted that they were focusing on very specific issues of corruption and government accountability, and thus appealed to perspectives across the political spectrum. It was in the United States that we saw a movement kicked off by revolutionaries that began by posing a direct challenge to the very nature of the economic system.

In part, this is simply because Americans really had no one else to blame. An Egyptian, a Tunisian, a Spaniard, a Greek, can all see the political and economic arrangements under which they live—whether U.S.-supported dictatorships, or governments completely subordinate to the reign of finance capital and free market orthodoxy—as something that's been imposed on them by outside forces, and which therefore could, conceivably, be shrugged off without a radical transformation of society itself. Americans have no such luxury. We did this to ourselves.

Or, alternately, if we did not do this to ourselves, we have to rethink the whole question of who "we" are. The idea of "the 99 percent" was the first step toward doing this.

A revolutionary movement does not merely aim to rearrange political and economic relations. A real revolution must always operate on the level of common sense. In the United States, it was impossible to proceed in any other way. Let me explain.

Earlier I pointed out that the U.S. media increasingly serves less to convince Americans to buy into the terms of the existing political system than to convince them that everyone does. This is true however only to a certain level. On a deeper level, there are very fundamental assumptions about what politics is, or could be, what society is, what people are basically like and what they want from the world. There's never absolute consensus here. Most people are operating with any number of contradictory ideas about such questions. But still, there is definitely a center of gravity. There are a lot of assumptions that are buried very deep.

In most of the world, in fact, people talk about America as the home of a certain philosophy of political life, which involves, among other things, that we are basically economic beings: that democracy *is* the market, freedom is the right to participate in the market, that the creation of an ever-growing world of consumer abundance is the only measure of national success. In most parts of the world this has come to be known as "neoliberalism," and it is seen as one philosophy among many, and its merits are a matter of public debate. In America we never really use the word. We can only speak about such matters through propaganda terms: "freedom," "the free market," "free trade," "free enterprise," "the American way of life." It's possible to mock such ideas—in fact, Americans often do—but to challenge the underlying foundations requires radically rethinking what being an American even means. It is necessarily a revolutionary project. It is also extraordinarily difficult. The financial and political elites running the country have put all their chips in the ideological game; they have spent a great deal more time and energy creating a world where it's almost more impossible to question the idea of capitalism than to create a form of capitalism that is actually viable. The result is that as our empire and economic system chokes and stumbles and shows all signs of preparing to give way all around us, most of us are left dumbfounded, unable to imagine that any-thing else could possibly exist.

———

One might object here: didn't Occupy Wall Street begin by challenging the role of money in politics—because, as that first flyer put it, "both parties govern in the name of the 1%," which has essentially bought out the existing political system? This might explain the resistance to working within the exist-ing political structure, but one might also object: in most parts of the world, challenging the role of money in politics is the quintessence of reformism, a mere appeal to the principle of good governance that would otherwise leave everything in place. In the United States, however, this is not the case. The reason tells us everything, I think, about what this country is and what it has become.

QUESTION 6

Why is it that in America, challenging the role of money in poli-tics is by definition a revolutionary act?

The principle behind buying influence is that money is power and power is, essentially, everything. It's an idea that has come to pervade every aspect of our culture. Bribery has become, as a philosopher might put it, an ontological principle: it defines our most basic sense of reality. To challenge it is therefore to challenge everything.

I use the word "bribery" quite self-consciously—and, again, the language we use is extremely important. As George Orwell long ago reminded us, you know you are in the presence of a corrupt political system when those who defend it cannot call things by their proper names. By these standards the contemporary United States is unusually corrupt. We maintain an empire that cannot be referred to as an empire, extracting tribute that cannot be referred to as tribute, justifying it in terms of an economic ideology (neoliberalism) we cannot refer to at all. Euphemisms and code words pervade every aspect of public debate. This is not only true of the right, with military terms like "collateral damage" (the military is a vast bureaucracy, so we expect them to use obfuscatory jargon), but on the left as well. Consider the phrase "human rights abuses." On the surface this doesn't seem like it's covering up very much: after all, who in their right mind would be in favor of human rights abuses? Obviously nobody; but there are degrees of disapproval here, and in this case, they become apparent the moment one begins to contemplate any other words in the English language that might be used to describe the same phenomenon normally referred to by this term.

Compare the following sentences:

- "I would argue that it is sometimes necessary to have dealings with, or even to support, regimes with unsavory human rights records in order to further our vital strategic imperatives."
- "I would argue that it is sometimes necessary to have dealings with, or even to support, regimes that commit acts of rape, torture, and murder in order to further our vital strategic imperatives."

Certainly the second is going to be a harder case to make. Anyone hearing it will be much more likely to ask, "Are these strategic imperatives really *that* vital?" or even, "What exactly is a 'strategic imperative' anyway?" There is even something slightly whiny-sounding about the term "rights." It sounds almost close to "entitlements"—as if those irritating torture victims are demanding something when they complain about their treatment.

For my own part, I find what I call the "rape, torture, and murder" test very useful. It's quite simple. When presented with a political entity of some sort or another, whether a government, a social movement, a guerrilla army, or really, any other organized group, and trying to decide whether they deserve condemnation or support, first ask "Do they commit, or do they order others to commit, acts of rape, torture, or murder?" It seems a self-evident question, but again, it's surprising how rarely—or, better, how selectively—it is applied. Or, perhaps, it might seem surprising, until one starts applying it and discovers conventional wisdom on many issues of world politics is instantly turned upside down. In 2006, for example, most people in the United States read about the Mexican government's sending federal troops to quell a popular revolt, initiated by a teachers' union, against a notoriously corrupt governor in the southern state of Oaxaca. In the U.S. media, this was universally presented as a good thing, a restoration of order; the rebels, after all, were "violent," having thrown rocks and Molotov cocktails (even if they did throw them only at heavily armored riot police, causing no serious injuries). No one to my knowledge has ever suggested that the rebels had raped, tortured, or murdered anyone; neither has anyone who knows anything about the events in question seriously contested the fact that forces loyal to the Mexican government had raped, tortured, and murdered quite a number of people in suppressing the rebellion. Yet somehow such acts, unlike the rebels' stone throwing, cannot be described as "violent" at all, let alone as rape, torture, or murder, but only appear, if at all, as "accusations of human rights violations," or in some similarly bloodless legalistic language.*

In the United States, though, the greatest taboo is to speak of the corruption itself. Once there was a time when giving politicians money so as to influence their positions was referred to as "bribery" and it was illegal. It was a covert business, if often pervasive, involving the carrying of bags of money and solicitation of specific favors: a change in zoning laws, the awarding of a construction contract, dropping the charges in a criminal case. Now soliciting bribes has been relabeled "fund-raising" and bribery itself, "lobbying." Banks rarely need to ask for specific favors if politicians, dependent on the flow of bank money to finance their campaigns, are already allowing bank lobbyists to shape or even write the legislation that is supposed to "regulate" their banks. At this point, bribery has become the very basis of our system of government. There are various rhetorical tricks used to avoid having to talk about this fact—the most important being allowing some limited practices (actually delivering sacks of money in exchange for a change in zoning laws) to remain illegal, so as to make it possible to insist that real "bribery" is always some *other* form of taking money in exchange for political favors. I should note

---

* An even more startling example: for many years and until quite recently, Somali pirates had never raped, tortured, or murdered anyone either, all the more remarkable considering their entire ability to operate as pirates depends on being able to convince potential victims they might do so.

that the usual line from political scientists is that these payments are not "bribes" unless one can prove that they changed a politician's position on a particular element of legislation. By this logic, if a politician is inclined to vote for a bill, receives money, and then changes his mind and votes against it, this is bribery; if however he shapes his view on the bill to begin with solely with an eye for who will give money as a result, or even allows this donor's lobbyists to write the bill for him, it is not. Needless to say these distinctions are meaningless for present purposes. But the fact remains that the average senator or congressman in Washington needs to raise roughly $10,000 a week from the time they take office if they expect to be reelected— money that they raise almost exclusively from the wealthiest 1 percent.* As a result, elected officials spend an estimated 30 percent of their time soliciting bribes.

All of this has been noted and discussed—even if it remains taboo to refer to any of it by its proper names. What's less noted is that, once one agrees in principle that it is acceptable to purchase influence, that there's nothing inherently wrong with paying people—not just one's own employees, but anyone, including the most prestigious and powerful—to do, and say, what you like, the morality of public life starts looking very different. If public servants can be bribed to take positions one finds convenient, then why not scholars? Scientists? Jour-

---

* Actually, over 80 percent of campaign contributions flow from the wealthiest 0.5 percent, and 60 percent from the wealthiest .01 percent. Of this, far and away the largest chunk comes from the financial sector. After that, business and law firms, and after that, health lobbyists—that is, pharmaceutical corporations and HMOs—then media, and then the energy sector (Federal Election Commission, Center for Responsive Politics, Public Campaign's "The Color of Money" Project).

nalists? Police? A lot of these connections began emerging in the early days of the occupation: it was revealed, for instance, that many of the uniformed police in the financial district, who one might have imagined were there to protect all citizens equally, spent a large portion of their working hours paid not by the city but directly by Wall Street firms;[15] similarly, one of the first *New York Times* reporters to deign to visit the occupation, in early October, freely admitted he did so because "the chief executive of a major bank" had called him on the phone and asked him to check to see if he thought the protests might affect his "personal security."[16] What's remarkable is not that such connections exist, but that it never seems to occur to any of the interested parties that there's anything that needs to be covered up here.

Similarly with scholarship. Scholarship has never been objective. Research imperatives have always been driven by funding from government agencies or wealthy philanthropists who at the very least have very specific ideas about what lines of questions they feel are important to ask, and usually about what sorts of answers it's acceptable to find to them. But starting with the rise of think tanks in the 1970s, in those disciplines that most affect policy (economics notably), it became normal to be hired to simply come up with justifications for preconceived political positions. By the 1980s, things had gone so far that politicians were willing to openly admit, in public forums, that they saw economic research as a way of coming up with justification for whatever it is they already wanted people to believe. I still remember during Ronald Reagan's administration being startled by exchanges like this one on TV:

ADMINISTRATION OFFICIAL: Our main priority is to enact
   cuts in the capital gains tax to stimulate the economy.
INTERVIEWER: But how would you respond to a host of recent economic studies that show this kind of "trickle-
   down" economics doesn't really work? That it doesn't
   stimulate further hiring on the part of the wealthy?
OFFICIAL: Well, it's true, the real reasons for the economic
   benefits of tax cuts remain to be fully understood.

In other words, the discipline of economics does not exist to
determine what is the best policy. We have already decided on
the policy. Economists exist to come up with scientific-sounding
reasons for us doing what we have already decided to do;
in fact, that's how they get paid. In the case of the economists
in the employ of a think tank, it's literally their job. Again, this
has been true for some time, but the remarkable thing is that,
increasingly, their sponsors were willing to actually *admit* this.

One result of this manufacture of intellectual authority is
that real political debate becomes increasingly difficult, because those who hold different positions live in completely different realities. If those on the left insist on continuing to debate
the problems of poverty and racism in America, their oppo-
nents would once more feel obliged to come up with counter-
arguments (e.g., poverty and racism are a result of the moral
failings of the victims). Now they are more likely to simply insist that poverty and racism no longer exist. But the same thing
happens on the other side. If the Christian right wants to
discuss the power of America's secular "cultural elite" those
on the left will normally reply by insisting there's isn't one;
when the libertarian right wishes to make an issue of the (very

real) historical connections between U.S. militarism and Federal Reserve policy, their liberal interlocutors regularly dismiss
them as so many conspiracy-theorist lunatics.

In America today "right" and "left" are ordinarily used to
refer to Republicans and Democrats, two parties that basically
represent different factions within the 1 percent—or perhaps,
if one were to be extremely generous, the top 2 to 3 percent of
the U.S. population. Wall Street, which owns both, seems
equally divided between the two. Republicans, otherwise, represent the bulk of the remaining CEOs, particularly in the military and extractive industries (energy, mining, timber), and
just about all middle-rank businessmen; Democrats represent
the upper echelons of what author and activist Barbara Ehren-
reich once called "the professional-managerial class," the
wealthiest lawyers, doctors, administrators, as well as pretty
much everyone in academia and the entertainment industry.
Certainly this is where each party's money is coming from—
and increasingly, raising and spending money is all these parties really do. What is fascinating is that, during the last thirty
years of the financialization of capitalism, each of these core
constituencies has developed its own theory of why the use of
money and power to create reality is inherently unobjectionable, since, ultimately, money and power are the only things
that really exist.

Consider this notorious quote from a Bush administration
aide, made to a *New York Times* reporter shortly after the invasion of Iraq:

> The aide said that guys like me were "in what we call the
> reality-based community," which he defined as people who
> "believe that solutions emerge from your judicious study of

discernible reality." . . . "That's not the way the world really works anymore," he continued. "We're an empire now, and when we act, we create our own reality."[17]

Such remarks might seem sheer bravado, and the specific remark refers more to military force than economic power—but in fact, for people at the top, when speaking off record, just as words like "empire" are no longer taboo, it's also simply assumed that U.S. economic and military power are basically identical. Indeed, as the reporter goes on to explain, there's an elaborate theology behind this kind of language. Since the 1980s, those on the Christian right—who formed the core of George W. Bush's inner circle—turned what was then called "supply-side economics" into a literally religious principle. The greatest avatar of this line of thought was probably conservative strategist George Gilder, who argued that the policy of the Federal Reserve creating money and transferring it directly to entrepreneurs to realize their creative visions was, in fact, merely a human-scale reenactment of God's original creation of the world out of nothing, by the power of His own thought. This view came to be widely embraced by televangelists like Pat Robertson, who referred to supply-side economics as "the first truly divine theory of money creation." Gilder took it further, arguing that contemporary information technology was allowing us to overcome our old materialistic prejudices and understand that money, like power, is really a matter of faith—faith in the creative power of our principles and ideas.[18] Others, like the anonymous Bush aide, extend the principle to faith in the decisive application of military force. Both recognize an intimate link between the two (as do the heretics of the right, Ayn Rand's materialist acolytes and Ron Paul–

style libertarians, who object to both the current system of money creation *and* its links to military power).

The church of the liberals is the university, where philosophers and "radical" social theorists take the place of theologians. This might appear a very different world, but during the same period, the vision of politics that took shape among the academic left is in many ways disturbingly similar. One need only reflect on the astounding rise in the 1980s, and apparent permanent patron saint status since, of the French poststructuralist theorist Michel Foucault, and particularly his argument that forms of institutional knowledge—whether medicine, psychology, administrative or political science, criminology, biochemistry for that matter—are always also forms of power that ultimately create the realities they claim to describe. This is almost exactly the same thing as Gilder's theological supply-side beliefs, except taken from the perspective of the professional and managerial classes that make up the core of the liberal elite. During the heyday of the bubble economy of the 1990s, an endless stream of new radical theoretical approaches emerged in academia—performance theory, Actor-Network Theory, theories of immaterial labor—all converging around the theme that reality itself is whatever can be brought into being by convincing others that it's there.* Granted, one's average enter-

---

* The poststructural theory, interestingly, has always had an odd blind spot for economics, and even more about military force; though when Michel Callon, one of the doyens of Actor-Network Theory, did turn to economics, he predictably argued that economists largely create the realities they purport to describe. This is actually true, but Callon completely neglects the role of government coercion in the process. So the left versions of power creating reality ignore exactly those elements—money and force of arms—that the right makes the centerpieces of their

tainment executive might not be intimately familiar with the work of Michel Foucault—most have probably barely heard of him, unless they were literature majors in college—but neither is the average churchgoing oil executive likely to be familiar with the details of Gilder's theories of money creation. These are both, as I remarked, the ultimate theological apotheoses of habits of thought that are pervasive within what we called "the 1 percent," an intellectual world where even as words like "bribery" or "empire" are banished from public discourse, they are assumed at the same time to be the ultimate basis of everything.

Taken from the perspective of the bottom 99 percent, who have little choice but to live in realities of one sort or another, such habits of thought might seem the most intense form of cynicism—indeed, cynicism taken to an almost mystical level. Yet all we are really seeing here is the notorious tendency of the powerful to confuse their own particular experiences and perspectives with the nature of reality itself—since, after all, from the perspective of a CEO, money really can bring things into being, and from the perspective of a Hollywood producer, or hospital administrator, the relation among knowledge, power, and performance really is all that exists.

There is one terrible irony here. For most Americans the problem is not the principle of bribery itself (much though most of them find it disgusting and feel politicians in particular are vile creatures), but that the 1 percent appear to have abandoned earlier policies of at least occasionally extending that bribery to the wider public. Since, after all, bribing the working

---

analysis. It's also interesting to note that just as the right has their materialist heresy, the left continues to have its own as well, in Marxism.

classes by, for instance, redistributing any significant portion of all this newly created wealth downward—as was common in the 1940s, 1950s, 1960s, and 1970s—is precisely what both parties' core constituencies are no longer willing to do. Instead, both Republicans and Democrats seem to have mobilized their activist "base" around a series of constituencies whose ultimate aspirations they have not the slightest intention of ever realizing: conservative Christians, for example, who will never really see abortion illegalized outright, or labor unions, who will never really see the legal hurdles placed in the way of organizing genuinely removed.

The answer to the initial question, then, is that in the United States, challenging the role of money in politics is necessarily revolutionary because bribery has become the organizing principle of public life. An economic system based on the marriage of government and financial interests, where money is transformed into power, which is then used to make more money again, has come to seem so natural among the core donor groups of both political parties that they have also come to see it as constitutive of reality itself.

How do you fight it? The problem with a political order based on such high levels of cynicism is that it doesn't help to mock it—in a way, that only makes matters worse. At the moment, the TV news seems divided between shows that claim to tell us about reality, which largely consist of either moderate right (CNN) to extreme right (FOX) propaganda, and largely satirical (*The Daily Show*) or otherwise performative (MSNBC) outlets that spend most of their time reminding us just how corrupt, cynical, and dishonest CNN and FOX actually are.

What the latter media says is true, but ultimately this only re-inforces what I've already identified as the main function of the contemporary media: to convey the message that even if you're clever enough to have figured out that it's all a cynical power game, the rest of America is a ridiculous pack of sheep.

This is the trap. It seems to me if we are to break out of it, we need to take our cue not from what passes for a left at all, but from the populist right, since they've figured out the key weak point in the whole arrangement: very few Americans ac-tually share the pervasive cynicism of the 1 percent.

One of the perennial complaints of the progressive left is that so many working-class Americans vote against their own economic interests—actively supporting Republican candi-dates who promise to slash programs that provide their fami-lies with heating oil, who savage their schools and privatize their Medicare. To some degree the reason is simply that the scraps the Democratic Party is now willing to throw its "base" at this point are so paltry it's hard not to see their offers as an insult: especially when it comes down to the Bill Clinton– or Barack Obama–style argument "we're not really going to fight *for* you, but then, why should we? It's not really in our self-interest when we know you have no choice but to vote for us anyway." Still, while this may be a compelling reason to avoid voting altogether—and, indeed, most working Americans have long since given up on the electoral process—it doesn't explain voting for the other side.

The only way to explain this is not that they are somehow confused about their self-interest, but that they are indignant at the very idea that self-interest is all that politics could ever be about. The rhetoric of austerity, of "shared sacrifice" to save one's children from the terrible consequences of government debt, might be a cynical lie, just a way of distributing even more wealth to the 1 percent, but such rhetoric at least gives ordinary people a certain credit for nobility. At a time when, for most Americans, there really isn't anything around them worth calling a "community," at least this is *something* they can do for everybody else.

The moment we realize that most Americans are not cynics, the appeal of right-wing populism becomes much easier to understand. It comes, often enough, surrounded by the most vile sorts of racism, sexism, homophobia. But what lies behind it is a genuine indignation at being cut off from the means for doing good.

Take two of the most familiar rallying cries of the populist right: hatred of the "cultural elite" and constant calls to "support our troops." On the surface, it seems these would have nothing to do with each other. In fact, they are profoundly linked. It might seem strange that so many working-class Americans would resent that fraction of the 1 percent who work in the culture industry more than they do oil tycoons and HMO executives, but it actually represents a fairly realistic assessment of their situation: an air conditioner repairman from Nebraska is aware that while it is exceedingly unlikely that his child would ever become CEO of a large corporation, it could possibly happen; but it's utterly unimaginable that she will ever become an international human rights lawyer or drama critic for *The New York Times*. Most obviously, if you wish to pursue a career that isn't simply for the money—a career in the arts, in politics, social welfare, journalism, that is, a life dedicated to pursuing some value other than money, whether that be the pursuit of truth, beauty, charity—for the first year or two, your employers will simply refuse to pay you. As I myself discovered on graduating college, an impenetrable bastion of unpaid internships places any such careers permanently outside the reach of anyone who can't fund several years' free residence in a city like New York or San Francisco—which, most obviously, immediately eliminates any child of the working class. What this means in practice is that not only do the children of this (increasingly in-marrying, exclusive) class of sophisticates see most working-class Americans as so many knuckle-dragging cavemen, which is infuriating enough, but that they have developed a clever system to monopolize, for their own children, all lines of work where one can both earn a decent living and also pursue something selfless or noble. If an air conditioner repairman's daughter does aspire to a career where she can serve some calling higher than herself, she really only has two realistic options: she can work for her local church, or she can join the army.

This was, I am convinced, the secret of the peculiar popular appeal of George W. Bush, a man born to one of the richest families in America: he talked, and acted, like a man that felt more comfortable around soldiers than professors. The militant anti-intellectualism of the populist right is more than merely a rejection of the authority of the professional-managerial class (who, for most working-class Americans, are more likely to have immediate power over their lives than CEOs), it's also a protest against a class that they see as trying to monopolize for itself the means to live a life dedicated to anything other than material self-interest. Watching liberals express bewilderment that they thus seem to be acting against their own self-interest—by not accepting a few material scraps they are offered by Democratic candidates—presumably only makes matters worse.

The trap from the perspective of the Republican Party is that by playing to white working-class populism in this way, they forever forgo the possibility of stripping away any significant portion of the Democratic Party's core support: African Americans, Latinos, immigrants, and second-generation children of immigrants, for whom (despite the fact that they are also overwhelmingly believing Christians and despite the fact that their children are so strongly overrepresented in the armed forces) this kind of anti-intellectual politics is simply anathema. Could one seriously imagine an African-American politician successfully playing the anti-intellectual card in the manner of George W. Bush? Such a thing would be unthinkable. The core Democratic constituencies are precisely those who not only have a more vivid sense of themselves as bearers of culture and community, but, crucially, for whom education is still a value in itself.

Hence the deadlock of American politics.

Now think of all the women (mostly, white women) who posted their stories to the "We Are the 99 Percent" page. From this vantage, it's hard to see them as expressing anything but an analogous protest against the cynicism of our political culture: even it takes the form of the absolute minimum demand to pursue a life dedicated to helping, teaching, or caring for others without having to sacrifice the ability to take care of their own families.* And after all, is "support our schoolteachers and

---

* Silvia Federici, in a little essay called "Women, Austerity and the Unfinished Feminist Revolution" (Occupy! #3, *n+1*, November 2011, pp. 32–34), moves in a similar direction when she makes the point that mainstream feminism has gone astray in placing all its emphasis on guaranteeing women's participation in the labor market, seeing this

nurses" any less legitimate a cry than "support our troops"? And is it a coincidence that so many actual former soldiers, veterans of the wars in Iraq and Afghanistan, have found themselves drawn to their local occupations?

By gathering together in the full sight of Wall Street, and creating a community without money, based on principles not just of democracy but of mutual caring, solidarity, and support, occupiers were proposing a revolutionary challenge not just to the power of money, but to the power of money to determine what life itself was supposed to be about. It was the ultimate blow not just against Wall Street, but against that very principle of cynicism of which it was the ultimate embodiment. At least for that brief moment, love had become the ultimate revolutionary act.

Not surprising, then, that the guardians of the existing order identified it for what it was, and reacted as if they were facing a military provocation.

QUESTION 7

Why did the movement appear to collapse so quickly after the camps were evicted in November 2011?

Pretty much the moment the camps were evicted in November 2011, the media began reporting Occupy's demise.

According to the narrative that soon became established in the U.S. media, things were already beginning to fall apart even

---

as intrinsically liberating, rather than the domain of what she—using a somewhat ungainly Marxist phrase—calls "the sphere of reproduction."

before the evictions. Supposedly, what had once been idealistic experiments began to fill with criminals, addicts, and homeless and crazy people; hygienic standards broke down; there was an epidemic of sexual assault. The famous photograph of the homeless derelict with his pants down, apparently preparing to relieve his bowels on a NYPD police car near Zuccotti Park, became the counterimage to the famous Tony Bologna pepper-spray video and was widely held out as an icon of just how low things were descending. (The fact that there's no evidence the person in question even was an occupier was treated as immaterial.) Most of these claims dissolve away the moment one examines them. For instance, despite claims of an epidemic of rape, the total number of occupiers accused of sexual assault—among hundreds of occupations—appears to have been exactly two. As Rebecca Solnit has pointed out, the United States has the highest rate of sexual assault against women of any country in the world, and the media hardly sees this as a moral crisis. Yet somehow the news story on Occupy was not that activists had managed to create an environment in the middle of the most dangerous American cities where the rate of assault against women had clearly precipitously declined, but a scandal that they had not eliminated such incidents altogether.

What's more, as she goes on to report of Oakland, California:

> Now here's something astonishing. While the camp was in existence, crime *went down 19%* in Oakland, a statistic the city was careful to conceal. "It may be counter to our statement that the Occupy movement is negatively impacting crime in Oakland," the police chief wrote to the mayor in an email that local news station KTVU later obtained

and released to little fanfare. Pay attention: Occupy was so powerful a force for nonviolence that it was already solving Oakland's chronic crime and violence problems just by giving people hope and meals and solidarity and conversation.[19]

Needless to say, no newspaper headlines loudly proclaiming "Violent Crime Drops Sharply During Occupation" ever appeared, and police continued to insist, despite the evidence of their own statistics, that exactly the opposite was the case.

Insofar as some camps did begin having internal troubles, it was not because of a lack of police—in fact, all were surrounded by police 24/7, so in theory they should have been the safest places in America—but precisely because police did everything in their power to bring it about. Many of the homeless ex-convicts who ended up settling in Zuccotti Park, for instance, reported having been actually bused to the location on release from Rikers Island by officers who told them that free food and lodging were available in the park. This is a common tactic. In Greece, just about everyone I talked to who'd been involved in the General Assembly at Syntagma Square told stories of pickpockets and drug dealers who'd been informed by the police that they would not be prosecuted for carrying out their trade among the protesters. In a way, the remarkable thing is that, under such pressures, most camps did remain relatively safe spaces and did not break down into the kind of Hobbesian chaos that the media, and municipal authorities, invariably claimed they were.

What was really happening here?

First of all, I think we have to understand that what happened did not occur in isolation. It has to be understood in its

global context. Occupy is, as I've repeatedly stressed, simply
the North American manifestation of a democratic rebellion
that began in Tunisia in January 2011, and by the end of that
year was threatening to call into question existing structures of
power everywhere.

One could hardly imagine that existing structures of power
would fail to be concerned by these developments, or try to
contain the danger to the established order, and clearly they did
not fail to do so. In fact, the United States sits at the center of
a whole apparatus of political, administrative, and "security"
mechanisms that have been put into place over the last generations largely to contain precisely this sort of danger, to ensure
that popular uprisings like these either do not occur or at least
do not make much difference and are quickly demobilized. In
the Middle East the United States performed a complex balanc-
ing act, allowing some democratic movements to be violently
suppressed (Bahrain is the most famous example) and attempting to co-opt or neutralize others through aid and NGOs. In
Europe there was a series of what can only be called financial
coups, with the political elite of the wealthy, northern countries effectively ousting elected governments in Greece and
Italy, and imposing "neutral technocrats" to push through austerity budgets, accompanied by increasingly sophisticated police operations against those gathered in their public squares.
In the United States, after two months of hesitation, police
began systematically clearing the encampments, often using
overwhelming militarized force, and, even more crucially, made
it clear to occupiers that from that time on any group of citizens who intended to re-create encampments, anywhere, would
be subject to immediate physical attack.

The U.S. government line has always been that none of this

was coordinated. We are supposed to believe that somehow, hundreds of municipal authorities all independently decided to evict their local camps, using the same pretexts (sanitation), employing the same tactics, all at the same time, and that all of them likewise decided that no camp would be set up after that, even if occupiers attempted to do so completely legally. This is of course absurd. Efforts to suppress the global justice movement back in 1999, 2000, and 2001 were clearly coordinated, and since September 11, 2001, the U.S. government has added several layers of new security bureaucracy with the express purpose of coordinating responses to anything perceived as a threat to public order. If those running such institutions were really just sitting back and paying no attention to the sudden appearance of a large, rapidly growing, and potentially revolutionary nationwide movement, they weren't doing their jobs.

How did they proceed? Well, again, we don't know, and presumably won't know for many years to come. It took us decades to learn the exact nature of FBI efforts to subvert the civil rights and peace movements in the 1960s. Still, the broad outlines of what must have happened are not particularly hard to reconstruct. Actually there's a fairly standard playbook employed by pretty much any government attempting to suppress a democratic movement, and this one clearly went very much by the book. Here's how it goes. First you try to destroy the moral authority of the radicals who actually drive the movement, by painting them as contemptible and (at least potentially) violent. Then you try to peel off their middle-class allies with a combination of calculated concessions and scare stories—or even, if a genuinely revolutionary situation seems imminent, the intentional creation of public disorder. (This is what Mubarak's government so famously did in Egypt when

they began releasing hardened criminals from prison and with-
drawing police protection from middle-class neighborhoods to
convince the residents there that revolution could only lead
to chaos.) Then you attack.

Back in 2000, I spent a good deal of time documenting
how this first stage worked in the wake of the WTO protests in
Seattle. At the time I was often working with activist media
liaisons, and we would have to deal with bursts of bizarre
claims that always seemed to suddenly appear on the horizon,
clearly deriving from multiple official sources, all at the same
time. During the summer of 2000, for example, there was one
week where suddenly everyone started saying that anti-
globalization protesters were all actually rich kids with trust
funds. Shortly thereafter we began to hear a list of ultraviolent
forms of behavior that protesters were supposed to have employed in Seattle—use of slingshots; throwing of Molotovs,
rocks, and excrement; water guns full of urine, bleach, or acid;
the use of crowbars to rip up sidewalks to secure projectiles to
throw at police. Warnings about such violent tactics soon
began regularly appearing in the newspapers before trade summits, often on the authority of experts sent to drill the local
police, creating a mood of looming panic—despite the fact that
during the Seattle protests themselves, no one had even suggested anyone had done anything of the sort. When such stories appeared in *The New York Times*, members of the local
Direct Action Network, myself included, actually picketed the
paper, and it was forced to issue a retraction after calling the
Seattle police, who confirmed that they had no evidence any of
these tactics had actually been deployed. Yet the stories kept
appearing anyway. While there's no way to know precisely

what was happening, the bits of evidence we could glean suggested they traced back to some sort of a network of private security companies that worked in liaison with police, right-wing think tanks, and possibly some sorts of police intelligence units. Before long, police chiefs in cities facing mobilizations started making up similar stories, which would invariably make splashy headlines for a few days, until we managed to establish the violent acts had never happened, by which time, of course, the entire subject was no longer considered newsworthy.

When you look at such smears in historical perspective, certain unmistakable patterns begin to emerge. The most dramatic is the constant juxtaposition of human body waste and men in uniform. I'm not sure I've ever seen a police slander against democracy protesters that did not contain at least one reference to someone hurling, or preparing to hurl, excrement. Presumably it all goes back to the success of the image of 1960s protesters spitting on returning veterans, one that lodged firmly in the popular imagination despite there being no evidence it actually happened, but even by the 1970s, lurid visions of hippies throwing shit had become a staple of the right-wing media, and always seemed to reappear right before the men and women in uniform are ordered to attack peaceful protesters—always, of course, without the slightest bit of documentary evidence. Videographers have caught thousands of images of police beating occupiers, journalists, and random passersby. No one has ever caught an image of an occupier hurling dung.

The emphasis on excrement is so effective because psychologically, it serves two purposes. The first is to win over the hearts and minds of the lower-ranking police officers who will actually be asked to swing the billy clubs against nonviolent idealists' heads,* and who, in the early days of Occupy, were often quite sympathetic on an individual basis. By January and February, when the repression had really become systematic, activists who had the opportunity to have long conversations with their arresting officers found it was impossible to convince them that occupiers had not been regularly pelting public employees with excrement.

The second effect is of course to destroy the moral authority of the activists in the eyes of the public: to paint them as both contemptible and violent. The photo of the homeless man squatting next to the police car seemed to service the first purpose quite handily. The problem with the second was—in New York in particular—there was simply no way to make a plausible claim that activists were attacking the police. So instead the line became, the police were obliged to step in to prevent activists from being violent to one another!

Really this was simply an extension of a symbolic strategy that appears to have been hatched in the very early weeks of the movement, when local authorities were struggling over how to come up with a pretext for criminalizing often largely middle-class citizens engaged in setting up tents. How could one really justify sending in heavily armed riot police against citizens who are mostly not even breaking any laws, but merely

* As I've written in the past, claiming that globalization protesters were really so many "trust fund babies" was perfectly calibrated to achieve the desired effect: it was a way of saying, "Don't think of what you are doing in defending this trade summit as a matter of protecting a bunch of fat cats who have contempt for you and everyone like you; think of it rather as an opportunity to beat up on their bratty children (but don't actually kill any of them, because you never know who their parents might be)."

violating certain municipal camping regulations? From the beginning, the solution was clear: sanitation. The camps were to be identified with filth. (The presence of often very meticulous sanitation working groups were of course considered irrelevant in this respect.) Already in the second or third week of occupation, activists in cities as far apart as Austin, Texas, and Portland, Oregon, were being informed that since the city was concerned about hygienic conditions, the camps would have to be completely cleared each day for special cleaning—a cleaning that then turned out to take four or five hours every day. From "den of filth," it was easy enough to carry over the imagery to "cesspool of violence, crime, and degradation." And, of course, when the camps were evicted, though mayors generally justified their actions by the need to protect everyone, including the campers, from crime, the official reason was in almost every case the need to provide access to public sanitation crews.

———

None of this directly answers the question of why the movement seemed to shrivel up so rapidly after the evictions. But it provides the necessary context.

The first thing to emphasize here is that we are talking about appearances. To say a movement *seemed* to shrivel up is not to say that it actually did. There is no doubt that the attacks on the camps, the destruction of occupiers' homes, kitchens, clinics, and libraries, the consequent creation in many cities of a refugee population of activists—many of whom had given up their jobs and homes to join the camps, and who suddenly found themselves on the streets or taking shelter in church basements, many traumatized, dealing with the psychological consequences of arrest, injury, imprisonment, and the loss of most of their worldly possessions—was sure to have its effects. At first the movement was thrown into enormous disarray. Recriminations abounded; indignation over issues of race, class, and gender that had largely been put aside during the heady days of the occupation seemed to emerge all at once. Everyone suddenly seemed to start fighting over money; in New York, more than half a million dollars had poured in; within a few months, it had all been spent providing accommodation and transport money (the churches charged us) for the hundreds who had been displaced. Some of the organizational forms, like the General Assembly, that had worked so beautifully in the camps proved entirely unsuited for the new situation. In most cities, GAs largely fell apart over the winter, though usually large working groups with some immediate practical purpose—in New York, the Direct Action working group, and various specific assemblies convoked to work on specific projects like the May Day mobilization—ended up doing most of the same work.

In retrospect, the collapse of the General Assembly model was hardly surprising: Most of us who had experience in the Global Justice Movement considered the idea something of a crazy experiment from the outset. We'd always assumed that for meetings of any real size, certainly any meeting involving thousands of people, the consensus process would only work if we adopted some kind of spokescouncil model, where everyone was arranged into groups with temporary "spokes" who alone could make proposals and participate in discussion (though this was always balanced by breakouts into smaller groups where everyone could tell their spokes what to say, or even replace them). The spokescouncil model had worked quite well during the mass mobilizations of 1999–2003. The remarkable thing about the GA approach was that it ever worked at all, which it did, when there was an actual face-to-face community to be maintained. None of us were particularly surprised when, as soon as the camps were cleared, the GAs fell apart.*

What really slowed things down, and led so many to believe the movement was collapsing, was an unhappy concatenation of several factors: the sudden change in police tactics, which made it impossible for activists to create any sort of free public space in an American city without being immediately physically assaulted; the abandonment by our liberal allies, who made no effort to make a public issue of this new policy; and a sudden media blackout, which ensured most Americans had no idea any of this was even happening. Maintaining a public space like Zuccotti Park was full of problems and by the end many organizers actually said they were a bit relieved that they no longer had to spend all their time worrying about the equivalent of zoning issues, and could start concentrating on planning direct actions and real political campaigns. They soon discovered that without a single center, one where anyone interested in the movement knew they could go at any time to get involved, express support, or just find out what was happening, this became much more difficult to do. But attempts to reestablish such a center were systematically stymied. An effort to convince Trinity Church, an erstwhile ally in lower Manhat-

---

* The tragedy in New York, at least, was that while a spokescouncil model was introduced, it was brought in what was widely seen as a top-down, divisive way at a moment of maximum conflict. There are currently efforts under way in New York to revive a spokescouncil model in a more democratic fashion.

tan, to let occupiers use a large deserted lot it was holding as a real estate investment failed; after appeals even from the likes of Desmond Tutu fell on deaf ears, several Episcopal bishops led a march to peacefully occupy the space. They were immediately arrested, and somehow, the entire story of their involvement never made it into the news. On the sixth-month anniversary of the original occupation, on March 17, former occupiers threw an impromptu party in Zuccotti Park. After about an hour, police attacked, which left several activists seriously injured and in the hospital; one band broke off and set up sleeping bags in Union Square, which, while a public park, had traditionally always remained open twenty-four hours a day. Within a few days, tables began to appear around them with Occupy literature, and a kitchen and library began to be set up. The city responded by declaring that from now on, the park would close at midnight, leading to what came to be called the "nightly eviction theater" as hundreds of riot police were assembled at eleven every evening to drive out the handful of campers with their sleeping bags at midnight. "No camping" regulations were enforced so aggressively that activists were arrested for placing blankets over themselves, or, in one case I myself witnessed, wrestled to the pavement and shackled for bending down to pet a dog (the police commander explained that in doing so the protester was too close to the ground).

During this period the level of violence involved in arrests increased dramatically. Even during the most peaceful protests, marchers who strayed off the sidewalk, or even seemed like they might be about to, found themselves tackled and having their heads repeatedly smashed against concrete. Police began deploying new, exotic tactics of intimidation, some of which appear to have been imported from abroad. For instance, in

Egypt, when some revolutionaries attempted a renewed occupation of Tahrir Square in November and December 2011,
police responded by a systematic campaign of sexual assault
against female protesters; female arrestees were not only beaten,
but stripped and groped, often ostentatiously in front of their
male counterparts. Egyptian friends told me the aim seemed
twofold: to maximally traumatize women activists, but also to
provoke male activists to violence in their defense. Similarly,
when attempts at reoccupation in New York began again in
March, we saw a sudden intense spate of police sexual attacks
on women protesters—something that had happened, at best,
only very occasionally before. I met one woman who told me
five different police had grabbed her breasts during one evening's eviction from Union Square (on one occasion, while another officer stood by blowing kisses); another screamed and
called the policeman fondling her a pervert, whereupon he and
his fellow officers dragged her behind police lines and broke
her wrists. Yet even when one well-known Occupy spokes-
woman appeared on Democracy Now! displaying a large hand-
shaped bruise across her chest, the media simply refused to
pick up the story. Rather, the new rules of engagement—that
anyone showing up at a large protest, however peaceful, should
just understand that this might mean being arrested, or put in
the hospital—were simply treated as a kind of "new normal,"
and any particular instance of police violence as no longer
newsworthy. Media sources did, dutifully, report the dwindling
numbers who showed up to such marches, which for obvious
reasons soon came to consist principally of hard-core activists
willing to accept beatings and imprisonment, now almost entirely bereft of the flocks of children and old people who had
accompanied, and so humanized, our earlier actions. While re-

porting the decreasing numbers at marches, the media refused
to report the reasons why.

———

So the real question is: how did these rules change, and why
was the effective repeal of the First Amendment (at least as it
applies to freedom of assembly) simply allowed to stand un-
contested? As every experienced activist knows, the rules of
engagement on the streets have everything to do with the quality and effectiveness of one's alliances.

One reason Occupy got so much attention in the media at
first—most of the seasoned activists I talked to agreed that we
had never seen anything like it—was that so many more mainstream activist groups so quickly endorsed our cause. I am referring here particularly to those organizations that might be
said to define the left wing of the Democratic Party: MoveOn
.org, for example, or Rebuild the Dream. Such groups were
enormously energized by the birth of Occupy. But, as I touched
on above, most also seem to have assumed that the principled
rejection of electoral politics and top-down forms of organization was simply a passing phase, the childhood of a movement
that, they assumed, would mature into something resembling a
left-wing Tea Party. From their perspective, the camps soon
became a distraction. The real business of the movement would
begin once Occupy became a conduit for guiding young activists into legislative campaigns, and eventually, get-out-the-vote
drives for progressive candidates. It took some time for them to
fully realize that the core of the movement was serious about
its principles. It's also fairly clear that when the camps were
cleared, not only such groups, but the liberal establishment

more generally, made a strategic decision to look the other way.

From the perspective of the radicals, this was the ultimate betrayal. We had made our commitment to horizontal principles clear from the outset. They were the essence of what we were trying to do. But at the same time, we understood that there has always been a tacit understanding, in America, between radical groups like ourselves, and their liberal allies. The radicals' call for revolutionary change creates a fire to the liberals' left that makes the liberals' own proposals for reform seem a more reasonable alternative. We win them a place at the table. They keep us out of jail. In these terms, the liberal establishment utterly failed to live up to their side of the bargain. Occupy succeeded brilliantly in changing the national debate to begin addressing issues of financial power, the corruption of the political process, and social inequality, all to the benefit of the liberal establishment, which had struggled to gain traction around these issues. But when the Tasers, batons, and SWAT teams arrived, that establishment simply disappeared and left us to our fate.

This might seem inevitable in retrospect, but it's not the way things have tended to work in the past. Obviously, the violent suppression of social movements is hardly new. One need only think of the Red Scare, the reaction to radical labor movements like the IWW, let alone the campaigns of outright assassination directed against the American Indian Movement or black radicals in the 1960s and early 1970s. But in almost every case, the victims were either working-class or nonwhite. On the few occasions where even much milder systematic repression is directed at any significant number of middle-class

white people—as during the McCarthy era, or against student
protesters during the Vietnam War—it quickly becomes a national scandal. And, while it would be wrong to call Occupy
Wall Street a middle-class white people's movement—it was
much more diverse than that—there is no doubt that very large
numbers of middle-class white people were involved in it. Yet
the government did not hesitate to attack it, often using highly
militarized tactics, often deploying what can only be called ter-
roristic violence—that is, if "terrorism" is defined as attacks on
civilians consciously calculated to create terror for political
ends. (I know this statement might seem controversial. But
when Los Angeles police, for example, open fire with rubber
bullets on a group of chalk-wielding protesters engaged in a
perfectly legal, permitted "art walk," in an obvious attempt to
teach citizens that participating in any Occupy-related activity
could lead to physical injury, it's hard to see how that word
should not apply.)

What had changed? One answer is that this was the first
American social movement to emerge since 9/11. Did the war
on terror really change the rules?

I must admit that when we first began the occupation, I was
somewhat surprised that the emotional aftermath of 9/11
wasn't something we had to deal with. Zuccotti Park might
have been two blocks away from Wall Street, but it was also
only two blocks away from Ground Zero, and I remember an-
ticipating all sorts of charges of sacrilege and disrespect for the
victims of terrorist attacks. These never materialized. But as we
were ultimately to discover, 9/11 changed the ground we were
working on in other, much more subtle ways. Yes, there was a
brief window where the Gandhian formula—delegitimating
power by maintaining scrupulous nonviolence, and then allow-

ing the world to witness just how brutal the state's reaction would nonetheless be—did, actually, seem to work. But it was very brief. It's not enough to note that, after the evictions, liberal organizations seem to have made a strategic decision not to make an issue of the violence. One also has to ask why they could get away with it—why their constituents were not sufficiently shocked by the violence to demand some sort of accounting. It's here where I think the real psychological effects of 9/11 can be seen.

The immediate wake of the terrorist attacks saw a major militarization of the American police. Billions were allocated to providing "anti-terrorist" equipment and training to police departments in otherwise underfunded municipalities like Dayton, Ohio, that clearly did not face terrorist threats of any kind. This helps explain the sometimes bizarre overreaction to many of our actions, as when a few dozen activists attempted to occupy a foreclosed home in New Jersey, or when we attempted to make our speeches on the steps of Federal Hall in Manhattan and were greeted by heavily armed SWAT teams. In another age, such overkill would have provoked outrage. In 2012, it went completely unremarked. How did middle-class liberals become so accepting of the militarization of the police? Largely, by their absolute, steadfast rejection of anything that might even suggest the possibility of violence on the part of protesters. Even if police executed what was clearly a pre-planned assault on peaceful protesters, say by firing tear-gas canisters directly at occupiers' heads—as did indeed happen several times in Oakland—the first response by both media and liberal commentators was always to ask whether any occupier, at any point, responded to that assault with anything other than passive resistance. If even one person kicked a tear-gas canister back in the cops' direction, the story would no longer be "police open fire on protesters" or even "marine veteran in critical condition after being shot in the head by tear-gas canister," but rather "protesters engage in clashes with police."

In one of the great ironies of history, the invocation of the spirit of Gandhi and Martin Luther King became the prime means of justifying the newfound militarization of American society, in a way that would surely have left either man, had they been alive to witness it, both astounded and horrified. Occupy is an extraordinarily nonviolent movement. It may well be the most nonviolent movement of its size in American history, and this despite the absence of peace codes, marshals, or official peace police. In the fall, there were at least five hundred occupations, with participants representing remarkably diverse philosophies, from evangelical Christians to revolutionary anarchists, and thousands of marches and actions—and yet the most "violent" acts attributed to protesters were four or five acts of window-breaking, basically less than one might expect in the wake of one not particularly rowdy Canadian hockey game. Historically, this is an extraordinary achievement. Yet has it ever been treated as such? Instead, the handful of windows themselves became a moral crisis. In the immediate wake of the evictions, when Americans first had the opportunity to process the full extent of what had happened—the mass arrests, beatings, the systematic destruction of homes and libraries—the liberal blogosphere was instead almost completely dominated by arguments about a piece called "The Cancer in Occupy," written by a former *New York Times* reporter turned OWS supporter named Chris Hedges, who argued that one or two incidents of window-breaking in Oakland were actually the work of a violent and fanatical anarchist

faction he called "the Black Bloc," and that the most important thing the movement could do was to expose and exclude
such elements lest they provide a pretext for police. The fact
that almost no statement in the piece was factually accurate
(Black Blocs are in fact a formation, not a group, and probably
95 percent of occupations hadn't even seen one) only seemed to
give everyone more excuse to argue about it. Before long, liberal commentators had formed a consensus that the real problem with Occupy was not any act of actual physical violence
that had taken place (these had pretty much all been carried
out by police) but the fact that some occupations contained
some elements that, while they had not committed any acts of
violence, felt that acts of damage to property *could* be justified.
To give a sense of the disparity: even in New York in March,
there was still endless discussion of a single café window that
may or may not have been broken by an activist associated
with a Black Bloc in Oakland during a march in November; as
a result, there was virtually no discussion of the first OWS-
associated window-breaking in New York itself, which occurred on March 17. The window in question—it was a shop
window in lower Manhattan—was broken by an NYPD officer, using an activist's head.

Just to give a sense how perverse this invocation of Gandhi
to justify state violence really is, we might recall the words and
actions of Gandhi himself. For most anarchists, Gandhi is an
ambivalent figure. On the one hand, his philosophy drew heavily on the anarchism of Tolstoy and Kropotkin. On the other,
he embraced a kind of masochistic puritanism and encouraged
a cult of personality whose implications can only be profoundly
inimical to the creation of a truly free society. He did condemn
all forms of violence. But he also insisted that passive acquies-

cence to an unjust social order was even worse. I remember one conference on OWS at the New School in New York in the wake of the evictions, where liberal pacifists kept reminding organizers that Gandhi had gone so far as "suspending his Quit India campaign when there was an incident of violence." What they didn't mention was that the incident in question involved Gandhi's own followers hacking twenty-two police officers to pieces and setting fire to the remains. It seems a pretty safe guess that if members of, say, Occupy Cleveland or Occupy Denver were discovered to have carved large numbers of police officers limb from limb, our movement would have stopped dead in its tracks as well, even without a charismatic leader to tell us to. In a world where such things were possible, the idea that Gandhi himself would have become worked up over a couple of broken windows is nothing short of insane. In fact, as a politician, Gandhi regularly resisted demands that he condemn those who engaged in more militant forms of anticolonial resistance—that is, when they were not part of his own movement. Even when it was a matter of guerrillas attacking police stations and blowing up trains, he would always note that while he believed nonviolence was the correct approach, these were good people trying to do what they believed to be the right thing. While opposing injustice nonviolently, he insisted, is always morally superior to opposing it violently, opposing injustice violently is still morally superior to doing nothing to oppose it at all.[20]

One could only wish those who claim to speak in the name of Gandhi would, occasionally, act like him.

But despite all this, was the movement indeed stopped dead in its tracks? Absolutely not. We had a rough six or eight months trying to find our footing in a radically new, and much more physically hostile, environment, without the benefit of sympathetic press. There were dramatic new campaigns: occupy foreclosed homes, occupy farms, rent strikes, educational initiatives. There were endless trainings in new street tactics, and a newfound emphasis on drama and comedy, partly just to keep spirits up in the face of repression. But mainly, there was a search for new alliances.

Once the liberals had largely abandoned us, the next step was to strengthen our ties with what we always considered our real allies: the unions, community organizations, and immigrant rights groups. In New York, Occupy's first really large initiative after the evictions was to take part in planning a nationwide May Day "general strike." This was always a risky undertaking since we all understood that we couldn't really organize a general strike in the traditional sense, and the media would almost certainly announce it was a failure. But having millions of people nationwide come out in the streets, to create a forum for the development of new initiatives, seemed like it would be victory enough. And while in New York we did manage to convince the leadership of pretty much every union in the city (including the Teamsters and Central Labor Council) to endorse a call for "revolutionary transformation," the final results were sobering. It turned out that union bureaucracies in particular are simply too vulnerable to pressure from above to make very effective allies. Just as in Bloombergville, union leaders talked enthusiastically about the idea of civil disobedience in the planning stages, then, at the last minute, balked:

ambitious plans to shut down the city gradually dissolved into a simple permitted march, to which the unions didn't even make much effort to turn out their rank and file, for fear they'd be assaulted by the NYPD.

By mid-May, most of the core organizers of Occupy Wall Street had come to the conclusion that it would be better to put aside the whole question of alliance-building and think about our base. What were the issues that had the most direct appeal to the real daily problems of occupiers, and to our friends and families? How could we organize campaigns that would take on those problems directly? We decided to organize a series of weekly open forums, each with a different theme—climate change, debt, police and prisons—to see which one took off. As it turned out, the debt forum was so enormously successful it instantly put all others in the shadows. A series of Debtor Assemblies was quickly thrown together, each bringing together hundreds of participants, many new to the movement, bursting with projects and ideas. By the time of writing, the emerging Strike Debt campaign—with campaigns with names like the Invisible Army, Rolling Jubilee, Debt Resistor's Operations Manual, and People's Bailout—are clearly the most exciting growth areas of the movement. Occupy has returned to its roots.

Of course, endless questions remain. Is it really possible to create a mass movement of debt resistance in America? How to overcome the feelings of shame and isolation that debt always seems to foster? Or, to put it a different way, how to provide a base of democratic support and a public forum for those millions of Americans (1 in 6, by some estimates) who are, effectively, already practicing civil disobedience against financial capitalism by refusing to pay their debts? It isn't obvious. For all we know, by the time this book appears, some new campaign will have emerged from some other city that will ultimately prove even more inspiring.

In social movement terms, a single year is nothing. Movements that aim for immediate, legislative goals tend to flicker quickly in and out of existence; in America, movements that have successfully aimed for a broad moral transformation of society (from the abolitionists to feminism) have taken much longer to see concrete results. But when they do, those results are deep and abiding. In one year, Occupy managed to both identify the problem—a system of class power that has effectively fused together finance and government—and to propose a solution: the creation of a genuinely democratic culture. If it succeeds, it is likely to take a very long time. But the effects will be epochal.

THREE

"THE MOB BEGIN TO THINK AND TO REASON"

The Covert History of Democracy

R eading accounts of social movements written by out-right conservatives can often feel strangely refreshing. Particularly when one is used to dealing with liberals. Liberals tend to be touchy and unpredictable because they claim to share the ideas of radical movements—democracy, egalitarianism, freedom—but they've also managed to convince themselves that these ideals are ultimately unattainable. For that reason, they see anyone determined to bring about a world based on those principles as a kind of moral threat. I noticed this during the days of the Global Justice Movement. There was a kind of mocking defensiveness on the part of many in the "liberal media" that was in its own way just as caustic as anything thrown at us by the right. As I read their critiques of the movement, it became clear to me that many senior members of the media, having gone to college in the 1960s, thought of themselves as former campus revolutionaries, if only through generational association. Within their work was an argument they were having with themselves; they were convincing themselves that even though they were now working for the establishment, they hadn't really sold out because their former revolutionary dreams were profoundly unrealistic, and actually, fighting for abortion rights or gay marriage is about as radical as one can realistically be. If you are a radical, at least with conservatives you know where you stand: they are your enemies. If they wish to understand you, it is only to facilitate your being violently suppressed. This leads to a certain clarity. It also means they often honestly do wish to understand you.

In the early days of Occupy Wall Street, the first major salvo from the right took the form of an essay in *The Weekly Standard* by one Matthew Continetti entitled "Anarchy in the U.S.A.: The Roots of American Disorder."[1] "Both left and right," Continetti argued, "have made the error of thinking that the forces behind Occupy Wall Street are interested in democratic politics and problem solving." In fact, their core were anarchists dreaming of a utopian socialist paradise as peculiar as the phalanxes of Charles Fourier or free love communes like the 1840s New Harmony. The author goes on to quote proponents of contemporary anarchism, mainly Noam Chomsky and myself:

> This permanent rebellion leads to some predictable outcomes. By denying the legitimacy of democratic politics, the anarchists undermine their ability to affect people's lives. No living wage movement for them. No debate over the Bush tax rates. Anarchists don't believe in wages, and they certainly don't believe in taxes. David Graeber, an anthropologist and a leading figure in Occupy Wall Street, puts it this way: "By participating in policy debates the

very best one can achieve is to limit the damage, since the very premise is inimical to the idea of people managing their own affairs." The reason that Occupy Wall Street has no agenda is that anarchism allows for no agenda. All the anarchist can do is set an example—or tear down the existing order through violence.

This paragraph is typical: it alternates legitimate insights with a series of calculated slurs and insinuations designed to encourage violence. It is true that anarchists did, as I said, refuse to enter the political system itself, but this was on the grounds that the system itself was undemocratic—having been reduced to a system of open institutionalized bribery, backed up by coercive force. We wanted to make that fact evident to everyone, in the United States and elsewhere. And that is what OWS did—in a way that no amount of waving of policy statements could ever have done. To say that we have no agenda, then, is absurd; to assert that we have no choice but to eventually resort to violence, despite the studious nonviolence of the occupiers, is the kind of statement one only makes if one is desperately trying to come up with justifications for violence oneself.

The piece went on to correctly trace the origins of the current global anticapitalist networks back to the Zapatista revolt in 1994, and, again correctly, to note their increasingly antiauthoritarian politics, their rejection of any notion of seizing power by force, their use of the Internet. Continetti concludes:

> An intellectual, financial, technological, and social infrastructure to undermine global capitalism has been developing for more than two decades, and we are in the middle of its latest manifestation. . . . The occupiers' tent cities are

self-governing, communal, egalitarian, and networked. They reject everyday politics. They foster bohemianism and confrontation with the civil authorities. They are the Phalanx and New Harmony, updated for postmodern times and plopped in the middle of our cities.

There may not be that many activists in the camps. They may appear silly, even grotesque. They may resist "agendas" and "policies." They may not agree on what they want or when they want it. And they may disappear as winter arrives and the liberals whose parks they are occupying lose patience with them. But the utopians and anarchists will reappear. . . . The occupation will persist as long as individuals believe that inequalities of property are unjust and that the brotherhood of man can be established on the earth.

You can see why anarchists might find this sort of thing refreshingly honest. The author makes no secret of his desire to see us all in prison, but at least he's willing to make an honest assessment of what the stakes are.

Still, there is one screamingly dishonest theme that runs throughout the *Weekly Standard* piece: the intentional conflation of "democracy" with "everyday politics," that is, lobbying, fund-raising, working for electoral campaigns, and otherwise participating in the current American political system. The premise is that the author stands in favor of democracy, and that occupiers, in rejecting the existing system, are against it. In fact, the conservative tradition that produced and sustains journals like *The Weekly Standard* is profoundly antidemocratic. Its heroes, from Plato to Edmund Burke, are, almost uniformly, men who opposed democracy on principle, and its readers are still fond of statements like "America is not a democracy, it's a republic." What's more, the sort of arguments Continetti breaks out here—that anarchist-inspired movements are unstable, confused, threaten established orders of property, and must necessarily lead to violence—are precisely the arguments that have, for centuries, been leveled by conservatives against democracy itself.

In reality, OWS *is* anarchist-inspired, but for precisely that reason it stands squarely in the very tradition of American popular democracy that conservatives like Continetti have always staunchly opposed. Anarchism does not mean the negation of democracy—or at least, any of the aspects of democracy that most Americans have historically liked. Rather, anarchism is a matter of taking those core democratic principles to their logical conclusions. The reason it's difficult to see this is because the word "democracy" has had such an endlessly contested history: so much so that most American pundits and politicians, for instance, now use the term to refer to a form of government established with the explicit purpose of ensuring what John Adams once called "the horrors of democracy" would never come about.[2]

As I mentioned at the beginning of the book, most Americans are unaware that nowhere in the Declaration of Independence or the Constitution does it say anything about the United States being a democracy.* In fact, most of those who took part in composing those founding documents readily agreed with the

* The same is true of all thirteen of the original state constitutions created after the Revolution.

seventeenth-century Puritan preacher John Winthrop, who wrote that "a democracy is, among most civil nations, accounted the meanest and worst of all forms of government."[3]

Most of the Founders learned what they did know about the subject of democracy from Thomas Hobbes's English translation of Thucydides' *History,* his account of the Peloponnesian War. Hobbes undertook this project, he was careful to inform his readers, to warn about the dangers of democracy. As a result, the founders used the word in its ancient Greek sense, assuming democracy to refer to communal self-governance through popular assemblies such as the Athenian agora. It was what we would now call "direct democracy." One might say that it was a system of rule by General Assemblies, except that these assemblies were assumed to always operate exclusively by the principle of 51 to 49 percent majority rule. James Madison for instance, made clear in his contributions to the Federalist Papers why he felt this sort of Athenian democracy was not only impossible in a great nation of his day, since it could not by definition operate over an extended geographical area, but was actively undesirable, since he felt history showed that any system of direct democracy would inevitably descend into factionalism, demagoguery, and finally, the seizure of power by some dictator willing to restore order and control:

A pure democracy, by which I mean a society consisting of a small number of citizens, who assemble and administer the government in person, can admit of no cure for the mischiefs of faction. . . . Hence it is that such democracies have ever been spectacles of turbulence and contention; have ever been found incompatible with personal security or the rights of property; and have in general been as short in their lives as they have been violent in their deaths.[4]

Like all the men we've come to know as Founding Fathers, Madison insisted that his preferred form of government, a "republic," was necessarily quite different:

> In a democracy the people meet and exercise the government in person; in a republic they assemble and administer it by their representatives and agents. A democracy, consequently, must be confined to a small spot. A republic may be extended over a large region.[5]

Now, this notion that republics were administered by "representatives" might seem odd at first glance, since they borrowed the term "republic" from ancient Rome, and Roman senators were not elected; they were aristocrats who held their seats by birthright, which meant they weren't really "representatives and agents" of anyone but themselves. Still, the idea of representative bodies was something the Founders had inherited from the British during the Revolution: the rulers of the new nation were precisely those who had been elected, by a vote of property-holding males, to representative assemblies like the Continental Congress, originally meant to allow a limited measure of self-governance under the authority of the king. After the revolution, they immediately transferred the power of government from King George III to themselves. As a result, the representative bodies meant to operate under the authority of the king would now operate under the authority of the people, however narrowly defined.

The custom of electing delegates to such bodies was nothing new. In England it went back to at least the thirteenth century. By the fifteenth century, it had become standard practice to allow men of property to select their parliamentary representatives by sending in their votes to their local sheriff (usually recorded on notched sticks). At that time it never would have occurred to anyone that this system had anything to do with "democracy."[6] Elections were assumed to be an extension of monarchical systems of government, since representatives were in no sense empowered to govern. They did not rule anything, collectively or as individuals; their role was to speak for ("represent") the inhabitants of their district before the sovereign power of the king, to offer advice, air grievances, and, above all, deliver their county's taxes. So while the representatives were powerless and the elections rarely contested, the system of elected representatives was considered necessary according to the prevailing medieval legal principle of consent: it was felt that while orders naturally came from above, and ordinary subjects should have no role in framing policy, those same ordinary subjects could not be held to be bound by orders to which they had not, in some broad sense, assented. True, after the English Civil War, Parliament did begin to assert its own rights to have a say in the disposal of tax receipts, creating what the framers called a "limited monarchy"—but still, the American idea of saying that the people could actually exercise sovereign power, the power once held by kings, by voting for representatives with real governing power, was a genuine innovation and immediately recognized as such.[7]

The American War of Independence had been fought in the name of "the people," and all the framers felt that the "whole body of the people" had to be consulted at some point to make their revolution legitimate—but the entire purpose of the Constitution was to ensure that this form of consultation was extremely limited, lest the "horrors of democracy" ensue. At the time, the common assumption among educated people was that there were three elementary principles of government that were held to exist, in different measure, in all known human societies: monarchy, aristocracy, and democracy. The framers agreed with ancient political theorists who held that the Roman Republic represented the most perfect balance between them. Republican Rome had two consuls (elected by the Senate) who filled the monarchical function, a permanent patrician class of senators, and, finally, popular assemblies with limited powers of their own. These assemblies selected from among aristocratic candidates for magistracies, and also chose two tribunes, who represented the interest of the plebeian class; tribunes could not vote or even enter the Senate (they sat just outside the doorway) but they were granted veto power over senatorial decisions.

The American Constitution was designed to achieve a similar balance. The monarchical function was to be filled by a president elected by the Senate; the Senate was meant to represent the aristocratic interests of wealth, and Congress was to represent the democratic element. Its purview was largely to be confined to raising and spending money, since the Revolution had, after all, been fought on the principle of "no taxation without representation." Popular assemblies were eliminated altogether. The American colonies, of course, lacked any hereditary aristocracy. But by electing a temporary monarch, and temporary representatives, the framers argued they could instead create what they sometimes explicitly called a kind of "natural aristocracy," drawn from the educated and propertied classes who had the same sober concern for the public welfare that they felt characterized the Roman senate of Cicero and Cincinnatus.

It is worthwhile, I think, to dwell on this point for a moment. When the framers spoke of an "aristocracy" they were not using the term metaphorically. They were well aware that they were creating a new political form that fused together democratic and aristocratic elements. In all previous European history, elections had been considered—as Aristotle had originally insisted—the quintessentially aristocratic mode of selecting public officials. In elections, the populace chooses between a small number of usually professional politicians who claim to be wiser and more educated than everyone else, and chooses the one they think the best of all. (This is what "aristocracy" literally means: "rule of the best.") Elections were ways that mercenary armies chose their commanders, or nobles vied for the support of future retainers. The democratic approach—employed widely in the ancient world, but also in Renaissance cities like Florence—was lottery, or, as it was sometimes called, "sortition." Essentially, the procedure was to take the names of anyone in the community willing to hold public office, and then, after screening them for basic competence, choose their names at random. This ensured all competent and interested parties had an equal chance of holding public office. It also minimalized factionalism, since there was no point making promises to win over key constituencies if one was to be chosen by lot. (Elections, by contract, fostered factionalism, for obvious reasons.) It's striking that while in the generations immediately before the French and American revolutions there was a lively debate among Enlightenment thinkers like Montesquieu and Rousseau on the relative merits of election and lottery, those creating the new revolutionary constitutions in the 1770s and 1780s did not consider using lotteries at all. The only use they found for lottery was in the jury system, and this was allowed to stand largely because it was already there, a tradition inherited from English common law. And even the jury system was compulsory, not voluntary; juries were (and still are) regularly informed that their role is not to consider the justice of the law, but only to judge the facts of evidence.

There were to be no assemblies. There was to be no sortition. The Founding Fathers insisted that sovereignty belongs to the people, but that—unless they rose up in arms in another revolution—the people could *only* exercise that sovereignty by choosing among members of a class of superior men—superior both because they were trained as lawyers, and because coming from the upper classes they were wiser and better able to understand the people's true interests than the people themselves were. Since "the people" would also be bound to obey the laws passed by the legislative bodies over which this new natural aristocracy presided, the Founders' notion of popular sovereignty was really not too far removed from the old medieval notion of consent to orders from above.

Actually, if one reads the work of John Adams, or the Federalist Papers, one might well wonder why such authors spent so much time discussing the dangers of Athenian-style direct democracy at all. This was, after all, a political system that had not existed for more than two thousand years and no major political figure of the time was openly advocating reestablishing it.

Here is where it becomes useful to consider the larger political context. There might not have been democracies in the eighteenth-century North Atlantic, but there were definitely men who referred to themselves as "democrats." In America, Tom Paine is perhaps the most famous example. During the same period in which the Continental Congress was beginning to contemplate severing relations with the English Crown, the term was undergoing something of a revival in Europe, where populists opposed to aristocratic rule increasingly began to refer to themselves as "democrats"—at first, it would seem, mainly for shock value, in much the same way that the gay rights movement defiantly adopted the word "queer." In most places, they were a tiny minority of rabble-rousers, not intellectuals; few propounded any elaborate theory of government. Most appear to have been involved in campaigns against noble or ecclesiastical privilege, and for very basic principles like equality before the law. When revolutions did break out, however, such men found their natural homes in the mass meetings and assemblies that always emerge in such situations—whether in New England town hall meetings or in the "sections" of the French revolutions—and many of them came to see such assemblies as potential building blocks for a new political order.[8] Since, unlike elected bodies, there were no property restrictions on voting at mass meetings, they tended to entertain far more radical ideas.

In the years immediately leading up to the American Revolution, the Patriots made much use of mass meetings, as well as calling up "the mob" or "mobility" (as they liked to call it) for mass actions like the Boston Tea Party. Often they were terrified by the results. On May 19, 1774, for example, a mass meeting was called in New York City to discuss a tax boycott to respond to the British closing of Boston Harbor—a meeting probably held not far from the present Zuccotti Park, and which apparently produced the very first proposal to convene a Continental Congress. We have an account of it from Gouverneur Morris, then chief justice of New Jersey, scion of the family that then owned most of what's now the Bronx. Morris describes watching as common mechanics and tradesmen who had taken the day off work ended up locked in a prolonged debate with the gentry and their supporters over "the future forms of our government, and whether it should be founded on aristocratic or democratic principles." As the gentry argued the merits of continuing with the existing (extremely conservative) English constitution, butchers and bakers responded with arguments from the Gracchi and Polybius:

> I stood in the balcony, and on my right hand were ranged all the people of property, with some few poor dependants, and on the other all the tradesmen, &c., who thought it worth their while to leave daily labor for the good of the country. The spirit of the English Constitution has yet a little influence left, but just a little. The remains of it, however, will give the wealthy people a superiority this time, but would they secure it, they must banish all schoolmasters, and confine all knowledge to themselves. This cannot be.
>
> The mob begin to think and to reason. Poor reptiles! it is with them a vernal morning, they are struggling to cast off their winter's slough, they bask in the sunshine, and ere noon they will bite, depend upon it. The gentry begin to fear this.[9]

So did Morris, who concluded from the event that full independence from Britain would be a very bad idea, lest, "I see it with fear and trembling, we will be under the worst of all possible dominions—a riotous mob."

Still, this conclusion seems rather disingenuous. What his account makes clear is it was not the irrational passions of "the mob" that frightened Morris, but precisely the opposite, the fact that so many of New York's mechanics and tradesmen could apparently not only trade classical references with the best of them, but frame thoughtful, reasoned arguments for democracy. *The mob begin to think and to reason.* Since there seemed no way to deny them access to education, the only remaining expedient was to rely on the force of British arms.

Morris ended the letter noting that the gentry put together a committee loaded with the wealthy to "trick" the ordinary people into thinking they had their best interests at heart. Unlike most of New York's propertied classes, he did eventually come over to the revolutionaries and ultimately went on to compose the final draft of the U.S. Constitution, although some of his strongest proposals at the Constitutional Convention, for instance, that senators should be appointed for life, were considered too conservative even for his fellow delegates, and were not ultimately adopted.

Even after the war, it was difficult to put the genie of democracy back in the bottle. Mobilizations, mass meetings, and threats of popular uprising continued. As before the Revolution, many of these protests centered on debt. After the war, there was a heated debate over what to do about the Revolutionary War debt. The popular demand was to let it inflate away into nothing and base the currency on paper notes issued by local "land banks" under public control. The Continental Congress took the opposite approach, following the advice of wealthy Philadelphia merchant Robert Morris (apparently no relation to Gouverneur) that wealthy speculators who'd bought up the debt at depreciated prices should be paid in full. This, he said, would cause wealth to flow "into the hands of those who would render it most productive"; at the same time, creating a single, central bank, on the model of the Bank of England, would allow the national debt to circulate as "new medium of commerce."[10] This system, of making government war debt the basis of the currency, was tried and true, and in a way it's the one we still have now in the Federal Reserve—but in the early days of the republic the ramifications for simple farmers who ended up effectively having to pay the debt were catastrophic. Thousands of returning Revolutionary War veterans would often find themselves greeted by "sheriff's wagons" arriving to seize their most valuable possessions. The result was waves of popular mobilizations and at least two major uprisings, one in western Massachusetts, one in rural Pennsylvania, and even calls, in some quarters, to introduce legislation to expropriate the largest speculators instead.*

---

* The uprisings are known to history as Shays' Rebellion, and even more condescendingly, the Whiskey Rebellion, though the latter name was consciously invented by Alexander Hamilton to dismiss the rebels as drunken hillbillies rather than, as Terry Bouton has demonstrated, citizens calling for greater democratic control. See Bouton, *Taming Democracy: "The People," the Founders, and the Troubled Ending of the American Revolution* (Oxford: Oxford University Press, 1997). There has been a wealth of recent research on the topic: notably, Woody Holton's *Unruly Americans and the Origin of the Constitution* (New York: Hill & Wang, 2007), and William Hogeland's *The Whiskey Rebellion* (New York: Simon & Schuster, 2006), and *Founding Finance: How Debt, Speculation, Foreclosures, Protests, and Crackdowns Made Us a Nation* (Austin: University of Texas Press, 2012). The intellectual tradition goes back at least to Charles Beard's famous *An Economic*

For men like Adams, Madison, or Hamilton, such projects bore a disturbing similarity to those of revolutionary movements of antiquity, with their calls to abolish debts and redistribute the land, and became prima facie evidence that America should never operate by a principle of majority rule. For instance, John Adams:

> If all were to be decided by a vote of the majority, the eight or nine millions who have no property, would not think of usurping over the rights of the one or two millions who have? . . .
>
> Debts would be abolished first; taxes laid heavy on the rich, and not at all on the others; and at last a downright equal division of everything be demanded, and voted. What would be the consequence of this? The idle, the vicious, the intemperate, would rush into the utmost extravagance of debauchery, sell and spend all their share, and then demand a new division of those who purchased from them. The moment the idea is admitted into society, that property is not as sacred as the laws of God, and that there is not a force of law and public justice to protect it, anarchy and tyranny commence.[11]

Similarly, for Madison, republican government was not just superior because it was capable of operating over a wide geographical range; it was better to have a government operating

---

Interpretation of the Constitution of the United States (New York: McMillan, 1913), which pointed out the Framers were almost exclusively bond-holders, though his original conclusions have been much further refined by subsequent research.

over a wide geographical range because if there ever was "a rage for paper money, for an abolition of debts, for an equal division of property, or for any other improper or wicked project,"[12] it was likely to occur on a local level—and a strong central government would ensure it could be quickly contained.

This, then, is what the nightmare vision of Athenian democracy seemed to mean for such men: that if the town hall assemblies and mass meetings of farmers, mechanics, and tradesmen that had formed in the years leading up to the Revolution became institutionalized, these—"abolition of debts . . . equal division of property"—were the sorts of demands they would likely make. Even more, they feared the specter of orgy, tumult, and indiscipline, where the sort of grave republicans who led Rome to glory and whom the Founders saw as their model would be cast aside for the vulgar passions of the masses. Another telling Adams quote about Athens: "From the first to the last moment of her democratical constitution, levity, gayety, inconstancy, dissipation, intemperance, debauchery, and a dissolution of manners, were the prevailing character of the whole nation."[13] Dr. Benjamin Rush, a physician and stalwart of Philadelphia's Sons of Liberty, actually felt that this democratic loosening of manners could be diagnosed as a kind of disease—thinking, here, particularly of the effects of "the changes in the habits of diet, and company, and manners, produced by annihilation of just debts by means of depreciated paper money":

> The excess of the passion for liberty, inflamed by the successful issue of the war, produced, in many people, opinions and conduct which could not be removed by reason nor restrained by government. . . . The extensive influence

which these opinions had upon the understandings, passions and morals of many of the citizens of the United
States, constituted a species of insanity, which I shall take
the liberty of distinguishing by the name of Anarchia.[14]

The reference to "depreciated paper money" is significant here.
One of the issues that drove the Federalists to convene the
Constitutional convention in the first place was not just the
threat of riots and rebellions against hard-money policies,
which could be militarily contained, but the fear that "democratic" forces might begin to take over state governments and
begin printing their own currency—both George Washington,
then the richest man in America, and Thomas Jefferson, had
personally lost considerable chunks of their personal fortunes
through such schemes. And this is precisely what had already
begun to happen in Pennsylvania, which had eliminated property qualifications for voting, and quickly saw the formation of
a populist legislature that, in 1785, first revoked the charter for
Robert Morris's central bank, and then began a scheme to create a system of public credit, with paper money designed to
depreciate in value over time, so as to relieve debtors and
thwart speculators. One of the leaders of the popular faction,
Quaker preacher Herman Husband—who men like Rush referred to as "the madman of Alleghenies"—openly argued that
such measures were justified because vast inequalities of wealth
made it impossible for freeborn citizens to participate in politics.* When the Framers assembled in Philadelphia in 1787,

* Husband had called for a relatively equal distribution of landed
  property as well, on the grounds that inequalities of property mitigate
  against democratic participation, and for voting districts small enough

Morris among them, they were determined to prevent the contagion from spreading. To get a sense of the flavor of the debate at the convention, we might consider its opening remarks, by Edmund Randolph, then governor of Virginia. Even outside of Pennsylvania, state constitutions did not contain sufficient safeguards against "government exercised by the people":

> Our chief danger arises from the democratic parts of our constitutions. It is a maxim which I hold incontrovertible, that the powers of government exercised by the people swallows up the other branches. None of the constitutions have provided sufficient checks against the democracy. The feeble senate of Virginia is a phantom. Maryland has a more powerful senate, but the late distractions in that state have discovered that it is not powerful enough. The check established in the constitution of New York and Massachusetts is yet a stronger barrier against democracy, but they all seem insufficient.*

The Canadian political scientist Francis Dupuis-Déri has carefully mapped out the way the word "democracy" was used by major political figures in the United States, France, and Canada during the eighteenth and nineteenth centuries and has discovered in every case exactly the same pattern. When the word

---

that representatives could regularly consult with their constituents. It is likely he was exactly who Adams was thinking of in his remarks about the dangers of majority vote.

* This passage is the opening epigraph of William Hogeland's *The Whiskey Rebellion,* which emphasizes the degree to which the resulting document was careful to avoid actual democracy.

first gains currency between 1770 and 1800, it is deployed almost exclusively as a term of opprobrium and abuse. The French revolutionaries disdained "democracy" almost as much as the American ones. It was seen as anarchy, the lack of government, and riotous chaos. Over time, a few begin to use the term, often as a provocation: as when Robespierre, at the height of the terror, began to refer to himself as a democrat, or when in 1800, Thomas Jefferson—who never mentioned the word "democracy" at all in his early writings,* but who ran against Adams as a radical, sympathetic with the organizers of debt uprisings and strongly opposed to central banking schemes—decided to rename his party the "Democratic-Republicans."

Still, it took some time before the term came into common use.

It was between 1830 and 1850 that politicians in the United States and France began to identify themselves as democrats and to use *democracy* to designate the electoral regime, even though no constitutional change or transformation of the decision-making process warranted this change in name. The shift in meaning first occurred in the United States. Andrew Jackson was the first presidential candidate to present himself as a democrat, a label by which he meant that he would defend

* In the twelve collected volumes of Jefferson's work the word "democracy" appears once, and only then in a quote by Samuel von Pufendorf about the legalities of treaties! Of course, Jefferson was the closest to an advocate of direct democracy as there was among the Founders, with his famous vision of dividing the country into thousands of "wards" small enough to afford public participation, allowing citizens to maintain the same sort of popular mobilization witnessed during the Revolution—but even these he referred to as small republics.

the interests of the little people (in particular, small Midwest farmers and laborers in the large Eastern cities) against the powerful (bureaucrats and politicians in Washington and the upper classes in large cities).[15]

Jackson was running as a populist—once again, against the central banking system, which he did temporarily manage to dismantle. As Dupuis-Déri observes, "Jackson and his allies were well aware that their use of *democracy* was akin to what would today be called political marketing"; it was basically a cynical ploy, but it was wildly successful—so much so that within ten years time all candidates of all political parties were referring to themselves as "democrats." Since the same thing happened everywhere—France, England, Canada—where the franchise was widened sufficiently that masses of ordinary citizens were allowed to vote, the result was that the term "democracy" itself changed as well—so that the elaborate republican system that the Founders had created with the express purpose of containing the dangers of democracy, itself was relabeled "democracy," which is how we continue to use the term today.

———

Clearly, then, the word "democracy" meant something different for ordinary Americans, as well as ordinary Frenchmen and Englishmen, than it did for members of the political elite. The question is precisely what. Owing to the limited nature of our sources—we have no way of knowing for instance, once the New York mob "began to think and reason," what arguments they actually put forth—we can really only guess. But I think we can reconstruct some broad principles.

First of all, when members of the educated classes spoke of

"democracy," they were thinking of a system of government, which traced back specifically to the ancient world. Ordinary Americans in contrast appear to have seen it, as we would say today, in much broader social and cultural terms: "democracy" was freedom, equality, the ability of a simple farmer or trades-man to address his "betters" with dignity and self-respect—the kind of broader democratic sensibility that was soon to so im-press foreign observers like Alexis de Tocqueville when they spoke of "Democracy in America" two generations later. The roots of this sensibility, like the real roots of many of the po-litical innovations that made the great eighteenth-century revo-lutions possible, are difficult to reconstruct. But they do not seem to lie where we are used to looking for them.

One reason we find it so difficult to reconstruct the history of these democratic sensibilities, and the everyday forms of or-ganization and decision making they inspired, is that we are used to telling the story in a very peculiar way. It's a story that only really took shape in the wake of World War I, when uni-versities in the United States and some parts of Europe began promulgating the notion that democracy was an intrinsic part of what they called "Western civilization." The idea that there even was something called "Western civilization" was, at the time, relatively new: the expression would have been meaning-less in the time of Washington or Jefferson. According to this new version of history, which soon became gospel to American conservatives, and is largely taken for granted by everyone else, democracy is really a set of institutional structures, based on voting, that was first "invented" in ancient Athens and has re-mained somehow embedded in a grand tradition that traveled from Greece to Rome to medieval England, making a detour through Renaissance Italy, and then finally lodging itself in the

North Atlantic, which is now its special home. This formulation is how former cold warriors like Samuel Huntington can argue that we are now engaged in a "war of civilizations," with the free and democratic West vainly trying to inflict its values on everyone else. As an historical argument, this is an obvious example of special pleading. The whole story makes no sense. First of all, about the only thing Voltaire, Madison, or Gladstone really had in common with an inhabitant of ancient Greece is that he grew up reading ancient Greek books. But if the Western tradition is simply an intellectual tradition, how can one possibly call it democratic? In fact, not a single surviving ancient Greek author was in favor of democracy, and for 2,400 years at least, virtually every author now identified with "Western civilization" was explicitly antidemocratic. When someone has the temerity to point this out, the usual response by conservatives is to switch gears and say that "the West" is a cultural tradition, whose unique love of liberty can already be witnessed in medieval documents like the Magna Carta and was just waiting to burst out in the Age of Revolutions. This makes a little better sense. If nothing else, it would explain the popular enthusiasm for democracy in countries like the United States and France, even in the face of universal elite disapproval. But, if one takes that approach, and says "the West" is really a deep cultural tradition, then other parts of the conventional story fall apart. For one thing, how can one say that the Western tradition begins in Greece? After all, if we're speaking in cultural terms, the people alive today most similar to ancient Greeks are obviously modern Greeks. Yet most of those who celebrate the "Western tradition" don't even think modern Greece is part of the West anymore—Greece apparently having defected back around A.D. 600 when they chose the wrong variety of Christianity.

In fact, as it's currently used, "the West" can mean almost anything. It can be used to refer to an intellectual tradition, a cultural tradition, a locus of political power ("Western intervention"), even a racial term ("the bodies discovered in Afghanistan appeared to be those of Westerners"), more or less depending on the needs of the moment.

It's not surprising then that American conservatives react so violently to any challenge to the primacy of "Western civilization"—since "Western civilization" is, essentially, something they made up. In fact for all its incoherence it might well be the only powerful idea they ever made up. In order to have any chance of understanding the real history of democracy, we have to put all this aside and start from scratch. If we do not see Western Europe as some special chosen land, then what, in the sixteenth, seventeenth, and eighteenth centuries, do we really see? Well, first of all, we see a group of North Atlantic kingdoms that were in almost every case moving *away* from earlier forms of popular participation in government, and forming ever more centralized, absolutist governments. Remember, until that time Northern Europe had been something of a backwater. During this period, European societies were not only expanding everywhere, with projects of overseas trade, conquest, and colonization across Asia, Africa, and the Americas, but they were also, as a result, being flooded with a dazzling welter of new and unfamiliar political ideas. Most European intellectuals who encountered these ideas were interested in using them to create even stronger centralized monarchies: like the German scholar Leibniz, who found inspiration in the example of China, with its cultural uniformity, national examination boards, and rational civil service, or Montesquieu, who became equally intrigued by the example of Persia. Others (John Locke, for example, or many of the other English political philosophers so beloved by the Founding Fathers) became fascinated by the discovery of societies in North America that appeared to be simultaneously far more egalitarian, and far more individualistic, than anything Europeans had previously imagined possible.

In Europe, tracts and arguments about the significance, and political and moral implications, of these newly discovered social possibilities abounded. In the American colonies, this was not a matter of mere intellectual reflection. The first European settlers in North America not only were in the paradoxical situation of being in direct contact with indigenous nations, and being obliged to learn many of their ways just to be able to survive in their new environment, at exactly the same time; they were also displacing and largely exterminating them. In the process—at least, according to the scandalized accounts of the leaders of early settler communities—they themselves, and especially their children, began acting more and more like Indians.

This is important since most debates over the influence of indigenous societies on American democracy largely miss the profoundly cultural transformation that resulted. There has been quite a lively debate on the topic since the 1980s. It's usually referred to in the scholarly literature as "the influence debate." While the scholars who kicked it off, historians Donald Grinde, himself a Native American, and Bruce Johansen, were making a much broader argument, the whole debate quickly became sidetracked over one very specific question: whether certain elements in the American Constitution, particularly its federal structure, were originally inspired by the example of the League of Six Nations of the Haudenosaunee, or Iroquois. This particular debate began in 1977, when Grinde pointed out that the idea of a federation of colonies seemed to have been first proposed by an Onondaga ambassador named Canassatego during negotiations over the Lancaster Treaty of 1744. Exhausted by having to negotiate with six different colonies, he snapped an arrow in half to show how easy it was to break it, then took a bundle of six arrows, and challenged his interlocutors to do the same. (This bundle of arrows still appears on the Seal of the Union of the United States, though with the number increased to thirteen.) Benjamin Franklin, who had taken part in the negotiations, did later propose the colonies adopt a federal system, though it was at first without success.

Grinde was not the first to suggest that Iroquois federal institutions might have had some influence on the U.S. Constitution. Similar ideas were occasionally proposed in the nineteenth century and, at the time, no one found anything particularly threatening or remarkable about it. When it was proposed again in the 1980s it set off a firestorm. Congress passed a bill recognizing the Haudenosaunee contribution and conservatives were up in arms at any suggestion that the Founders were influenced by anything but the tradition of "Western civilization." Almost all scholars of Native American descent embraced the notion, but they also emphasized that this was simply one example of a broader process of settlers being influenced by the freedom-loving ways of indigenous societies. Meanwhile, both (nonnative) anthropologists who studied the Six Nations and American constitutional historians insisted on focusing exclusively on the constitutional question, and rejected the argument out of hand. This meant insisting that despite the fact that many of the Founders had taken part in treaty negotiations with the Haudenosaunee federation, and despite the fact that this was the only federal system with which any of them had direct experience, that experience played no role whatsoever in their thinking when they pondered how to create a federal system themselves.

On the face of it, this seems an extraordinary claim. The reason it's possible to make it is that when the authors of the Federalist Papers did openly discuss the advantages and disadvantages of different sorts of federal systems, they did not mention the one they had seen, but rather others they'd only read about: the organization of Judaea in the time of the Book of Judges, the Achaean League, the Swiss Confederacy, the United Provinces of the Netherlands. When they did refer to indigenous peoples, they ordinarily referred to them as "the American savages," who were perhaps to be occasionally celebrated as exemplars of individual liberty but whose political experience was strictly irrelevant for that very reason. John Adams, for instance, compared them to the ancient Goths, a people unusual, he held, in that they actually could support a largely democratic system of government without it being plunged into violent unrest. This was possible for both peoples, he concluded, because they were too scattered and indolent to have accumulated any significant amount of property, and therefore did not need institutions designed to protect wealth.

Still, the entire constitutional debate was something of a sideshow. It's a way of keeping everything focused on the reading habits of the educated gentry, and the kinds of arguments and allusions they considered appropriate to employ in public debate. For instance, it's clear that the Founders were well aware of Canassatego's metaphor of the arrows—after all, they put the image on the seal of their new republic—it never seems to have occurred to any to so much as allude to it in their published writings, speeches, or debates. Even New York's butchers and wainwrights knew that when debating with the gentry, they had to adorn their arguments with plenty of classical references.

If we want to explore the origins of those democratic sensibilities that caused ordinary New Yorkers to feel sympathetic to the idea of democratic rule in the first place, or even to find where people actually had direct, hands-on experience in collective decision making that might have influenced their sense of what democracy might actually be like, we not only have to look beyond the sitting rooms of the educated gentry. In fact, we soon find ourselves in places that might seem, at first, genuinely startling. In 1999, one of the leading contemporary historians of European democracy, John Markoff, published an essay called "Where and When Was Democracy Invented?" In it there appears the following passage:

> That leadership could derive from the consent of the led, rather than be bestowed by higher authority, would have been a likely experience of the crews of pirate vessels in the early modern Atlantic world. Pirate crews not only elected their captains, but were familiar with countervailing power (in the forms of the quartermaster and ship's council) and contractual relations of individual and collectivity (in the form of written ship's articles specifying shares of booty and rates of compensation for on-the-job injury).[16]

He makes the remark very much in passing but in a way it's a very telling example. If existing ship constitutions are anything to go by, the typical organization of eighteenth-century pirate ships was remarkably democratic.[17] Captains were not only elected, they usually functioned much like Native American war chiefs: granted total power during chase or combat, but otherwise treated like ordinary crewmen. Those ships whose captains were granted more general powers also insisted on the crew's right to remove them at any time for cowardice, cruelty, or any other reason. In every case, ultimate power rested in a general assembly, which often ruled on even the most minor matters, always, apparently, by a majority show of hands.

This isn't surprising if one considers the pirates' origins. Pirates were generally mutineers, sailors often originally pressed into service against their will in port towns across the Atlantic, who had mutinied against tyrannical captains and "declared war against the whole world." They often became classic social bandits, wreaking vengeance against captains who abused their crews, and releasing or even rewarding those against whom they found no complaints. The makeup of crews was often extraordinarily heterogeneous. According to Marcus Rediker's *Villains of All Nations,* "Black Sam Bellamy's crew of 1717 was 'a Mix'd Multitude of all Country's,' including British, French, Dutch, Spanish, Swedish, Native American, African American, and two dozen Africans who had been liberated from a slave ship."[18] In other words, we are dealing with a collection of people in which there was likely to be at least some firsthand knowledge of a very wide range of directly democratic institutions, ranging from Swedish *things* (councils) to African village assemblies to Native American federal structures, suddenly finding themselves forced to improvise some mode of self-government in the complete absence of any state. It was the perfect intercultural space of experiment. There was likely to be no more conducive ground for the development of new democratic institutions anywhere in the Atlantic world at the time.

Did the democratic practices developed on Atlantic pirate ships in the early part of the eighteenth century have any influence, direct or indirect, on the evolution of democratic constitutions in the North Atlantic world sixty or seventy years later? It's possible. There's no doubt that the typical eighteenth-century New York mechanic or tradesman had spent plenty of time trading pirate stories over a pint at dockside bars. Sensationalist accounts of the pirates did circulate widely and it's likely that men like Madison or Jefferson had read them, at least as children. But it's impossible to really know if such men culled any ideas from such accounts; if such stories had influenced them in any way, it would have been the last influence they would ever have openly acknowledged.

One might even speculate about the existence of a kind of broad democratic unconscious that lay behind many of the ideas and arguments of the American Revolution, ideas whose origins even ordinary citizens felt uncomfortable with, since they were so firmly associated with savagery and criminality. The pirates are just the most vivid example. Even more important in the North American colonies were the societies of the frontier. But those early colonies were far more similar to pirate ships than we are given to imagine. Frontier communities might not have been as densely populated as pirate ships, or in as immediate need of constant cooperation, but they were spaces of intercultural improvisation, and, like the pirate ships, largely outside the purview of any states. It's only recently that historians have begun to document just how thoroughly entangled the societies of settlers and natives were in those early days,[19] with settlers adopting Indian crops, clothes, medicines, customs, and styles of warfare. They engaged in trading, often living side by side, sometimes intermarrying, while others lived for years as captives in Indian communities before returning to their homes having learned native languages, habits, and mores. Most of all, historians have noted the endless fears among the leaders of colonial communities and military units that their subordinates were—in the same way that they had taken up the use of tomahawks, wampum, and canoes— beginning to absorb Indian attitudes of equality and individual liberty.

The result was a cultural transformation that affected almost every aspect of settler life. For instance, Puritans felt that corporal punishment was absolutely essential in the raising of children: the birch was required to teach children the meaning of authority, to break their will (tainted by original sin), in much the way one breaks a horse or other animal—in the same way as, they also held, the birch was required in adult life to discipline wives and servants. Most Native Americans in contrast felt that children should never be beaten, under any circumstances. In the 1690s, at the same time as the famous Boston Calvinist minister Cotton Mather was inveighing against pirates as a blaspheming scourge of mankind, he was also complaining that his fellow settlers, led astray by the ease of the climate in the New World and relaxed attitudes of its native inhabitants, had begun to undergo what he called "Indianization"—refusing to apply corporal punishment to their children, and thus undermining the principles of discipline, hierarchy, and formality that should govern relations between masters and servants, men and women, or young and old:

> Though the first English planters in this country had usually a government and a discipline in their families and had a sufficient severity in it, yet, as if the climate had taught us to Indianize, the relaxation of it is now such that it is wholly laid aside, and a foolish indulgence to children is become an epidemical miscarriage of the country, and like to be attended with many evil consequences.[20]

In other words, insofar as an individualistic, indulgent, freedom-loving spirit first began emerging among the colonists, the early Puritan Fathers laid it squarely at the feet of the Indians—or, as they still called them at the time, "the Americans," since the settlers then still considered themselves not American but English. One of the ironies of the "influence debate" is that in all the sound and fury over the Iroquois influence on the federal system, this was what Grinde and Johansen were really trying to emphasize: that ordinary Englishmen and Frenchmen settled in the colonies only began to think of themselves as "Americans," as a new sort of freedom-loving people, when they began to see themselves as more like Indians.

What was true in towns like Boston was all the more true on the frontiers, especially in those communities often made up of escaped slaves and servants who "became Indians" outside the control of colonial governments entirely,[21] or island enclaves of what historians Peter Linebaugh and Marcus Rediker have called "the Atlantic proletariat," the motley collection of freedmen, sailors, ship's whores, renegades, Antinomians, and rebels who developed in the port cities of the North Atlantic world before the emergence of modern racism, and from whom much of the democratic impulse of the American—and other—revolutions seems to have first emerged.[22] Men like Mather would have agreed with that as well: he often wrote that Indian attacks on frontier settlements were God's punishment on such folk for abandoning their rightful masters and living like Indians themselves.

If the history were truly written, it seems to me that the real origin of the democratic spirit—and most likely, many democratic institutions—lies precisely in those spaces of improvisation just outside the control of governments and organized churches. I might add that this includes the Haudenosaunee themselves. The league was originally formed—we don't know precisely when—as a kind of contractual agreement among the Seneca, Onondaga, Cayuga, Oneida, and Mohawk (the sixth tribe, the Tuscarora, joined later) to create a way of mediating disputes and making peace; but during their period of expansion in the seventeenth century it became an extraordinary jumble of peoples, with large proportions of the population adopted war captives from other indigenous nations, captured settlers, and runaways. One Jesuit missionary at the height of the seventeenth century Beaver Wars complained that it was almost impossible to preach to the Seneca in their own language, since so many were barely fluent in it! Even during the eighteenth century, for instance, while Canassatego, the ambassador who first suggested a federation to the colonists, was born to Onondaga parents, the other main Haudenosaunee negotiator with the colonists at this time, Swatane, was actually French—or, anyway, originally born to French parents in Quebec. Like all living constitutions, the league was constantly

changing and evolving, and no doubt much of the careful architecture and solemn dignity of its council structure was the
product of just such a creative mix of cultures, tradition, and
experience.

———

Why do conservatives insist that democracy was invented in
ancient Greece, and that it is somehow inherent in what they
call "Western civilization"—despite all the overwhelming evidence to the contrary? In the end, it's just a way of doing what
the rich and powerful always do: taking possession of the fruits
of other people's labor. It's a way of staking a property claim.
And property claims must be defended. This is why, if whenever someone like Amartya Sen appears (as he has recently
done) to make the obvious point that democracy can just as
easily be found in village councils in southern Africa, or India,
one can count on an immediate wave of indignant responses in
conservative journals and web pages arguing that he has completely missed the point.

Generally speaking, if you can find a concept—truth, freedom, democracy—that everyone agrees is a good thing, then
you can be sure that no one will agree on precisely what it is.
But the moment you ask *why* most Americans, or most people
generally, like the idea of democracy, the conventional story
not only falls apart, it becomes completely irrelevant.

Democracy was not invented in ancient Greece. Granted,
the word "democracy" was invented in ancient Greece—but
largely by people who didn't like the thing itself very much.
Democracy was never really "invented" at all. Neither does it
emerge from any particular intellectual tradition. It's not even
really a mode of government. In its essence it is just the belief

that humans are fundamentally equal and ought to be allowed to manage their collective affairs in an egalitarian fashion, using whatever means appear most conducive. That, and the hard work of bringing arrangements based on those principles into being.

In this sense democracy is as old as history, as human intelligence itself. No one could possibly own it. I suppose, if one were so inclined, one could argue it emerged the moment hominids ceased merely trying to bully one another and developed the communication skills to work out a common problem collectively. But such speculation is idle; the point is that democratic assemblies can be attested in all times and places, from Balinese seka to Bolivian ayllu, employing an endless variety of formal procedures, and will always crop up wherever a large group of people sat down together to make a collective decision on the principle that all taking part should have equal say.

One of the reasons it is easy for political scientists to ignore such local associations and assemblies when speaking of the history of democracy is that in most such assemblies, things never come down to a vote. The idea that democracy is simply a matter of voting—which the Founders, too, assumed—also allows one to think of it as an innovation, some sort of conceptual breakthrough: as if it had never occurred to anyone in previous epochs to test support for a proposal by asking people to all put up their hands, scratch something on a potsherd, or have everyone supporting a proposal stand on one side of a public square. But even if people throughout history have always known how to count, there are good reasons why counting has often been avoided as a means of reaching group decisions. Voting is divisive. If a community lacks means to compel its members to obey a collective decision, then probably the stupidest thing one could do is to stage a series of public contests in which one side will, necessarily, be seen to lose; this would not only allow decisions that as many as 49 percent of the community strongly oppose, it would also maximize the possibility of hard feelings among that part of the community one most needs to convince to go along despite their opposition. A process of consensus finding, of mutual accommodation and compromise to reach a collective decision everyone at least does not find strongly objectionable, is far more suited to situations where those who have to carry out a decision lack the sort of centralized bureaucracy, and particularly, the means of systematic coercion, that would be required to force an angry minority to comply with decisions they found stupid, obnoxious, or unfair.

Historically, it is extremely unusual to find both of these together. Throughout most of human history, egalitarian societies were precisely those that did not have some military or police apparatus to force people to do things they did not wish to do (all those sekas and ayllus referred to above); where the means of compulsion did exist, it never occurred to anyone that ordinary people's opinions were in any way important.

Where do we find voting, then? Sometimes in societies where spectacles of public competition are considered normal— such as ancient Greece (ancient Greeks would make a contest out of anything)—but mainly in situations where everyone taking part in an assembly is armed or, at least, trained in the use of weapons. In the ancient world, voting occurred mainly within armies. Aristotle was well aware of this: the constitution of a Greek state, he observed, largely depends on the chief arm of its military: if it's a cavalry, one can expect an aristocracy, if it's heavy infantry, voting rights will be extended to those wealthy men who can afford armor, if it's light troops, archers, slingers, or a navy (as in Athens), one can expect democracy. Similarly, in Rome, popular assemblies that also relied on majority vote were based directly on military units of one hundred men, called centuries. Underlying the institution was the rather commonsensical idea that if a man was armed, his opinions had to be taken into account. Ancient military units often elected their own officers. It's also easy to see why majority voting would make sense in a military unit: even if a vote was 60–40, both sides are armed; if it did come down to a fight, one could see immediately who was most likely to win. And this pattern applies, broadly, more or less across the historical record: in the 1600s, for instance, Six Nations councils—which were primarily engaged in peacemaking—operated by consensus, but pirate ships, which were military operations, used majority vote.

All this is important because it shows that the aristocratic fears of the wealthy early Patriots—who when they thought of their nightmare vision "democracy" thought of an armed populace making decisions by majority show of hands—were not entirely unfounded.

———

Democracy, then, is not necessarily defined by majority voting: it is, rather, the process of collective deliberation on the principle of full and equal participation. Democratic creativity, in turn, is most likely to occur when one has a diverse collection of participants, drawn from very different traditions, with an urgent need to improvise some means to regulate their common affairs, free of a preexisting overarching authority.

In today's North America, it's largely anarchists—

proponents of a political philosophy that has generally been opposed to governments of any sort—who actively try to develop and promote such democratic institutions. In a way the anarchist identification with this notion of democracy goes back a long way. In 1550, or even 1750, when both words were still terms of abuse, detractors often used "democracy" interchangeably with "anarchy," or "democrat" with "anarchist." In each case, some radicals eventually began using the term, defiantly, to describe themselves. But while "democracy" gradually became something everyone felt they had to support (even as no one agreed on what precisely it was), "anarchy" took the opposite path, becoming for most a synonym for violent disorder.

What then is anarchism?

Actually the term means simply "without rulers." Just as in the case of democracy, there are two different ways one could tell the history of anarchism. On the one hand, we could look at the history of the word "anarchism," which was coined by Pierre-Joseph Proudhon in 1840 and was adopted by a political movement in late-nineteenth-century Europe, becoming especially strongly established in Russia, Italy, and Spain, before spreading across the rest of the world; on the other hand, we could see it as a much broader political sensibility.

The easiest way to explain anarchism in either sense is to say that it is a political movement that aims to bring about a genuinely free society—and that defines a "free society" as one where humans only enter those kinds of relations with one another that would not have to be enforced by the constant threat of violence. History has shown that vast inequalities of wealth, institutions like slavery, debt peonage, or wage labor, can only exist if backed up by armies, prisons, and police. Even deeper structural inequalities like racism and sexism are ultimately based on the (more subtle and insidious) threat of force. Anarchists thus envision a world based on equality and solidarity, in which human beings would be free to associate with one another to pursue an endless variety of visions, projects, and conceptions of what they find valuable in life. When people ask me what sorts of organization could exist in an anarchist society, I always answer: any form of organization one can imagine, and probably many we presently can't, with only one proviso— they would be limited to ones that could exist without anyone having the ability, at any point, to call on armed men to show up and say "I don't care what you have to say about this; shut up and do what you're told."

In this sense there have always been anarchists: you find them pretty much any time a group of people confronted with some system of power or domination imposed over them object to it so violently that they begin imagining ways of dealing with each other free of any such forms of power or domination. Most such projects remain lost to history but every now and then evidence for one or another crops up. In China around 400 B.C., for example, there was a philosophical movement that came to be known as the "School of the Tillers," which held that both merchants and government officials were both useless parasites, and attempted to create communities of equals where the only leadership would be by example, and the economy would be democratically regulated in unclaimed territories between the major states. Apparently, the movement was created by an alliance between renegade intellectuals who fled to such free villages and the peasant intellectuals they encountered there. Their ultimate aim appears to have been to gradually draw off defectors from surrounding kingdoms and thus, eventually, cause their collapse. This kind of encouragement of mass defection is a classic anarchist strategy. Needless to say they were not ultimately successful, but their ideas had enormous influence on court philosophers of later generations. And in the cities, anarchist ideas gave rise to notions that the individual should not be bound by any social conventions and that all technology should be rejected in order to return to an imagined primitive utopia—a pattern that was to repeat itself many times through world history. Those individualist and primitivist ideas, in turn, had an enormous influence on the Taoist philosophy of Lao Tzu and Chuang Tzu.[23]

How many similar movements have there been throughout human history? We cannot know. (We only happen to know about the Tillers because they also compiled manuals of agricultural technology so good they were read and recopied for thousands of years.) But really all the Tillers were doing was an intellectually self-conscious version of what, as James Scott has recently shown in his "anarchist history of Southeast Asia," millions of people in that part of the world have been doing for centuries: flee from the control of nearby kingdoms and try to set up societies based on a rejection of everything those states represent; then try to convince others to do the same.[24] There are likely to have been many such movements winning free spaces of one sort or another from different states. My point is that such initiatives have always been around. For most of human history, rejection has been more likely to take the form of flight, defection, and the creation of new communities than of revolutionary confrontation with the powers-that-be. Of course, all this is much easier when there are distant hills to run away to and states that had difficulty extending their control over wide stretches of terrain. After the industrial revolu-

tion, when radical workers' movements began to emerge across
Europe, and some factory workers in places like France or
Spain began to espouse openly anarchist ideas, this option was
no longer available. Anarchists instead embraced a variety of
strategies, from the formation of alternative economic enter-
prises (co-ops, mutualist banking), workplace strikes and sabo-
tage, and the general strike, to outright insurrection.

Marxism emerged as a political philosophy around the
same time and, in its early days especially, aspired to the same
ultimate goal as anarchism: a free society, the abolition of all
forms of social·inequality, self-managed workplaces, the dissolution of the state. But from the debates surrounding the
creation of the First International onwards there was a key difference. Most Marxists insisted that it was necessary first to
seize state power—whether by the ballot or otherwise—and
use its mechanisms to transform society, to the point where, the
argument usually went, such mechanisms would ultimately become redundant and simply fade away into nothingness. Even
back in the nineteenth century, anarchists pointed out this was
a pipe dream. One cannot, they argued, create peace by training for war, equality by creating top-down chains of command,
or, for that matter, human happiness by becoming grim joyless
revolutionaries who sacrifice all personal self-realization or
self-fulfillment to the cause. Anarchists insisted that it wasn't
just that the ends do not justify the means (though the ends do
not, of course, justify the means) but that you will never achieve
the ends at all unless the means are themselves a model for the
world you wish to create. Hence the famous anarchist call to
begin "building the new society in the shell of the old" with
egalitarian experiments ranging from nonhierarchical schools
(like the Escuela Moderna in Spain or the Free School move-

ment in the United States) to radical labor unions (CGT in France, CNT in Spain, IWW in North America) to an endless variety of communes (from the Modern Times collective in New York in 1851 to Christiania in Denmark in 1971; the kibbutz movement in Israel, which was originally largely anarchist-inspired, being perhaps the most famous and successful spin-off from such experiments).

Sometimes, too, around the turn of the nineteenth century, individual anarchists would strike directly against world leaders or robber barons (as they were then called) with assassinations or bombings: in the period from roughly 1894 to 1901 there was a particularly intense spate, which led to the deaths of one French president, one Spanish prime minister, and U.S. president William McKinley, as well as attacks on at least a dozen other kings, princes, secret police chiefs, industrialists, and heads of state. This is the period that produced the notorious popular image of the anarchist bomb thrower, which has lingered in the popular imagination ever since. Anarchist thinkers like Peter Kropotkin and Emma Goldman often struggled with what to say about such attacks, which were often carried out by isolated individuals who were not actually part of any anarchist union or association. Still, it's worthy of note that anarchists were perhaps the first modern political movement to (gradually) realize that, as a political strategy, terrorism, even when it is not directed at innocents, doesn't work. For nearly a century now, in fact, anarchism has been one of the very few political philosophies whose exponents never blow anyone up (indeed, the twentieth-century political leader who drew most from the anarchist tradition was Mohandas K. Gandhi). Yet for the period of roughly 1914 to 1989, during which time the world was continually either fighting or preparing for world wars, anarchism went into something of an eclipse for precisely that reason: to seem "realistic" in such violent times a political movement had to be capable of organizing tank armies, air-craft carriers, and ballistic missile systems, and that was one thing at which Marxists could often excel, but everyone recognized that anarchists—rather to their credit, in my opinion—would never be able to pull off. It was only after 1989, when the age of great-war mobilizations seemed to have come to an end, that a global revolutionary movement based on anarchist principles—the Global Justice Movement—reappeared.

———

There are endless varieties, colors, and tendencies of anarchism. For my own part, I like to call myself a "small-a" anarchist. I'm less interested in figuring out what sort of anarchist I am than in working in broad coalitions that operate in accord with anarchist principles: movements that are not trying to work through or become governments; movements uninterested in assuming the role of de facto government institutions like trade organizations or capitalist firms; groups that focus on making our relations with each other a model of the world we wish to create. In other words, people working toward truly free societies. After all, it's hard to figure out exactly what kind of anarchism makes the most sense when so many questions can only be answered further down the road. Would there be a role for markets in a truly free society? How could we know? I myself am confident, based on history,[25] that even if we did try to maintain a market economy in such a free society—that is, one in which there would be no state to en-force contracts, so that agreements came to be based only on trust—economic relations would rapidly morph into something libertarians would find completely unrecognizable, and would soon not resemble anything we are used to thinking of as a "market" at all. I certainly can't imagine anyone agreeing to work for wages if they have any other options. But who knows, maybe I'm wrong. I am less interested in working out what the detailed architecture of what a free society would be like than in creating the conditions that would enable us to find out.

We have little idea what sort of organizations, or for that matter, technologies, would emerge if free people were unfettered to use their imagination to actually solve collective problems rather than to make them worse. But the primary question is: how do we even get there? What would it take to allow our political and economic systems to become a mode of collective problem solving rather than, as they are now, a mode of collective war?

Even anarchists have taken a very long time to come around to grappling with the full extent of this problem. When anarchism was part of the broader workers' movement, for example, it tended to accept that "democracy" meant majority voting and Robert's Rules of Order, relying on appeals to solidarity to convince the minority to go along. Appeals to solidarity can be very effective when one is locked in life-or-death conflict of one sort or another, as revolutionaries usually were. The CNT, the anarchist labor union in Spain of the 1920s and 1930s, relied on a principle that when a workplace voted to strike, no member who had voted against striking was bound by the decision; the result was, almost invariably, 100 percent compliance. But again, strikes were quasi-military operations. Local rural communes tended to fall back, as rural communities everywhere do, on some sort of de facto consensus.

In the United States, on the other hand, consensus, rather than majority voting, has often been used by grassroots organizers who were not, explicitly, anarchists: SNCC, the Student Nonviolent Coordinating Committee, which was the horizontal branch of the civil rights movement, operated by consensus, and SDS, Students for a Democratic Society, claimed in their constitutional principles to operate by parliamentary procedure, but in fact tended to rely on consensus in practice. Most of those who participated in such meetings felt the process used at the time was crude, improvised, and often extremely frustrating. Part of it was just because Americans, for all their democratic spirit, mostly had absolutely no experience of democratic deliberation. There's a famous story from the civil rights movement of a small group of activists trying to come to a collective decision in an emergency situation, unable to attain consensus. At one point, one of them gave up and pulled out a gun and aimed it directly at the facilitator. "Either make a decision for us," he said, "or I'll shoot you." The facilitator replied, "Well I guess you'll just have to shoot me then." It took a very long time to develop what might be called a culture of democracy, and when it did emerge, it came from surprising directions: spiritual traditions, Quakerism, for instance, and feminism.

The American Society of Friends, the Quakers, for instance, had spent centuries developing their own form of consensus decision making as a spiritual exercise. Quakers had also been active in most grassroots American social movements from Abolitionism onward, but until the 1970s they were not, for the most part, willing to teach others their techniques for the precise reason that they considered it a spiritual matter, a part of their religion. "You rely on consensus," George Lakey, a famous Quaker pacifist activist once explained, "when you have a shared understanding of the theology. It is not to be imposed on people. Quakers, at least in the '50s, were anti-proselytizing."[26] It was really only a crisis in the feminist movement—which started using informal consensus in small consciousness-raising groups of usually around a dozen people, but found themselves running into all sorts of problems with cliques and tacit leadership structures when those became larger in size—that eventually inspired some dissident Quakers (the most famous was Lakey himself) to pitch in and begin disseminating some of their techniques. These techniques, in turn, now infused with a specifically feminist ethos, came to be modified when adopted for larger and more diverse groups.[27]

This is just one example of how what has now come to be called "Anarchist Process"—all those elaborate techniques of facilitation and consensus finding, the hand signals and the like—emerged from radical feminism, Quakerism, and even Native American traditions. In fact, the particular variety employed in North America should really be called "feminist process" rather than "anarchist process." These methods became identified with anarchism precisely because anarchists recognized them to be forms that could be employed in a free society, in which no one could be physically coerced to go along with a decision they found profoundly objectionable.*

---

* With a few die-hard exceptions. I should note here that the first mass use of consensus process, in the antinuclear movement of the late 1970s and early 1980s, was often quite rocky—partly out of simple lack of experience, partly out of purism (it was only later that modified consensus for larger groups came into common use)—and many who went through the experience, most famously libertarian socialist Murray Bookchin, who promoted the idea of communalism, came out strongly against consensus and for majority rule.

Consensus is not just a set of techniques. When we talk about process, what we're really talking about is the gradual creation of a culture of democracy. This brings us back to rethinking some of our most basic assumptions about what democracy is even about.

If we return to the writings of men like Adams and Madison or even Jefferson in this light, it's easy to see that, elitist though they were, some of their criticisms of democracy deserve to be taken seriously. First of all, they argued that instituting a system of majoritarian direct democracy among white adult males in a society deeply divided by inequalities of wealth would likely lead to tumultuous, unstable, and ultimately bloody results, to the rise of demagogues and tyrants. Here they were probably right.

Another argument they made is that only established men of property should be allowed to vote and hold office because only they were sufficiently independent and therefore free of self-interest that they could afford to think about the common good. This latter is an important argument and deserves more attention than it has usually been given.

Obviously, the way it was framed was nothing if not elitist. The profound hypocrisy of arguing that the common people lacked education or rationality come through clearly in the writings of men like Gouverneur Morris, who was willing to admit, at least in a private letter to a fellow member of the gentry, that it was the opposite idea—that ordinary people had acquired education and were capable of framing rational arguments—that terrified him most of all.

But the real problem with arguments based on the pre-

sumed "irrationality" of the common people was in the underlying assumptions about what constituted "rationality." One
common argument against popular rule in the early republic
was that the "eight or nine millions who have no property" as
Adams put it, were incapable of rational judgment because
they were unused to managing their own affairs. Servants and
wage laborers, let alone women and slaves, were accustomed
to taking orders. Some among the elites held this to be because
they were capable of nothing else; some simply saw it as the
outcome of their habitual circumstances. But almost all agreed
that if such people were given the vote, they would not think
about what was best for the country but immediately attach
themselves to some leader—either because that leader bought
them off in some way (promised to abolish their debts, or even
directly paid them), or just because following others is all they
knew how to do. An excess of liberty, therefore, would only
lead to tyranny as the people threw themselves to the mercies
of charismatic leaders. At best, it would result in "factionalism," a political system dominated by political parties—almost
all the framers were strongly opposed to the emergence of a
party system—battling over their respective interests. Here
they were right: while major class warfare didn't ensue—partly
because of the existence of the escape hatch of the frontier—
factionalism and political parties immediately followed once
an even modestly expanded franchise began to be put into
place in the 1820s and 1830s. The fears of the elites were not
entirely misplaced.

The notion that only men with property can be fully rational, and that others exist primarily to follow orders, traces
back at least to Athens. Aristotle states the matter quite explicitly in the beginning of his *Politics*, where he argues that

only free adult males can be fully rational beings, in control of their own bodies, just as they are in control over others: their women, children, and slaves. Here then is the real flaw in the whole tradition of "rationality" that the Founders inherited. It's not ultimately about self-sufficiency, being disinterested. To be rational in this tradition has everything to do with the ability to issue commands: to stand apart from a situation, assess it from a distance, make the appropriate set of calculations, and then tell others what to do.[28] Essentially, it is the kind of calculation one can make *only* when one can tell others to shut up and do as they are told, not work with them as free equals in search of solutions. It's only the habit of command that allows one to imagine that the world can be reduced to the equivalent of mathematical formulae, formulae that can be applied to any situation, regardless of its real human complexities.

This is why any philosophy that begins by proposing that humans are, or should be, rational—as cold and calculating as a lord—invariably ends up concluding that, really, we're the opposite: that reason, as Hume so famously put it, is always, and can only be, the "slave of the passions." We seek pleasure; therefore we seek property, to guarantee our access to pleasure; therefore, we seek power, to guarantee our access to property. In every case there's no natural end to it; we'll always seek more and more and more. This theory of human nature is already present in the ancient philosophers (and is their explanation why democracy can only be disastrous), and recurs in the Christian tradition of Saint Augustine in the guise of original sin, and in the atheist Thomas Hobbes's theory of why a state of nature could only have been a violent "war of all against all," and again, of course, of why democracy must necessarily be disastrous. The creators of the eighteenth-century republican constitutions shared these assumptions as well. Humans were really incorrigible. So for all the occasional high-minded language, most of these philosophers were ultimately willing to admit that the only real choice was between utterly blind passions and the rational calculation of the interests of an elite class; the ideal constitution, therefore, was one designed to ensure that such interests checked each other and ultimately balanced off.

This has some curious implications. On the one hand, it is universally held that democracy means little without free speech, a free press, and the means for open political deliberation and debate. At the same time, most theorists of liberal democracy—from Jean-Jacques Rousseau to John Rawls—grant that sphere of deliberation an incredibly limited purview, since they assume a set of political actors (politicians, voters, interest groups) who already know what they want before they show up in the political arena. Rather than using the political sphere to decide how to balance competing values, or make up their minds about the best course of action, such political actors, if they think about anything, consider only how best to pursue their already existing interests.[29]

So this leaves us with a democracy of the "rational," where we define rationality as detached mathematical calculation born of the power to issue commands, the kind of "rationality" that will inevitably produce monsters. As the basis for a true democratic system, these terms are clearly disastrous. But what is the alternative? How to found a theory of democracy on the kind of reasoning that goes on, instead, between equals?

One reason this has been difficult to do is that this sort of reasoning is actually more complex and sophisticated than simple mathematical calculation, and therefore doesn't lend it-self to the quantifiable models beloved of political scientists and those who assess grant applications. After all, when one asks if a person is being rational, we aren't asking very much: really, just whether they are capable of making basic logical connections. The matter rarely comes up unless one suspects someone might actually be crazy or perhaps so blinded by pas-sion that their arguments make no sense. Consider, in contrast, what's entailed when one asks if someone is being "reason-able." The standard here is much higher. Reasonableness im-plies a much more sophisticated ability to achieve a balance between different perspectives, values, and imperatives, none of which, usually, could possibly be reduced to mathematical formulae. It means coming up with a compromise between positions that are, according to formal logic, incommensura-ble, just as there's no formal way, when deciding what to cook for dinner, to measure the contrasting advantages of ease of preparation, healthiness, and taste. But of course we make such decisions all the time. Most of life—particularly life with others—consists of making reasonable compromises that could never be reduced to mathematical models.

Another way to put this is that political theorists tend to assume actors who are operating on the intellectual level of an eight-year-old. Developmental psychologists have observed that children begin to make logical arguments not to solve problems, but when coming up with reasons for what they al-ready want to think. Anyone who deals with small children on a regular basis will immediately recognize that this is true. The ability to compare and coordinate contrasting perspectives on the other hand comes later and is the very essence of mature intelligence. It's also precisely what those used to the power of command rarely have to do.

The philosopher Stephen Toulmin, already famous for his models of moral reasoning, made something of an intellectual splash in the 1990s when he tried to develop a similar contrast between rationality and reasonableness: though he started his analysis on the basis for rationality as deriving not from the power of command, but from the need for absolute certainty. Contrasting the generous spirit of an essayist like Montaigne, who wrote in the expansive Europe of the sixteenth century and assumed that truth is always situational, with the well-nigh paranoid rigor of René Descartes, who wrote a century later when Europe had collapsed into bloody wars of religion and who conceived a vision of society as based on purely "rational" grounds, Toulmin proposed that all subsequent political thought has been bedeviled by attempts to apply impossible standards of abstract rationality to concrete human realities. But Toulmin wasn't the first to propose the distinction. I myself first encountered it in a rather whimsical essay published in 1960 by the British poet Robert Graves called "The Case for Xanthippe."

For those who lack the classical education of New York's early butchers and bakers,* Xanthippe was Socrates' wife, and has gone down in history as an atrocious nag. Socrates' equanimity in enduring (ignoring) her is regularly held out as a proof of his nobility of character. Graves begins by pointing

---

* One does sometimes worry that the Gouverneur Morrises of the world have ultimately been successful in preventing such knowledge from reaching most of the population.

out: why is it that for two thousand years, no one seems to have asked what it might have actually been like to be married to Socrates? Imagine you were saddled with a husband who did next to nothing to support a family, spent all his time trying to prove everyone he met was wrong about everything, and felt true love was only possible between men and underage boys? You wouldn't express some opinions about this? Socrates has been held out ever since as the paragon of a certain unrelenting notion of pure consistency, an unflinching determination to follow arguments to their logical conclusions, which is surely useful in its way—but he was not a very reasonable person, and those who celebrate him have ended up producing a "mechanized, insensate, inhumane, abstract rationality" that has done the world enormous harm. Graves writes that as a poet, he feels no choice but to identify himself more with those frozen out of the "rational" space of Greek city, starting with women like Xanthippe, for whom reasonableness doesn't exclude logic (no one is actually *against* logic) but combines it with a sense of humor, practicality, and simple human decency.

With that in mind, it only makes sense that so much of the initiative for creating new forms of democratic process—like consensus—has emerged from the tradition of feminism, which means (among other things) the intellectual tradition of those who have, historically, tended not to be vested with the power of command. Consensus is an attempt to create a politics founded on the principle of reasonableness—one that, as feminist philosopher Deborah Heikes has pointed out, requires not only logical consistency, but "a measure of good judgment, self-criticism, a capacity for social interaction, and a willingness to give and consider reasons."[30] Genuine deliberation, in short. As a facilitation trainer would likely put it, it requires the ability to listen well enough to understand perspectives that are fundamentally different from one's own, and then try to find pragmatic common ground without attempting to convert one's interlocutors completely to one's own perspective. It means viewing democracy as common problem solving among those who respect the fact they will always have, like all humans, somewhat incommensurable points of view.

This is how consensus is supposed to work: the group agrees, first, to some common purpose. This allows the group to look at decision making as a matter of solving common problems. Seen this way, a diversity of perspectives, even a radical diversity of perspectives, while it might cause difficulties, can also be an enormous resource. After all, what sort of team is more likely to come up with a creative solution to a problem: a group of people who all see matters somewhat differently, or a group of people who all see things exactly the same?

As I've already observed, spaces of democratic creativity are precisely those where very different sorts of people, coming from very different traditions, are suddenly forced to improvise. One reason is because in such situations, people are forced to reconcile divergent assumptions about what politics is even about. In the 1980s, a group of would-be Maoist guerrillas from urban Mexico descended to the mountains of the Mexican southwest, where they began to create revolutionary networks, first by beginning women's literacy campaigns. Eventually, they became the Zapatista Army of National Liberation, who initiated a brief insurrection in 1994—not, however, to overthrow the state, but to create a liberated territory in which largely indigenous communities could begin experimenting with new forms of democracy. From the beginning, there were constant differences between the originally urban intellectuals, like the famous Subcomandante Marcos, who assumed democracy meant majority vote and elected representatives, and Mam, Cholti, Tzeltal, and Tzotzil speakers, whose communal assemblies had always operated by consensus, and preferred to see a system where, if delegates had to be selected, they could be recalled the moment communities no longer felt they were conveying the communal will. As Marcos recalled, they soon found there was no agreement about what "democracy" actually meant:

> The communities are promoting democracy. But the concept seems vague. There are many kinds of democracy. That's what I tell them. I try to explain to them: "You can operate by consensus because you have a communal life." When they arrive at an assembly, they know each other, they come to solve a common problem. "But in other places it isn't so," I tell them. "People live separate lives and they use the assembly for other things, not to solve the problem."
>
> And they say, "no," but it means "yes, it works for us."
>
> And it indeed does work for them, they solve the problem. So they propose that method for the Nation and the world. The world must organize itself thus. . . . And it is very difficult to go against that because that is how they solve their problems.[31]

Let us take this proposal seriously. Why shouldn't democracy be a matter of collective problem solving? We might have very different ideas about what life is ultimately about, but it's perfectly apparent that human beings on this planet share a large number of common problems (climate change comes most readily to mind as a pressing and immediate one, but there are any number of them) that we would do well to work together to try to solve. Everyone seems to agree that in principle it would be better to do this democratically, in a spirit of equality and reasonable deliberation. Why does the idea that we might actually do so seem like such a utopian pipe dream?

Perhaps instead of asking what the best political system is that our current social order could support, we should be asking, What social arrangements would be necessary in order for us to have a genuine, participatory, democratic system that could dedicate itself to solving collective problems?*

It seems kind of an obvious question. If we are not used to asking it, it's because we've been taught from an early age that the answer is itself unreasonable. Because the answer, of course, is anarchism.

In fact, there is reason to believe the Founders were right: one cannot create a political system based on the principle of direct, participatory democracy in a society such as their own, divided by vast inequalities of wealth, the total exclusion of the bulk of the population (in early America, women, slaves, indigenous people), and where most people's lives were organized

---

* It wouldn't have to be based on a system of strict consensus, by the way, since, as we'll see, absolute consensus is unrealistic in large groups—let alone on a planetary scale! What I am talking about is just what I say: an approach to politics, whatever particular institutional form it takes, that similarly sees political deliberation as problem solving rather than as a struggle between fixed interests.

around the giving and taking of orders. Nor is it possible in a society such as our own, in which 1 percent of the population controls 42 percent of the wealth.

If you propose the idea of anarchism to a roomful of ordinary people, someone will almost inevitably object: but of course we can't eliminate the state, prisons, and police. If we do, people will simply start killing one another. To most, this seems simple common sense. The odd thing about this prediction is that it can be empirically tested; in fact, it frequently has been empirically tested. And it turns out to be false. True, there are one or two cases like Somalia, where the state broke down when people were already in the midst of a bloody civil war, and warlords did not immediately stop killing each other when it happened (though in most respects, even in Somalia, a worst-case hypothesis, education, health, and other social indicators had actually improved twenty years after the dissolution of the central state!).[32] And of course we hear about the cases like Somalia for the very reason that violence ensues. But in most cases, as I myself observed in parts of rural Madagascar, very little happens. Obviously, statistics are unavailable, since the absence of states generally also means the absence of anyone gathering statistics. However, I've talked to many anthropologists and others who've been in such places and their accounts are surprisingly similar. The police disappear, people stop paying taxes, otherwise they pretty much carry on as they had before. Certainly they do not break into a Hobbesian "war of all against all."

As a result, we almost never hear about such places at all. When I was living in the town of Arivonimamo in 1990, and wandering about the surrounding countryside, even I had no idea at first that I was living in an area where state control had effectively disappeared (I think part of the reason for my impression was that everyone talked and acted as if state institutions were still functioning, hoping no one would notice). When I returned in 2010, the police had returned, taxes were once again being collected, but everyone also felt that violent crime had increased dramatically.

So the real question we have to ask becomes: what is it about the experience of living under a state, that is, in a society where rules are enforced by the threat of prisons and police, and all the forms of inequality and alienation that makes possible, that makes it seem obvious to us that people, under such conditions, would behave in a way that it turns out they don't actually behave?

The anarchist answer is simple. If you treat people like children, they will tend to act like children. The only successful method anyone has ever devised to encourage others to act like adults is to treat them as if they already are. It's not infallible. Nothing is. But no other approach has any real chance of success. And the historical experience of what actually does happen in crisis situations demonstrates that even those who have not grown up in a culture of participatory democracy, if you take away their guns or ability to call their lawyers, can suddenly become extremely reasonable.[33] This is all that anarchists are really proposing to do.

FOUR

HOW CHANGE HAPPENS

The last chapter ended with a long-term, philosophical perspective; this one aims to be more practical.

It would be impossible to write a how-to guide for nonviolent uprisings, a modern-day *Rules for Radicals*. If there is one rule that always applies to civil resistance, it is that there are no strict rules. Movements work best when they best adapt themselves to their particular situations. The best democratic process depends on the nature of the community involved, its cultural and political traditions, the number of people taking part, the experience level of the participants, and, of course, what they are trying to accomplish—among any number of other immediate practical concerns. Tactics have to remain flexible: if movements do not constantly reinvent themselves, they soon shrivel and die.

Then there's the obvious, but often misunderstood, fact that the kind of tactics appropriate to one community might be completely inappropriate to others. After the OWS evictions, there was a raging debate, as I've mentioned, over Black Blocs. Black Blocs are formations, mainly composed of anarchists or other anti-authoritarians, that come to actions dressed in masks and identical black hoodies, partly as a display of revolutionary solidarity, but also to indicate the presence of people willing to engage in more militant action should it be required. In America, they tend to consider themselves nonviolent but also to define "violence" as damage to living beings; they are often willing to engage in symbolic attacks on corporate property, and sometimes even to fight back in limited ways if directly assaulted by police. Just as often, though, "militant tactics" might just be a matter of spray painting slogans, or linking arms or forming a shield wall to protect more vulnerable protesters from police.

As I mentioned earlier, the very presence of Black Blocs is often treated by liberal commentators as itself a form of violence. One common argument is that such formations, by their very presence, end up alienating the very working-class communities that the larger movements are meant to draw in, or giving police a pretext to attack nonviolent protesters. But the truth is that in 90 percent of occupations, no one has employed Black Bloc tactics at all, and the one that saw the largest bloc— Occupy Oakland—had its own specific, local reasons. Oakland is a city marked by decades of extreme police brutality and militant resistance from the poor—especially within the African-American community (the Black Panthers, after all, did come out of Oakland). Where in most cities Black Bloc tactics could easily alienate the larger movement from working-class communities, in Oakland militant tactics are more likely to be seen as a sign of working-class solidarity.

As I learned in my days in the Global Justice Movement in

2000, heated arguments about tactics are often really arguments about strategy in disguise. For instance, after the Seattle
WTO actions in November 1999, the question we all debated
was "Is it ever okay to break a window?" But the underlying
argument was really about whom the Global Justice Movement in the United States should really be mobilizing, and for
what purposes: educated middle-class consumers who might
be brought around to support fair trade policies—the sorts of
people who might recoil from any signal of violence—or potentially revolutionary elements who didn't need to be convinced that the system was violent and corrupt, but did need to
be convinced that it was possible to successfully strike against
it—the sorts of people who might find a broken window or
two inspiring. The debate was never fully settled and such strategic questions also seem out of place here—at least, it's hardly
my role to weigh in on what part of the population should be
mobilizing, other than to say all those organizing in their own
communities, whoever they are, should think about how to act
in a spirit of solidarity with all other members of the 99 percent.

Rather, I will concentrate on a series of practical ideas and
suggestions, born of my own decade-long experience in horizontal organizing, and my direct experience with Occupy itself.

CONSENSUS

There is a great deal of debate about whether consensus is even
possible in larger groups, when it is appropriate for consensus-
based groups to fall back on voting and to what purpose, but
these debates are often marked by confusion as to what consensus actually means. Many for example assume, fairly stub-

bornly, that consensus process is simply a unanimous voting system—and then proceed to debate whether such a system "works," presumably, as opposed to a system where all decisions take the form of a majority vote. From my perspective at least, such debates miss the point. The essence of consensus process is just that everyone should be able to weigh in equally on a decision, and no one should be bound by a decision they detest. In practice, this might be said to boil down to four principles:

- Everyone who feels they have something relevant to say about a proposal ought to have their perspectives carefully considered.
- Everyone who has strong concerns or objections should have those concerns or objections taken into account and, if possible, addressed in the final form of the proposal.
- Anyone who feels a proposal violates a fundamental principle shared by the group should have the opportunity to veto ("block") that proposal.
- No one should be forced to go along with a decision to which they did not assent.

Over the years, different groups or individuals have developed systems of formal consensus process to ensure these ends. These can take a number of different forms. But one doesn't necessarily need a formal process. Sometimes it's helpful. Sometimes it's not. Smaller groups can often operate without any formal procedures at all. In fact, there is an endless variety of ways one might go about making decisions in the spirit of those four principles. Even the often debated question of whether or not the process of considering a proposal ends in a

vote through some sort of formal show of hands, or other af-
firmation of consensus, is secondary: what's crucial is the process that leads to decision. Ending with a vote tends to be
problematic not because there is anything intrinsically wrong
with showing hands, but because it makes it less likely that all
perspectives will be fully taken into account. But if a process is
created that ends in a vote yet also allows all perspectives to be
satisfactorily addressed, there's really nothing wrong with it.

Let me give some practical examples of what I mean here.

One common problem facing new groups is how one
chooses a decision-making process to begin with. It can seem
to be a bit of a chicken-egg conundrum. Does one need to
take a vote to decide whether to operate by consensus, or to
require a consensus that the group should operate by majority
vote? What's the default?

To figure this out, it might be helpful to take a step back
and think about the nature of the group itself. We're used to
thinking of groups as collections of people with some kind of
formal membership. If you agree to join a group that already
has a set of rules—a labor union, or for that matter an amateur
softball league—you are, by the very act of joining, also agreeing to be bound by those rules. If it is a group that operates
by majority vote, that means you are agreeing to be bound by
majority decisions. If it is a vertical group with a leadership
structure, it means you're agreeing to do what the leaders say.
You still have recourse: if you object to a decision, you can
quit, or refuse to comply, which might cause the group to reconsider the decision but is more likely to mean you'll be pe-
nalized in some way, or expelled. But the point is there is some
kind of sanction. The group can coerce behavior through the
threat of punishment.

But if you're talking about an activist meeting or public assembly, as opposed to a group composed of formal members, none of this is true. No one at a public meeting has agreed to anything. They are just a bunch of people sitting in a room (or standing in a public square). They are not bound by a majority decision unless they all agree to be. And even if they do agree, if a participant later finds a decision so objectionable he or she changes his or her mind, there's not much the group can do about it. No one is really in a position to force anyone to do anything. And if it's a horizontal or anarchist-inspired group, no one wishes to be in such a position.

So how does such a group decide if they want to operate by majority vote or some other form of consensus? Well, first, everyone would have to agree to it. If there is no such agreement then it is fair to say that "everyone should have equal say and no one can be forced to do anything they strongly object to." That becomes the general principle of any decision making.

This doesn't mean that one should never call for a majority show of hands at all. Most obviously, it's often the best way to find out critical information, such as, "If we held an event at 1 P.M. on Monday, how many of you would be able to come?" Similarly, if there is a technical matter where it seems clear that no question of principle is likely to arise ("Should we table this discussion for now," or, "Shall we meet on Tuesday or on Wednesday?") a facilitator might simply ask if everyone is willing to be bound by a majority decision on that question and be done with it. More often, though, a facilitator will just ask for a show of hands as a "nonbinding straw poll" or "temperature check," that is, just to get a sense of how people are feeling in the room. This can just be by a simple show of hands or a more subtle system where everyone either waves hands up in the air for approval, down for disapproval, and horizontal for uncertainty. While nonbinding, such tests can often give all the information you need to know: if sentiment is running strongly against a proposal, the person who submitted it might then withdraw it.

When one is dealing with nontrivial questions, though, the four principles become more important. So how do you find consensus on more complex issues? There is a fairly standardized four-step procedure that has been developed over the years to ensure that proposals can be continually refashioned in a spirit of compromise and creativity until they reach a form most likely to be amenable to everyone. There's really no need to be religious about it: there are lots of possible variations. And it's important to remember that while those coming to a meeting might be presumed to have agreed to the basic principles, they have not agreed to any particular formal rules of procedure, so the procedures should adapt to the desires of the group. But generally speaking it goes something like this:

1. someone makes a **proposal** for a certain course of action
2. the facilitator asks for **clarifying questions** to make sure everyone understands precisely what is being proposed
3. the facilitator asks for **concerns**
   a. during the discussion those with concerns may suggest **friendly amendments** to the proposal to address the concern, which the person originally bringing the proposal may or may not adopt
   b. there may or may not be a **temperature check** about the proposal, an amendment, or the seriousness of a concern

   c. in the course of this the proposal might be scotched, reformulated, combined with other proposals, broken into pieces, or tabled for later discussion.

4. the facilitator **checks for consensus** by:

   a. asking if there are any **stand-asides**. By standing aside one is saying "I don't like this idea, and wouldn't take part in the action, but I'm not willing to stop others from doing so." It is always important to allow all those who stand aside to have a chance to explain why they are doing so.

   b. asking if there are any **blocks**. A block is *not* a "no" vote. It is much more like a veto. Perhaps the best way to think of it is that it allows anyone in the group to temporarily don the robes of a Supreme Court justice and strike down a piece of legislation they consider unconstitutional; or, in this case, **in violation of the fundamental principles of unity or purpose of being of the group.***

There are various ways of dealing with a block. The easiest is simply to drop the proposal. The facilitator might encourage the blocker to meet up with those who brought the proposal, to join the relevant working group for instance, and see if they can come up with some kind of reasonable compromise. Sometimes, especially if others feel the block isn't justified (e.g., "I don't think it's anti-Semitic to have the next meeting on Friday

---

* I should note that the usual language in Occupy Wall Street is that a block has to be based on a "moral, ethical, or safety concern that's so strong you'd consider leaving the movement were the proposal to go forward."

even though it's a Jewish holiday. Most of us are Jewish and we don't care!"*), there might be some process for challenging a block: for instance, asking if at least two other members of the group are willing to sustain it. (We sometimes speak of "consensus minus one" or "consensus minus two" to describe such a situation.) Or, if it is a large group, it is usually a good idea to have some fallback: if there is a strong feeling that most people want to go ahead, regardless of a block, one can turn to a supermajority vote. During our first August 2 meeting for Occupy Wall Street, for instance, we decided on a version of "modified consensus" where we could in the event of a logjam fall back on a two-thirds majority, but later, a few days into the actual occupation, the General Assembly agreed on moving to a 90 percent fallback on the grounds that, with the movement growing so rapidly, the earlier system would allow proposals to pass that were opposed by hundreds or even thousands of participants. It is important though not to fall back on this automatically: if someone blocks, the most likely reason is a failure of process, that is, a legitimate concern was raised and not addressed. In that case, the group might do well to go back and reconsider the proposal. But, especially in a very large

---

* As the reader might suspect this refers to a specific incident: an Orthodox Jewish newcomer to a Direct Action Network meeting objected to our plan to meet on several proposed dates on the grounds they were Jewish holidays, to the exasperation of several others—there were only twelve of us left after a very long meeting—and one African-American activist indicated she was inclined to block on the grounds holding the meeting on that date would be discriminating on the basis of religion. Someone finally had to explain, quietly, that she was actually the only non-Jewish person remaining in the room.

group, one will have to fall back on such expedients now and then.

There are a few areas of consensus process that often cause problems or confusion that I will try to clarify a bit here.

One is that one cannot very well base a block on a group's principles of unity unless that group actually has principles of unity. Thus it's always a good idea to come to some sort of agreement about why the group exists and what it is trying to accomplish as quickly as possible. It is best to keep these principles simple. It is also crucial, in framing them, to remember that any activist group exists to *do* something, to change the world in some way. So the principles should reflect both what the group is trying to accomplish and the manner in which it goes about trying to accomplish it—and the two (the ends and means) should be in as much harmony with each other as they can possibly be. But the smartest thing to do when it comes to defining the group is to keep it simple. It is much easier to write, "We oppose all forms of social hierarchy and oppression," for instance, than to try to list every form of social hierarchy and oppression you think exists.

One good thing about having principles of unity is not just that it clarifies blocking, but that it makes it possible for well-meaning participants to periodically remind everyone why they're all there. This can be almost unimaginably helpful in resolving conflict, because, in moments of passionate conflict, people have a remarkable ability to forget why they got together in the first place. Which leads to another point: there's nothing wrong with conflict, provided people do remember why they're all there. This is another misconception about consensus. "But conflict is the essence of politics," one often hears.

"How can you try to eliminate it?" Obviously you can't. Nor should you try to. Some of the confusion comes from the fact that in America (unlike many other places) activists were first introduced to consensus through the tradition of Quakerism, which has meant that for most activists, their first experience of consensus is rooted in gentle and, frankly, bourgeois sensibilities. Everyone is expected to be, at least superficially, *extremely* nice. After the macho histrionics of so much late 1960s radicalism, where jumping on chairs and pounding one's fist was considered a normal way to behave, Quaker- and feminist-inspired consensus was a useful corrective. But before long, a desperately needed feminist emphasis on mutual listening, respect, and nonviolent communication began shading into a distinctly upper-middle-class cocktail-party-style emphasis on politeness and euphemism, on avoiding any open display of uncomfortable emotions at all—which is in its own way just as oppressive as the old macho style, especially for those who were not themselves of upper-middle-class origins.

While the bourgeois style has hardly been put to rest, in recent years there's been a shift away from it. The best facilitation trainers, for example, have realized it's much better to say in effect: yes, we are passionate people, we are here because we care deeply and have strong emotions; displays of anger and frustration are just as important (and legitimate) as those of humor and love. Rather than trying to suppress all these things, we should instead understand that for a group to accomplish its goals, conflict between friends and allies ought to be encouraged, provided everyone remembers that this is, ultimately, a lovers' quarrel. What that means in practice is that while it is perfectly legitimate to doubt the wisdom of another's words or deeds during a meeting, or even to express outrage at their words and deeds, one must always give them the benefit of the doubt for honesty and good intentions. This can often be extremely difficult to do. Often one might have every reason to suspect that one's interlocutors are not behaving honestly and do not have good intentions. One might even suspect they're an undercover cop. But one could be wrong. And just as the surest way to guarantee people will act like children is to treat them like children, the surest way to guarantee people will start behaving irresponsibly during a meeting is to treat them as if they already are. Therefore, challenging though it is, everyone must be on guard for such behavior, and immediately call it out. It's fine to tell someone they're being an idiot, if you genuinely think they are. It's not okay to say they're intentionally trying to wreck the movement.

If it turns out they are intentionally trying to wreck the movement, there are ways to deal with that. If someone does turn out to be a cop, or a Nazi, or is actively trying to block the group from achieving its purposes, or is just a stark raving lunatic, there has to be some way to get rid of them—though usually this has to happen outside the meeting. One problem we had in New York is that, even when people declared their purpose was to disrupt a meeting, they were often nonetheless allowed to take part. We eventually found the best way to deal with such people was by the equivalent of shunning: whatever they say, whatever they do, simply do not react. The approach was first developed, quite spontaneously, when using the People's Microphone: if someone began saying something others found offensive, everyone would simply stop repeating it, and eventually, if the speaker continued in the same offensive vein, they found no one could hear anything they had to say.

There are always boundaries, acknowledged or otherwise.

If unacknowledged they become visible the moment someone breaks them. Just as "diversity of tactics" is based on the tacit assumption that no one would ever show up to a demo with a car bomb or rocket-propelled grenade, so assertions that no activist should be expelled from a meeting do assume certain parameters. I recently attended a Spokescouncil in New York where everyone had been engaged in a long debate over whether there should be a "community agreement" and a shared principle that if anyone violates that agreement, they should be asked to voluntarily leave. The proposal was meeting concerted opposition when, suddenly, someone noticed one of the delegates was holding a plaque saying "Aryan Identity Working Group." He was immediately surrounded by people— many of those who had just been loudly insisting such a rule was oppressive—who successfully forced him to leave.

This is only one of the various tools that have been developed over the years among activist groups to make consensus process work. There are many others (icebreakers, go-rounds, popcorn, fishbowls . . .) and detailed resources already exist on how to use them (they're easily accessible on the web through a simple Google search). My own personal favorite guide on facilitation and process is by activist and author Starhawk, but there are many according to taste. There are also different models of organization (General Assemblies and Spokescouncils, for instance), each with its own merits. There is no single right way, exactly, or road map for how these models can be scaled up to organize all of society on a directly democratic basis. The beauty of consensus process is that it *is* so various and adaptable. So here are some practical considerations and common misunderstandings about the basic principles of consensus, which, hopefully, will make it easier for interested readers to participate in a process of figuring such things out for themselves:

A QUICK CONSENSUS FAQ

Q: **But doesn't all this "consensus process" just come down to manipulation by a tacit or hidden leadership clique?**

A: If you operate by consensus without any rules at all, then, yes, inevitably a tacit leadership will emerge—at least, as soon as your group grows larger than eight or nine people. The writer and activist Jo Freeman pointed this out back in the 1970s during the early years of the feminist movement. What we now call "consensus process" was created largely to address this problem in the wake of Freeman's critique.

The role of the facilitator is a perfect example here. The easiest way to know you're dealing with bad process is that the same person is (a) running the meeting, and (b) making all the proposals. In any horizontal group there will be a clear understanding that the facilitator doesn't herself bring forward any proposals. He or she is just there to listen and become the medium through which the group can think. Usually, in fact, even the role of facilitator is broken up and divided among several people: one person to actually keep the meeting running, another to keep stack (count of those who've asked to speak), another to keep time, another as vibes watcher to ensure energy isn't flagging and no one is feeling left out. This makes it even harder for a facilitator to manipulate debate, even unconsciously. Facilitators rotate, which allows the group to constantly maintain gender balance among facilitators, as well as in stacks.

This doesn't mean there won't be cliques, especially in very large groups, or that some people won't end up with much more influence than others. The only real solution is for the group to maintain constant vigilance against the rise of cliques.

Q: But if you're saying such influential cliques will tend to emerge, wouldn't simply recognizing the fact that there really are leaders, and therefore creating a formal leadership structure, at least be better than having a secret unaccountable leadership no one acknowledges?

A: Actually, no. People who do more work will, of course, have more influence. This does give a certain advantage to those who have more time on their hands. Inevitably, some will start coordinating together and this will mean some people have privileged access to information. This is the real problem. In any egalitarian group, information tends to become the limited resource: if hierarchies develop, it'll be because some people have ways of finding out what's happening that others do not. Formalizing this by declaring those with privileged access to information a "leadership" is not going to ameliorate the problem, it will only make it worse. The only way to ensure that this group doesn't actually start imposing their will on others, even without intending to, is to create mechanisms that ensure that information is as widely available as possible, and constantly reminding the most active members that there is no formal leadership structure and no one has the right to impose their will.

Similarly, declaring members of an informal leadership clique to be members of a "coordinating committee," but allowing everyone else to decide whether to reappoint them every six months or so, does not make them "more accountable," as is often suggested (contrary to all experience); it clearly makes them less. One might well ask why anyone would imagine otherwise.*

Q: I'll allow that consensus works well enough in a small group or neighborhood or community where everyone knows one another, but how can it work in a large group of strangers where there's no initial foundation of trust?

A: We shouldn't romanticize community. True, people who have lived together all their lives in, say, a rural village are more likely to share perspectives than those who live in a large, im-

---

* In fact, the reasons hark back to a widespread prejudice, born of liberal political theory, against anything that might look like "arbitrary power." For at least a century, the predominant justification for government use of force against its own citizens is that this is only abusive if it doesn't follow explicit, well-publicized rules. The implication is that any way of exercising power, even by influence, is objectionable if it isn't formally recognized and the powers explicitly spelled out. As a result, informal power (even if nonviolent) is somehow considered more of a threat to human freedom even than violence itself. Ultimately, of course, this is a kind of utopianism: it's quite impossible for there to really be clear and explicit rules covering all political action.

personal metropolis, but they are also more likely to be bitter enemies. The fact that they can nonetheless come to consensus is a testimony to humans' ability to overcome hatred for the sake of the common good.

As for meetings between strangers: if one just assembled a random group of people off the street and forced them to attend a meeting against their will, probably they would be unable to find much common ground (other than in forming a plot to escape). But no one comes to a meeting of their own free will unless they want to get something out of it, a common goal everyone is there to achieve. If they don't get sidetracked and constantly bear in mind what they came for, they can, generally speaking, overcome their differences.

Q: If you have a fallback on a 66 percent, or 75 percent, or even 90 percent vote in larger meetings, why call this "modified consensus"? Isn't that just a supermajority voting system? Why not just be honest and call it that?

A: It's not actually the same thing. What's crucial to consensus is the process of synthesis, of reworking proposals to the point where the largest possible percentage of participants likes it, and the smallest percentage objects. Sometimes in larger groups you will find that despite this someone will block, and there will be fundamental disagreements about whether that block is a genuine expression of the group's basic principles. In that case you have the option of going to a vote. But as anyone who has actually sat through a meeting based on, say, two-thirds voting can attest, if you just go to a vote immediately, the whole dynamic will be different because there is never the presumption that everyone's perspective is equally valuable. Anyone whose views would appear to represent less than a third of the people of the meeting can simply be ignored.

Q: **What to do if people abuse the system?**

A: There are people who are, for whatever reasons, too damaged or disturbed to take part in a democratic assembly. There are others who can be accommodated, but who are so disruptive and difficult, who demand such constant attention, that indulging them would mean devoting so much more time to their thoughts and feelings than those of everyone else in the group that it undermines the principle that everyone's thoughts and feelings should have equal weight. If a person is continually disruptive, there should be a way to ask that person to leave. If they refuse, the next step is generally to reach out to their friends or allies to help convince them. If that's not possible, the best approach is to make a collective decision to systematically ignore them.

Q: **Isn't the insistence on consensus stifling of creativity and individuality? Doesn't it promote a kind of bland conformity?**

A: Yes, if done badly. Anything can be done badly. Consensus process is often done very badly. But this is mostly because so many of us are new to it. We're effectively inventing a democratic culture from scratch. When done right, there's no other process so supportive of individualism and creativity, because it is based on the principle that one should not even try to convert others entirely to one's point of view, that our differences are a common resource to be respected, rather than an impediment to pursuing common goals.

The real problem here is when consensus is a decision-making process by groups that are already based on sharp inequalities of power (either recognized or not) or that already have a culture of conformism—to take an extreme example, the way consensus is practiced within a Japanese corporation, or even an American one like Harley-Davidson. In cases like this, there's no doubt that demanding "consensus" can make all this even worse. But in cases like this we're not really talking about consensus at all, in the terms being laid out here, but rather, forced unanimity. There is no more effective way to destroy the radical potential of such democratic procedures than to force people to pretend to use them when actually they're not.

Q: Is it reasonable to expect people to constantly attend fourteen-hour meetings?

A: No, it is completely unreasonable to expect that. Obviously no one should be forced—even by moral pressure—to attend meetings they don't want to. But neither do we want to divide into one class of leaders who have time to attend long meetings, and another class of followers who never get to weigh in on key decisions. In traditional societies that have been practicing consensus for centuries, the usual solution is to make meetings fun: introduce humor, music, poetry, so that people actually enjoy watching the subtle rhetorical games and attendant dramas. (Here again, Madagascar provides my favorite example. The kind of rhetoric deployed in meetings is so appreciated there that I have seen particularly skilled orators come out and perform it as a form of entertainment between sets by rock bands at music festivals.) But of course these are societies where most people have a lot more time on their hands (not to mention don't have TV or social media to distract them). In a contemporary urban context, the best solution, when one is not at a moment of initial ferment when everyone is thrilled to be taking part at all, is simply not to have fourteen-hour meetings. Be assiduous with time limits: allocate ten minutes for this item of discussion, five for that, no more than thirty seconds for each speaker. Constantly remind speakers there's no need to repeat what someone else has said. But most important, do not bring proposals before a larger group unless there is a compelling reason. This is absolutely essential. In fact it's so important I will give it an entire section of its own.

DO NOT SUBMIT A PROPOSAL FOR CONSENSUS UNLESS THERE IS A COMPELLING REASON TO DO SO

Consensus process only works if it is combined with a principle of radical decentralization.

I really can't stress this enough. If there is any silver lining to the cumbersome nature of formal consensus process, it's precisely this: that it discourages people bringing proposals before a General Assembly or Spokescouncil or other large group unless they really have to. It's always better, if possible, to make decisions in smaller groups: working groups, affinity groups, collectives. Initiative should rise from below. One should not feel one needs authorization from anyone, even the General Assembly (which is everyone), unless it would be in some way harmful to proceed without.

Let me give an example.

At one point when we were still meeting in Tompkins

Square Park, before the actual occupation began, the Outreach group came very close to quitting en masse when they proposed a two-line description of the nature and purposes of the Occupy Wall Street group to be used in flyers, only to see it blocked at General Assembly. The woman who was point person for Outreach at the time could barely disguise her exasperation, and finally sought me out—as the presumed process maven—to see if there was some way to mediate. I thought about it for a moment and asked: "Well, why did you bring the text to the group at all?"

"Because I figured it would be better to have everyone approve the way they were being described to others. But it looks like whatever language we come up with, no matter how minimal, someone will object to it. I mean, that was a *really* unobjectionable statement we came up with!"

"Are you sure they're not objecting to the fact that you brought it before the group at all?"

"Why would they do that?"

"Well, okay, let's think about it this way. You're the Outreach group. You're a working group that has been empowered by the General Assembly to do outreach. Well, I guess you could argue, then, if you are empowered to do outreach, you have therefore also been empowered to do those things it is necessary to do in order to do outreach. Like, say, coming up with some way to describe the group. So I don't think there's any real reason you should have to ask the group's approval unless you think there's something sufficiently controversial in there that you want to check. I mean, I wasn't there: was it controversial?"

"No. I thought if there was a problem it was because it was actually pretty bland."

Which is what happens if you think you need approval for anything.

After this conversation I hunted down the person who had originally blocked the language and discovered that he completely agreed with my assessment. He blocked because he wanted to establish that working groups should decide such matters for themselves. (The main problem, then, wasn't a difference about process at all; it was that the blocker hadn't properly explained it.)

———

As a general rule of thumb: decisions should be made on the smallest scale, the lowest level, possible.* Do not ask for higher approval unless there's a pressing need to. But when does a need become pressing? What are the criteria for deciding who really ought to have the opportunity to weigh in on a question, and who doesn't?

It you look at it this way, much of the history of radical thought—and particularly radical democratic thought—turns on exactly this question. Who gets to make the decisions and why? It has largely taken the form of a debate between two principles: one is often referred to as workers' self-organization, or just workers' control; the other we can just call direct democracy.

In the past the concept of workers' control has most often been applied, as its name suggests, to the organization of workplaces, but as a basic principle, it can be applied anywhere. The

* Within the European Union, this principle is referred to by the atrocious jargon-term "subsidiarity." As far as I know there's no better word for it but I couldn't bring myself to use that one.

basic principle boils down to the idea that anyone actively engaged in a certain project of action should be able to have an
equal say in how that project is carried out. This is the principle, for instance, that lies behind theorist Michael Albert's proposed system of participatory economics (or parecon), which
tried to answer the question: what kind of work organization
allows for a genuinely democratic workplace? His answer was
"balanced job complexes"—organizations in which everyone
would have to do a certain share of physical, mental, and administrative labor. The basic idea of workers' control is that if
you're involved in a project, you should have an equal voice in
how it's executed.

The second principle, that of direct democracy, is that
everyone *affected* by a project of action should have a say in
how it is conducted. Obviously the implications here are
quite different. If such a notion were formalized, it would lead
to some form of democratic communal assemblies in order to
gather together the opinions of everyone who had a stake in
the project. But things need not become so formalized. In many
circumstances it's probably critical that they aren't. In Madagascar, where people have been operating by consensus for
a very long time, there is what is called the "fokon'olona"
principle, which is hard to translate, since sometimes it's translated as "public assembly" and sometimes just as "everybody."
French colonists tended to assume that fokon'olona were local
political institutions that could be turned into extensions of
their administration; later Malagasy governments often attempted to make them the grassroots cells for local democracy.
It never really works, and it's largely because these aren't formal bodies at all, but assemblies brought together around a
particular problem—resolving a dispute, distributing irrigation

water, deciding whether to build a road—uniting anyone whose lives are likely to be affected by the decision made.

While there are some who have tried to present these two principles—direct democracy and workers' control—as a stark choice, a truly democratic society would likely have to rely on a combination of both. If there were a paper mill in a small town, there's no reason everyone in the town whose life was somehow affected by the mill would need or want to weigh in on its vacation policies; there's every reason they might wish to be consulted on what the mill was pouring into the local river.

In the case of an activist group, when we ask this question, we are really asking about the role of working groups. Every Occupy General Assembly had these; by November 2011, the New York City General Assembly already had over thirty of them. Some were permanent and structural: Media, Facilitation, Housing, Accounting, Direct Action. Some were permanent and thematic: Alternative Banking, Ecology, Transgender Issues. Some were organized around specific actions or campaigns and might therefore be either permanent or temporary: Occupy Foreclosed Homes and Oakland Solidarity March would be examples. Action working groups will themselves tend to have their own structural working groups: media, outreach, transportation, and so forth.

Working groups are created by the General Assembly or larger group, in order to fulfill a specific task or carry out some kind of work: research, education, whatever it may be. Sometimes this happens because there's a generally recognized need ("Is anyone willing to take responsibility for sanitation issues for the camp?"), sometimes because a group of people has an idea ("Some of us want to create a group to think about how sanitation systems would work in an egalitarian society"). The

New York City GA operates by the principle that anyone wishing to create a working group needs to assemble at least five initial members and submit the request to the group. Some requests have been blocked.

Anyone is free to meet in a room and discuss anything they like, of course: what the GA is doing when it approves a working group is empowering it to act in the name of the GA. It's basically a form of delegation. It doesn't create vertical hierarchies because working groups are open to anyone. In fact, when a General Assembly or action planning meeting breaks out into working groups during the course of a meeting, this is actually a way of ensuring no one takes on too much influence, since it's physically impossible to take part in more than one at the same time. In principle, even point people, who volunteer to be the person to contact if you want to reach members of the working group, ought to be rotated. At Spokescouncils, where only one "spoke" from each working group can take part in the formal discussion (other members are encouraged to attend and whisper in his or her ear or consult discreetly), no one can speak for the same group twice in a row. Still, once the work has been divvied up, or once an existing group has been authorized to pursue some project, there comes to question of how often one needs to check back for approval. The general rule really ought to be: only when it's obvious it would be wrong to do otherwise. If there's any reason to doubt you have to check, just go ahead and do it, you probably don't.

DIRECT ACTION, CIVIL DISOBEDIENCE, AND CAMPING

The original inspiration of Occupy Wall Street was the tradition not just of direct democracy, but of direct action. From an anarchist perspective, direct democracy and direct action are—or ought to be—two aspects of the same thing: the idea that the form of our action should itself offer a model, or at the very least a glimpse of how free people might organize them-selves, and therefore what a free society could be like. In the early twentieth century it was called "building the new society in the shell of the old," in the 1980s and 1990s it came to be known as "prefigurative politics." But when Greek anarchists declare "we are a message from the future," or American ones claim to be creating an "insurgent civilization," these are really just ways of saying the same thing. We are speaking of that sphere in which action itself becomes a prophecy.

The original conception of OWS reflected this anarchist sensibility in several different ways. Most obviously, the refusal to make demands was, quite self-consciously, a refusal to rec-ognize the legitimacy of the existing political order of which such demands would have to be made. Anarchists often note that this is the difference between protest and direct action: protest, however militant, is an appeal to the authorities to behave dif-ferently; direct action, whether it's a matter of a community setting up an alternative education system or making salt in defiance of the law (an example from Gandhi's famous salt march), trying to shut down a meeting or occupy a factory, is a matter of proceeding as one would if the existing structure of power did not exist. Direct action is, ultimately, the defiant in-sistence on acting as if one is already free.

(Everyone is perfectly well aware the power structure does exist. But acting this way denies any moral authority to their inevitable, usually violent, response.)

The refusal to ask for permits was in the same spirit. As we kept pointing out to one another in the early days of meeting in

Tompkins Square Park, New York codes are so restrictive that any unpermitted assembly of more than twelve people in a public park is technically illegal (it's one of those laws that are never actually enforced except against political activists): therefore, even our meetings were at the very least a form of civil disobedience.

This raises another important distinction: between civil disobedience and direct action, which is often, mistakenly, thought to be simply a difference of militancy (civil disobedience is assumed to be a matter of blockading things, direct action, of blowing them up). Civil disobedience means refusal to comply with an unjust law, or legally valid, but unjust, order. As such, an act of civil disobedience can also be a direct action: as when one, say, burns one's draft card, on the principle that one would not have draft cards in a free society, or insists on one's right to be served at a segregated lunch counter. But an act of civil disobedience does not have to be a direct action, and ordinarily acts of civil disobedience do not question the legal order itself: only specific laws or policies. In fact they often explicitly aim to work within that legal system. This is why those engaged in civil disobedience so often welcome arrest: it allows them a platform to challenge the law or policy either legally or in the court of public opinion.

A little-known bit of history might help illustrate this. One of the inspirations for the mobilizations that led to the actions against the World Trade Organization in Seattle in 1999 was a Gandhian farmers' group based in the Indian state of Karnataka called the KRSS (it stands for Karnataka State Farmers' Association), which was best known for an action in 1995 where hundreds of farmers methodically dismantled a local Kentucky Fried Chicken franchise that they considered the first wave of an invasion of cheap bioengineered junk food about to destroy Indian agriculture. As the example suggests, they saw property destruction as a perfectly legitimate means of nonviolent resistance. In the late 1990s, their president, M. D. Nanjundaswamy, launched a campaign to disseminate mass nonviolent civil disobedience to Europe and America, and spent a good deal of time working with the early Global Justice Movement. The KRSS action against Kentucky Fried Chicken was one of the inspirations for what came to be known as "the ritual trashing of the McDonald's" that came to be a regular feature of European actions, and, ultimately the attacks on Starbucks and other chains in Seattle. Yet Swamy (as he is universally known by the activists) ended up objecting strongly to such tactics. Not because he considered attacks on storefronts a form of violence. Obviously not: like the Kentucky Fried Chicken action, he felt they were perfectly consonant with the Gandhian tradition. What he objected to was the fact that the activists who damaged the buildings did not then remain in front of them until the police arrived and voluntarily turn themselves over for arrest. "You must confront the unjust law!" But the people who attacked fast-food outlets in Europe and America were anarchists; they completely agreed with the KRSS critique of fast food as a state-supported engine of ecological and social devastation, their existence made possible by a whole legal apparatus of trade treaties and "free trade" legislation; but it never occurred to them it would be possible to address this, or find any kind of justice, within the legal system.

The original occupations were both direct actions and acts of civil disobedience. After all, we were well aware that a good case could be made that the regulations on assembly we were violating were unconstitutional. The Bill of Rights was created in part in reaction to old British colonial abuses like the banning of popular assemblies, and was essentially forced on a reluctant Constitutional Convention by popular pressure so as to protect exactly this kind of political activity. The wording of the First Amendment is also pretty unambiguous. "Congress shall make no law . . . abridging the freedom of speech, or of the press; or the right of the people peaceably to assemble, and to petition the Government for a redress of grievances." Since having to ask the police permission to speak is the definition of *not* having freedom of speech, and having to ask the police permission to publish something is the definition of *not* having freedom of the press, it is difficult to make a logical case that a law saying one needs to ask permission of the police to assemble is not a violation of the freedom to assemble.* For most of American history no one even tried. Permit laws were considered obviously unconstitutional until the 1880s, right around the time of the emergence of modern corporate capitalism, and were created explicitly for use against the emerging labor movement. It wasn't because judges changed their minds about the intent of the First Amendment; they just decided they no longer cared. The laws were further tightened in the 1980s and 1990s to ensure that nothing like the antiwar mobilizations of the 1960s and 1970s could ever again take place.

---

* Particularly since the Constitution contains no corresponding rights to freedom of traffic flow, or freedom from nuisance, which are the principles usually held to justify abridgements on freedom of assembly: the famous "time, place, and manner" qualifications used by the courts to justify police restriction on freedom of assembly. The text of the First Amendment refers to Congress, but it has been held since *Gitlow v. New York* in 1925 to apply to all legislative bodies in the United States, as well as to municipal ordinances.

If there was any legal claim that an anarchist could actually agree with, then, it was the demand to be allowed a space to engage in self-organized political activity—since, after all, this is just a matter of asking the state to leave us alone. Even Georgia Sagri, nothing if not an anarchist, was willing to put that forward when we were initially brainstorming what to put on any hypothetical list of demands.

The idea of occupying a public space was directly inspired by the revolutions in the Middle East—the role of Tahrir Square most famously—as well as Syntagma Square in Athens and the reclaimed public spaces in Spanish cities like Barcelona and Madrid. But the model was also perfect strategically because it allowed a common ground between liberals and others working in the tradition of civil disobedience who wished to democratize the system, and anarchists and other antiauthoritarians who wished to create spaces entirely outside the system's control. Both could agree that the action was legitimate based on a moral order prior to the law: since those practicing civil disobedience felt they were answering to universal principles of justice on which the law itself was founded, and anarchists felt the law itself lacked all legitimacy. The peculiar thing is that the exact nature of this prior moral order—by which one can declare some laws, or all laws, unjust—is generally unclear to all involved. Rarely can anyone spell it out as a set of propositions. One might conclude this decidedly weakens their claim of legitimacy, but in fact, those who defend the legal system have precisely the same problem, and in many ways it's even worse, since according to most legal theory the legitimacy of the entire system rests not only on a decidedly murky prior notion of justice, but also on past acts of armed insurrection. This is the fundamental incoherence in the very foundations of the modern state. It's sometimes referred to as "the paradox of sovereignty." Basically it goes something like this: the police can use violence to, say, expel citizens from a public park because they are enforcing duly constituted laws. Laws gain their legitimacy from the Constitution. The Constitution gains its legitimacy from something called the "people." But how did "the people" actually grant this legitimacy to the Constitution? As the American and French revolutions make clear: basically, through acts of illegal violence. (Washington and Jefferson after all were clearly guilty of treason under the laws under which they grew up.) So what gives the police the right to use force to suppress the very thing—a popular uprising—that granted them their right to use force to begin with?

For anarchists the answer is simple: nothing. This is why they hold that the idea of a democratic state based on a state monopoly of force makes no sense. For liberals, the idea of a state monopoly on force creates a real problem. For starters, it's a practical problem. If we grant that the "people" have a right to resist unjust authority, which is, after all, how the United States came into being in the first place, then how do we distinguish, in any given instance, "the people" from a mere rampaging mob? Historically, the answer has tended to be: "retrospectively, depending on who won." But applied consistently this would mean that if those being cleared from the park successfully resisted the police with automatic weapons, they would have more right to it than if they did not (at least, if in doing so they sparked a national uprising)—a formulation that might appeal to many Second Amendment purists, but whose might-makes-right implications would hardly be appealing to most liberals. Unsurprisingly, they take the opposite direction.

But this creates a secondary moral problem. Liberals tend to object, on moral grounds, to anything that even looks like a rampaging mob, under any circumstances. So how do the people resist unjust authority, which, we all agree, they must and should do and have done in the past? The best solution anyone has come up with is to say that violent revolutions can be avoided (and therefore, violent mobs legitimately suppressed) if "the people" are understood to have the right to challenge the laws through nonviolent civil disobedience. Those with the courage to confront the legal order on matters of conscience thus become "the people."* As liberal constitutional scholars like Bruce Ackerman point out, this is how fundamental constitutional change has typically come about in the United States, and presumably in most other liberal democracies as well: through social movements willing to break the law. Or, to put it in more anarchist terms: no government has ever granted a new freedom to those it governed all of its own accord. Such new freedoms as have been won have always been taken by those who feel they are operating on principles that go beyond the law and respect for duly constituted authority.

———

From this perspective, one can begin to understand why the strategy of occupation became such a stroke of unintentional collective genius. It was an act of defiance that could appeal to anyone, from liberals to anarchists. Like the great convergences of the Global Justice Movement—in Seattle, Prague,

* In much the way, one might even say, that those with the courage to block a proposal clearly favored by a majority in a consensus meeting take on a special constitutional role as well.

Washington, Quebec—it aimed to juxtapose an image of true democracy against the squalid power system that currently wished to pass itself off as such (back then that implicated the world trade bureaucracies that no one was supposed to even know about). But there was a crucial difference. The great mobilizations of 1999–2001 were essentially parties. That's how they framed themselves, anyway: they were "carnivals against capitalism," and "festivals of resistance." For all the dramatic images of the Seattle Black Bloc breaking Starbucks windows, what most people remember from the movement is the giant puppets, which came accompanied by clowns, brass bands, pagan priestesses, radical cheerleaders, and "Pink Blocs" in tutus armed with feather dusters tickling the police, comic-opera Roman armies waddling along wrapped in inflatable armor tumbling through barricades. Their aim was to make a mockery of the pretensions of the elite to any kind of sober wisdom, to "break the spell" of consumerism and provide a glimpse of something more enticing. Compared to the current round of mobilization, it was both more militant, and more whimsical. OWS, in contrast, is not a party, it's a community. And it's less about fun, or not so much primarily about fun, as it is about caring.

Each camp quickly developed a few core institutions: if it was any size, at least there would be a free kitchen, medical tent, library, media/communications center where activists would cluster together with laptops, and information center for visitors and new arrivals. General Assemblies would be convened at regular hours: say, every 3 P.M. for general discussion, and every 9 P.M. for technical matters specific to the camp. In addition there were working groups of every sort meeting and operating at all times: an Art and Entertainment working group, Sanitation working group, Security working group, and so on. The issues that came up in organizing were so endlessly complex that one could (and I imagine someday people will) write whole books on this subject alone.

It's significant though that the very center of everything tended to consist of two institutions: the kitchen and the library. The kitchens got a lot of the attention. Partly this was because, inspired by the example of the Egyptian labor unions who had sent pizzas to fellow union activists occupying Wisconsin's statehouse some months before, hundreds of people across North America and beyond reached for their credit cards and began phoning in orders for pizzas. (By week three, one local pizzeria had already created a pie especially for us: dubbed the "Occu-pie," it consisted, they said, of "99 percent cheese, 1 percent pig.") Much of the food was Dumpster-dived, all of it was offered free. But the libraries that cropped up everywhere were if anything even more potent symbols, especially for a population whose core was indebted former students. Libraries were immensely practical but also perfectly symbolic: libraries provide free loans, no interest, no fees—and the value of what they are lending, of words, images, above all, ideas, is not based on a principle of limited good, but actually increases with their dissemination.

It's a difficult business creating a new, alternative civilization, especially in the midst of the coldest and most unfriendly streets of major American cities, full of the sick, homeless, and psychologically destroyed, and in the very teeth of a political and economic elite whose thousands of militarized police are making abundantly clear they do not want you to be there. There are any number of sticky issues that came up quickly. There were questions of communal versus private space: when a park becomes dense with personal tents, communal space often vanishes. There are questions of security, of course, but also of how to deal with the inevitable strategies of the authorities of encouraging dangerous elements of the criminal classes to take residence in, or prey upon, the communities. And then there's the question of the relation of such liberated spaces to the surrounding communities, and using them as a platform for much broader projects of political action. So many of these variables shift case by case that it seems best, in a book like this, to focus instead on questions that will always crop up in some form or another.

Thus I'm going to begin with that one omnipresent feature of American life: the police.

TACTICS: DEALING WITH POLICE

Tell it to the marines.

—AMERICAN PROVERB

One of the key decisions we made in the early planning for the occupation was not to have a formal police liaison, or liaison team. This was the decision that really locked in our direct action strategy, and set the stage for everything that followed. Other occupations took a different course, and did create liaisons. As far as I know, in every case it was a disaster.

Why is that? One would imagine that particularly in a movement dedicated to nonviolence, there would be no reason not to open up lines of communication. But in fact in order to create an autonomous space—and this goes not just for permanent spaces like camps, but any space in which people intend to create their own form of order—certain very clear lines have to be drawn.

Those who argue the opposite often begin by declaring that "the police are part of the 99 percent"—that if we claim to represent everyone, it is hypocritical to refuse all dealings with a specific section of the American working class. Yes, taken from a purely socioeconomic perspective, almost all police officers are indeed "part of the 99 percent." Few of even the most corrupt senior-ranking officers pull in more than $340,000 a year. The fact that most are also among the roughly 15 percent of the American workforce that are still union members does make a difference as well. I have often observed that police officers will almost always treat pickets and street actions carried out by anyone they see as part of the labor movement quite differently than they will almost any other sort of protest. I've been active in the IWW (Industrial Workers of the World), which is a largely anarchist union for many years, and it never fails to strike me how the exact same young people who are immediately attacked or preemptively arrested if they so much as show up in masks during a globalization protest would be treated with kid gloves if they engaged in much more militant activity—even when wearing almost identical clothes—on a picket line. I keenly remember one occasion in the warehouse district of an American city, listening to an officer stroll up to an IWW picket line after we'd sabotaged several trucks, saying, "Hey, the owner claims one of you guys is messing with his vehicles but he says he didn't see which. Maybe you should just take off for a half hour, come back, and that way, if he claims now he knows who did it, I can just say, 'How do you know now if you didn't know then?'" (The irony was many of the picketers on this occasion were Black Bloc veterans, dressed in largely Black Bloc clothing, some actually waving anarcho-syndicalist flags. The next day, though, the warehouse owner just paid off the commanding officer and his men drove us all off from a perfectly legal picket with sticks, resulting in several injuries.) In a company town like New Haven, even student activists are treated with kid gloves if they're protesting the local university, because they're assumed to be working with the unions.

However, this is true mostly in cases when police have discretion: when protesters confront only an individual officer, or a low-ranking commander with only a few men under his charge. Occupiers in New York discovered there was a sharp class division even within the police. Many street officers, the blue-shirts, expressed sympathy and support. The white-shirts, or commanding officers, were quite a different story; many, in fact, were in the direct pay of Wall Street corporations. But even this misses the point: which is that when push comes to shove, even the white-shirts are just following orders.

"Dealing with the police" does not mean chatting with individual officers; some protesters, occupiers, even Black Bloc anarchists will always do this and there's no way one could stop them, or any reason, really, one would want to try. But "the police" are not a collection of individuals acting in accord with their personal feelings, judgments, or moral assessments. They are a group of government functionaries who, as part of the terms of their employment, have agreed to set their personal opinions and feelings aside—at least in any circumstance where they receive direct orders—and to do as they are told. They are part of an administrative bureaucracy marked by a top-down chain of command, and even the highest-ranking officers, with the most discretion, are only there to carry out the orders of political authorities whom they must obey. In such circumstances, their personal feelings are utterly irrelevant. I have spoken to many activists at the WTO protests in Seattle who saw riot police crying behind their visors, so upset were they when given orders to attack obviously peaceful young idealists. They attacked them anyway. Often they didn't do it particularly well. But neither did they disobey orders.

Not only are police trained and vetted so as to be reliable in this regard, the entire existing political and economic system depends on this reliability. The reader will recall what I said in the last chapter about anarchist forms of organization: that they are any form that would not have to rely, in the event of a challenge, on the ability to call in people with weapons to say "shut up and do what you're told." The police are precisely those people with weapons. They are essentially armed administrators, bureaucrats with guns. This role—that of upholding existing institutional arrangements, and especially property arrangements and the ability of some people to give unchallengeable orders—is much more important, ultimately, than any supposed concern with public order or even public safety. It might not seem that way, but it becomes clear when the institutional order is in any way directly threatened. When there is a political challenge to the system, a large protest or act of civil disobedience, one witnesses increasingly extreme behavior— the use of agents provocateurs to encourage protesters to attack police so they can be arrested, or even suggesting they acquire explosives and blow up bridges, police actions designed to create panic and strife, massive and violent assaults on crowds when only one or two individuals in the crowd commit some illegal act, often the equivalent of a parking violation,

mass arrests that by definition must sweep up innocent passersby, use of tear gas or other chemical agents in public places.
All of these acts show that when protest begins to be truly effective, police will invariably be ordered to act as a political
force, with the aim of suppressing political opposition even at
the expense of seriously endangering, injuring, or traumatizing
members of the public.

Thus while the police as individuals are part of the 99 percent, as an institutional structure they are the most basic support for that entire structure of institutional authority that
makes the wealth and power of the 1 percent possible. There is
absolutely nothing wrong with dealing with police in a friendly
and respectful way as individuals—it is clearly the right thing
to do, not just because it's good to be friendly and respectful to
everyone, but even from a strategic perspective: when regimes
do crumble and fall, when revolutionaries actually win the day,
it's always because the soldiers or police sent to shoot them
refuse to do so. But we should also remember: that's the endgame. In the meantime, we need to remember that we're never
likely to get anywhere near that endgame if we engage with the
police as an institutional structure, and maintain ourselves
within the overall structure of power they represent.

Note that I say "structure of power," not "structure of
law." On most such issues, legality is largely irrelevant. After
all, almost every aspect of our lives is in theory governed by
laws and regulations many of which we're barely even aware
of; almost everyone in America violates ten or twenty such a
day; if a policeman really wanted to just rough up some random citizen, kick them in the testicles, break a tooth or thumb
perhaps, they could in almost any case find a justifiable excuse
to do so. (In fact, it's a notorious activist paradox that police

have much more discretion to visit random violence if they are not trying to ultimately convict the victim of any crime, since if the victim is in fact guilty of something, and will face trial, any violation of codes of conduct by the arresting officer might prejudice a conviction; if the police aren't aiming for a conviction anyway, from a legal standpoint there's really no reason not to physically abuse them. The very worst that could happen, in the case of a national scandal, would be the loss of a few weeks' pay.) This is why if police wish to enforce unstated racial codes—to harass African Americans who go into the "wrong" neighborhood—they can usually do so legally, simply by enforcing rules that are not enforced on white people. Similarly with activists.

That law has very little to do with the matter becomes apparent the moment members of a group *do* decide to engage with the police as an institutional structure, by appointing a police liaison and beginning to negotiate. After all, if it were simply a matter of each side acting within the law, what would there be to negotiate about? It would just be a matter of exchanging information about what the legal rules are, what the occupiers, or marchers, intend to do, and then allow the police to protect those members of the public who intend to protest. This is never what happens. In fact, the first thing police commanders will do is create their own, impromptu rules, based on translating their sheer power (they are allowed to hit you, you are not allowed to hit them; they can arrest you, you cannot arrest them) into a larger structure of authority.

Let me give an unusually clear example. In New York, it is the custom of police to use metal barriers to create narrow pens, and then try to contain all picketers and protesters inside them. It's very demoralizing for protesters. It's also fairly obviously unconstitutional. What's more, police commanders seem to be aware that it is: at least no one to my knowledge has ever been arrested for refusal to enter a pen (though protesters who have refused to enter pens have occasionally been arrested on other, made-up charges). The very first thing the police do if there are protest marshals is to tell the marshals that they are not themselves obliged to enter the pens, but that the police consider it the responsibility of the marshals to make sure everyone else stays inside. In other words, if there is a structure of authority, police will immediately grant those who are in it special privileges (which they have just invented) and try to make them an extension of their authority, effectively an unofficial extension of their own chain of command. I have experienced this myself when I've volunteered to be a marshal; refusal to beg or bully other protesters into getting inside pens will immediately be greeted by accusations that "you're not doing your job!"—as if by agreeing to be a marshal, one has effectively volunteered to work for the police.

If there is no structure of authority within the group, the police commander in charge will, just as inevitably, try to see if one can be created. Liaisons will be granted special privileges, and commanders will try to make informal, extralegal arrangements with them that they will be expected—made to feel honor-bound, if possible—to enforce, with the knowledge that others in de facto authority will then have to support them and a formal top-down structure will gradually come into place. Here's another personal experience, this time from the other side: during the early days of Occupy Austin, one activist (I remember him as a dreadlocked libertarian hippie much given to meditation, who seemed to be close to most of the core members of the facilitation team) volunteered at an early General Assembly to act as liaison with police, or, as he said he preferred to call them, "peace officers." The proposal was not approved but he decided to take on the role anyway. One of the very first issues when occupiers established themselves in front of City Hall was about tents: could we establish a camp? The legalities were ambiguous. Some occupiers immediately tried, the police appeared menacingly; most of us surrounded the tent prepared for nonviolent civil disobedience. Our self-appointed liaison sprang into action, sought out the commander, and reappeared a short while later saying he'd negotiated a compromise: we could keep the one tent for symbolic purposes, so long as we did not raise any more.

Many—I'd dare say most—of the occupiers assumed that this was just a way of saving face, since the police clearly didn't want to have to attack peaceful campers on their first day, and were feeling out our willingness to resist. So the next day, a small group of more experienced activists decided the obvious thing was to slowly expand our liberated territory in the most nonconfrontational way possible, and discreetly raised another, small tent by its side. One grows by accretion, constantly pushing at the borders. This was the approach taken in Zuccotti Park as well, where it proved successful. Here, however, the activists raising the tent found themselves besieged by friends of the self-appointed liaison, who declared that this was a betrayal of the trust that had been placed in him by the police commander the day before. The vibes watcher at the General Assembly employed the People's Microphone to collectively demand we take the tent down, one woman tried to call in the police (who themselves appeared uninterested in the tent) to arrest us, another man appeared declaring "I am a combat veteran and I am going to tear this tent down!" and only stopped trying to shove his way past the activists who had raised the tent (who by now were trying to lock arms in passive resistance) when it became clear he was endangering a small child who was inside. While the camp's security team eventually de-escalated the overt confrontation, the tent did ultimately come down, and no further attempts to raise others were made; subsequent attempts to at least establish the principle that nonviolent fellow occupiers should not be threatened with violence or arrest were ignored by the facilitation team (or even met with objections that those who acted in such a way as to make the police more likely to attack, thus endangering children, were themselves being violent!). Once the police and City Council, in turn, observed that unity in the camp was broken, and those more committed to civil disobedience had been marginalized, they realized they once again had the initiative and began imposing all sorts of new restrictions: on tables, on the serving of food, on staying overnight, until within a few weeks the occupation in front of City Hall had been cleared entirely.

The reason this story is worth recounting at length is because it illustrates so clearly that we are not talking about a legal order, but a balance of political forces, where each side was essentially improvising, trying to get a sense of the state of the game and what they could get away with at any given moment. Appealing to the letter of the law—which was rarely clear-cut—was just one weapon among many that each side could deploy, alongside appealing to the public (whether via the media, or directly), to the threat of force (truncheons, handcuffs, chemical weapons in the case of the police, civil disobedience such as blockades in the case of the occupiers), to political allies of one sort or another, or even to conscience.

The police strategy was, from the beginning, clearly political, and presumably based on instructions from above: they aimed to minimize any disruption caused by the camp and clear it out as soon as possible. (It later came out that they had also sent undercovers to join the camp, to try to convince occupiers to engage in more militant tactics—blockades using lockboxes—knowing that Texas had recently passed laws making it easy to obtain felony convictions against anyone adopting them.) Making one strategic concession (the one tent) and using that as a wedge was a perfect strategy, as it made it possible for the authorities to create a cadre within the occupation that was essentially willing to act as an extension of the police's power, to translate the mere threat of force ("the police will attack us!") into moral authority ("we promised!"), and thus ultimately either control, or easily break up, the occupation. It is absolutely essential never to allow this translation of threats of violence into morality. The only way to oppose the threat of physical force is by moral force, and moral force has to be based, first of all, in solidarity. The moment some people participating in an action feel they have more of a moral commitment to those who are threatening to attack them than they do to another activist, the game is basically over.

————

It is best, in fact, to think of all occupations and street actions as a kind of war. I know this sounds extreme, but years of reflection and experience have driven me to the conclusion that there's really no more appropriate way to describe what happens. I should emphasize: this is not in any way a call for violence. It is always best not to hurt other human beings if one can possibly avoid it, and in the contemporary United States, one is rarely in a situation where violence is the only option.* However, there are two sides to any conflict, and in any street action, one side does show up prepared for a war: armed, backed up by SWAT teams, helicopters, and armored vehicles, making it known from the beginning that they are prepared to use violence in the pursuit of political ends. Neither is it, generally speaking, up to someone conducting an unauthorized march whether that force will actually be deployed. Certainly, if the protesters begin trashing vehicles or setting fires, one can pretty much guarantee the police will begin throwing people against walls and handcuffing them. But it will often happen anyway. In fact, it may well happen less in, say, a march where police think there is the possibility of real violence breaking out on the part of the marchers, but in which it has not yet happened, than in one where they think the marchers are unlikely to offer any sort of resistance at all. It all depends on a whole series of calculations about the likely reaction of protesters, communities, media, and important institutions. The rules of engagement between occupiers and police are continually being negotiated and renegotiated.

A few examples from Zuccotti Park might prove illustrative:

---

* I was once at an activist roundtable on violence and nonviolence in Quebec, and one ultra-militant began his intervention by asking "Why do we assume nonviolence is always better than violence if there's a choice?" I replied, "Because it's really difficult to have to spend your life trying to get around with no legs." Which is the almost inevitable consequence if bombs start going off.

- According to one journalist who interviewed numerous police and city officials in the early days of Occupy Wall Street, one of the main concerns of those giving the street officers their orders was the presence of Guy Fawkes–masked members of the hackers collective Anonymous in Zuccotti Park. Most, he said, were genuinely worried that if they attacked the camp and expelled the protesters, Anonymous would hack their bank and credit card accounts, and the fear of this played a major role in their decision to hold off from doing so.

- New York mayor Bloomberg's first attempt to expel the occupation from the newly renamed Liberty Park on October 14, 2011, proved an embarrassing failure. After he announced his plan to clear the space for a "cleaning," activists mobilized on all possible fronts simultaneously: thousands arrived prepared to defend the camp through nonviolent civil disobedience; at the same time, legal teams prepared injunctions, potentially sympathetic members of the media were called in, and unions and other allies mobilized political allies in the city legislature. Finally, the mayor backed off. It was not any one approach, but the combined weight of so many different ones, that ultimately forced him to do so.

- The 1 A.M. raid on November 12, 2012, that did evict the occupation appears to have been based on a nationwide political decision, and it was planned as a sudden surprise attack, using overwhelming force, with all media banned from the scene. It also simply ignored legal authority. By 2 A.M., the occupiers' legal team had secured a judicial order to halt the eviction until the legalities were clarified;

Bloomberg ignored the court order until he could find a judge that would rule in his favor. It was during the period that the raid was, technically, illegal, for instance, that the Liberty Park library was seized and systematically destroyed.

What these examples make clear is that we are dealing with a balance of political forces that has almost nothing to do with law. If the police are able, as they were in Austin, they negotiate arrangements, backed by the threat of force, that stand independent of any laws and regulations. If they are not able to do this, as they were not in New York, their first move is to make sure everyone knows they are willing and able to make illegal arrests. The Anonymous example above also demonstrates that the lines of force might exist largely in the imagination—hackers can't really do most of the things that they do in the movies—but that the game of politics is largely a psychological war of bluffs and feints, even at the same time as it is a moral conflict. And as the final example illustrates, local victories might prove ephemeral if one is not able to mobilize the same sort of forces on a national or even international level.

Debates within the movement are almost never really about whether to be nonviolent, but rather over what form of nonviolence to employ. (Within the faith community, these debates are often referred to as the difference between the Gandhi/Martin Luther King tradition of nonviolence, which eschews damage to property, and the Daniel Berrigan or Plowshares Eight tradition, which holds that certain types of damage to state or corporate property can be a legitimate way of preventing greater harm.) What I would like to propose are a few principles we need to think more about when considering tactics.

First, here are some principles to consider on a broader level: just as we need to think about what sort of social arrangements would allow us to create a truly democratic society, we need to think about what sort of tactics would best allow us to maintain the democratic nature of the movement. The question is rarely framed this way, but it should be. One example of a social movement that considered it quite explicitly was the 2006 popular uprising in Oaxaca, Mexico, where the conclusion was that *either* a strategy of armed uprising, or of pure Gandhian nonviolence, would necessarily have to rely on charismatic leaders and military-style discipline that would ultimately undermine any genuine participatory democracy. Conversely, it makes sense that right-wing political movements, such as the Tea Party, which had no problems at all with top-down forms of authority, combined scrupulous attention to legality with threats of outright armed insurrection.

Second is a practical point. That middle zone, between actual uprising and ritualized Gandhian nonviolence, is also a zone of maximum creativity and improvisation and that is entirely to our advantage. On the streets, creativity is our greatest tactical advantage. This is why the clowns and spiral dance rituals and women in tutus armed with feather dusters were so effective during the Global Justice Movement. The police (speaking again of the police as an institution, not as individual officers) are not very bright. This is especially true when masses of them are arranged in riot gear. In such a circumstance, the most effective method of dealing with police is always to do something they have not been trained to respond to. This is the cost of that sort of military discipline that allows otherwise decent human beings to engage in a baton charge against non-violent protesters: in order to be able to do what one is told, one has to agree to do *only* what one is told. The other cost is that those in charge of training riot police seem to feel that in order to be psychologically able to engage in violence against activists, police have to be trained how to respond, not to the tactics that they are actually likely to face, but to forms of extreme violence that activists never really engage in at all. After Seattle, for instance, there were squads of police trainers circulating through America instructing police in cities preparing for trade summits in how to deal with activists hurling Molotov cocktails, human excrement, and lightbulbs full of acid or ammonia, firing ball bearings from slingshots, or armed with squirt guns full of bleach and urine. In fact no activist at Seattle or any subsequent summit had ever done any of these things. But it appears that commanders felt it was more important to convince the police that activists were the moral equivalent of Bond villains than to prepare them for the tactics they would actually have to face. As a result, many police found the actual experience profoundly confusing, and were forced to constantly radio back for orders. On more than one occasion in those years, I witnessed groups of surrounded activists escape arrest when police lines fell into momentary confusion when confronted with clowns on high bicycles or theatrical troupes. On other occasions I've seen lines of riot police who had been methodically beating back a line of activists stop dead in their tracks, like so many robots, when the activists did nothing more than all simultaneously sit down.

Third, the political question of power, and the balance of forces I've been describing, is best considered as one of how to create a space where such creative nonviolent action is possible. Here another recent Mexican example is telling: the 1994 Zapatista uprising in Chiapas. This was an area where, for centuries, it was impossible for indigenous people to mobilize politically without seeing their organizers arrested, tortured, or assassinated. In January 1994, largely indigenous rebels seized the provincial capital and engaged in a twelve-day shooting war against the Mexican army; a war that ended with a truce, whereon the rebels hid their weapons in the jungle and embarked on a campaign of organizing autonomous, self-governing communities and have been engaging in direct action tactics against the Mexican state and local elites ever since. In other words, they used precisely as much outright violence as they had to in order to put themselves in a position not to have to use violence anymore. Aside from its more obvious disadvantages, violence is boring and predictable. Hollywood movies and similar forms of entertainment are determined to convince us otherwise, but actually it's true. This is why historically it has always been the preferred tactic of the stupid. Violence is basically a form of active stupidity, a way of clapping one's hands over one's ears and refusing to be reasonable. For this very reason, it is the state's preferred arena for dealing with any sort of real challenge to its legitimacy. But the moment one changes the lines of force so the actual conflict is not simply one of violence, we have tilted the field in our favor.

The space for nonviolent political action in contemporary North America is much wider than 1990s Chiapas, but it has been narrowing steadily since the 1960s. When the president of Columbia University invited police onto campus to retake student-occupied buildings in 1968, this was considered a shocking breach of the tacit understanding that universities do not call in military-style force against their own students. When, as I described earlier, a handful of students attempted occupations at the New School and NYU in 2009, they were

almost immediately overwhelmed by special police antiterrorism squads with high-tech weapons and equipment. Even more
important, there was no outcry on the part of the media. In
fact, the national media made no mention of the events at all.
They weren't even newsworthy. The use of overwhelming military force against nonviolent students inside their own university had, by that time, come to be considered perfectly normal.

The key political question, then, has to be: how to reopen
this space. This is actually one reason why the language of occupation is so important. Many have objected to the apparent
military origins of the term "occupation." True, in Europe, it's
commonplace to talk about squatters "occupying" an apartment building, or workers "occupying" a factory, but in the
United States we're much more used to hearing about "occupied France" in World War II, the "occupied territories" of the
West Bank, or of U.S. forces occupying Baghdad. None are
particularly inspiring examples. But in fact what we are doing
is an occupation. The military analogy is appropriate. It's not
even really an analogy. We are seizing space and defending it by
means of various lines of force: moral, psychological, and
physical. The key is that once we do liberate this space, we always, immediately, transform it into a space of love and caring.
Indeed, the power of that image of love and caring was our
primary weapon: as evidenced by the fact that it took a sustained campaign on the part of the mainstream media to replace images of democracy, community, and feeding the hungry
with largely concocted images of violence and sexual assault,
in order to be able to justify the coordinated police attacks that
were eventually able to dislodge them.

Now let's turn from questions of tactics to questions of strategy. Of course, as I emphasized at the beginning, the two can never really be divorced. Questions of tactics are always questions of strategy.

But this also means one cannot rule definitively on such matters because at the moment there is no absolute consensus within the movement about what the strategic horizon ultimately is. We have on board everyone from liberals interested in driving the Democratic Party to the left so as to return to something more like New Deal–style capitalism, to anarchists who ultimately wish to dismantle the state and capitalism entirely. The very fact that they have been able to work so well together at all has been a minor miracle. At some point, difficult decisions will have to be made.

One thing I have written about tactics makes clear that the Occupy movement is ultimately based on what in revolutionary theory is often called a dual power strategy: we are trying to create liberated territories outside of the existing political, legal, and economic order, on the principle that that order is irredeemably corrupt. It is a space that operates to what extent it is possible, outside the apparatus of government and its claims of a monopoly on the legitimate use of force. But in contemporary North America, we are hardly yet in a position of declaring liberated neighborhoods or territories in which we can solve our own problems through purely democratic means. How, then, can we pursue this strategy in a way that will bring concrete benefits to the kind of people who posted their stories to "We Are the 99 Percent"?

In part, this is a question of alliances. It is one thing to say one will not engage in an inherently corrupt system. It is quite another to say one will not even engage with those who do.

The latter would mean limiting ourselves to creating tiny utopian enclaves that could have no immediate effect on anyone
else's lives. However, the moment one begins to engage with
institutionally powerful supporters—unions, NGOs, political
parties or party-affiliated groups, even celebrities—one runs
the danger of compromising one's own internal democracy. It
started as soon as people like Roseanne Barr, Joseph Stiglitz,
and Michael Moore began appearing in Zuccotti Park to offer
their support. Everyone was glad to see them, but they obviously weren't about to limit their participation to collective
discussions via the People's Microphone. Their mode was
to make speeches. It was very difficult, at first, to prevent the
speechifying from becoming infectious. This was a little thing,
but gives a sense of the problems. This tension intensified
when liberal groups like MoveOn.org, with paid, experienced,
full-time employees, vertical habits, and often political and
legislative agendas about which they were not always entirely
forthcoming, decided to throw in their support. Again, one
does not wish to refuse support when it's critical to help expand and create tools to coordinate the movement, but there
were endless challenges in ensuring that those structures of co-
ordination remain horizontal, especially when dealing with
well-meaning organizers who have never even heard of "horizontality" and may consider any meticulous concern with internal democracy a peculiar self-indulgence. Even money can
be a problem. In the first month or two of the Wall Street occupation, about a half a million dollars' worth of contributions
flowed in. This money caused so many disputes and problems
that many activists wished they could simply get rid of it
somehow: many proposed the whole wad should be somehow
spent on one giant project (an Occupy blimp?); eventually,

after the evictions, almost all of it ended up being used to pay churches to put up hundreds of evictees until they could find other places to stay. The fact that the effects of money were so corrosive does not reflect an intrinsic problem with democratic process, I think, so much as the fact that activists' every experience of dealing with money and organizations whose lifeblood is money have been suffused with completely different habits and imperatives. Yet again, it's not as if one can avoid the world of money entirely.

Most of these problems can be dealt with, and eventually will, by the creation of various sorts of firewalls: mental and organizational. Larger strategic questions are much stickier, but it might be helpful to throw out some examples of approaches that have been attempted elsewhere in recent years, and have proved relatively effective, so as to get a sense of what kind of directions there are to take.

Let us imagine that a movement like Occupy does succeed in creating a network of liberated spaces: either by reestablishing the camps that were so systematically dismantled in 2011 (though it's pretty clear that in the current situation, the government would never allow this) or by starting from a different sort of space, public buildings, for example. In either case the ultimate aim would be to create local assemblies in every town and neighborhood, as well as networks of occupied dwellings, occupied workplaces, and occupied farms that can become the foundations of an alternative economic and political system. How then could that network of liberated spaces and alternative institutions relate to the existing legal and political system?

There are a number of potential models. None corresponds exactly to anything that is likely to happen in the United States, but they provide a way to think about the problem.

- **The Sadr City Strategy:** One obvious question is how to defend these spaces, since one must expect there will be a systematic attempt to wipe them out. In the Middle East the solution is to create armed militias. While this is hardly likely to happen anytime soon in the contemporary United States (at least on the part of left-wing groups), the experience of groups like the Sadrists in Iraq is nonetheless instructive. The Sadrists are a populist Islamist movement with a mass working-class base that, even during the years of U.S. military occupation, proved remarkably successful in creating zones of self-governance in Iraqi cities and towns. One reason they were so effective is that they understood that the key to any such dual-power strategy was to begin by creating institutions that no one could possibly object to—in their case, a network of free clinics for pregnant and nursing mothers—and then gradually building up a security apparatus, and larger social infrastructure, to protect it. The next step is to try to negotiate clear, and scrupulously respected, borders between zones under one's own control, and zones still under the control of the ostensible government.

  While brilliantly successful in creating autonomous institutions in the very teeth of foreign military occupation, the example of the Sadrists, or Hezbollah in Lebanon, which pursued a broadly similar approach, also shows that any such dual-power approach quickly encounters limits. For one thing, if one is engaging in armed resistance, even if one's strategy is basically defensive, one's followers will pretty much inevitably end up using violence in all sorts of other ways—and violence takes on a logic of its own. Military discipline is required, which of course limits any possibility of democratic experiment, and puts the focus on charismatic leaders, and any such movement has a tendency, as the course of least resistance, to become the political voice of some specific fairly culturally uniform group. All of these factors, along with the endless problems that follow from governing neighborhoods, make the temptation to enter formal politics eventually irresistible. After all, if one does not eschew organized violence or operate on horizontal principles, there's no particular reason not to enter into state institutions. As a result, just about every example of such an approach in the Middle East has ultimately led to the creation of a political party.

Obviously I'm not suggesting that any of this could be a model for a movement like Occupy, but it's an excellent example to start from, partly because the original strategy (starting from the women's health clinics) was really quite ingenious, but mainly because it shows that it's always precisely the groups that do not eschew the use of guns and bombs that seem to find it easiest to end up absorbed into structures of government.

- **The San Andrés strategy:** A very different approach was taken by the Zapatistas in the years immediately following their twelve-day insurrection in December 1994. As noted above, the uprising was quickly ended by a truce, and whatever its original aims, mainly served to open up a space for rebel communities to create their own autonomous institutions, and to engage in various forms of nonviolent direct action (the Zapatistas soon became famous for organizing events like "invasions" of Mexican army camps by thousands of unarmed indigenous women carrying babies).

The Zapatistas made a decision not to enter the formal political process in Mexico, but to begin creating a different kind of political system entirely. The question remained how to formally engage with existing structures of power. The solution was to engage in formal negotiations for a peace treaty—they came to be known as the San Andrés Accords—which would, rather than compromise the newly created structures of local-level democracy, instead provide a reason to legitimate, develop, and expand them, since Zapatista negotiators (who were selected as recallable delegates by their communities) insisted that every stage of negotiations was subject to comprehensive democratic consultation, approval, and review. The negotiation process itself became, in other words, the perfect firewall. The fact that everyone knew the government was almost certainly negotiating in bad faith, without the slightest intention of enforcing the treaty, was a secondary consideration.

It's interesting to think about what a parallel strategy might look like for Occupy Wall Street: that is, a mode of engagement with the existing political structure that rather than compromising its directly democratic process would actually help foster and develop it. One obvious approach might be an attempt to promote one or more constitutional amendments, which has already been proposed in some quarters: for example, for eliminating money from political campaigns, or an abolition of corporate personhood. There are parallels to that, too: in

Ecuador, for example, indigenous groups that mobilized to put a moderate left-of-center economist named Rafael Correa in power insisted, as their expected payback, that they play a major role in writing a new constitution. One could anticipate a lot of problems here, particularly since one is working within the confines of a constitutional structure that was, as noted in the last chapter, largely designed to prevent direct democracy, but if nothing else, it would be far easier to create firewalls in this sort of process than if one was dealing directly with elected officials.

• **The El Alto strategy:** The case of Bolivia is one of the few examples I know of where the two approaches to dual power—using autonomous institutions as the base to win a role in government, and maintaining them as a directly democratic alternative completely separate from government—have been effectively combined. I call it the "El Alto strategy" after the largely indigenous city outside the capital, famous for its directly democratic institutions and traditions of direct action (popular assemblies in El Alto had, for instance, taken control of and were administering the city's water system, among other utilities), and which is also the current home of the country's first indigenous president, former farmers' union leader Evo Morales. The same social movements that are largely responsible for putting Morales in power, having led a series of largely nonviolent insurrections against various predecessors, and mobilized for his election, nonetheless insist on maintaining the ability to rise up against, and similarly overthrow, him at any time. The logic is quite explicit, and often echoed by elected officials from Morales's own party: government is not, and cannot be, a truly democratic institution. It has its own top-down logic, stretching from the demands of international capital and trade organizations from above, or the very nature of bureaucracies backed up by the power of police. Elected officials will therefore almost inevitably end up, at least in some circumstances, under enormous pressure to do the exact opposite of what their constituents elected them to do. Maintaining dual-power institutions provides a check on this, and even puts politicians like Morales in a stronger negotiating position when dealing with, say, foreign governments and corporations, or his own bureaucracy, since he can honestly claim that in certain areas his hands are tied—he has no choice but to answer to his constituents.

Needless to say in the United States we are nowhere near this point, but it's useful to bear in mind as one future horizon of possibility. If there is a lesson here, I think it is that it would be unwise to even consider making forays into electoral politics until we have established the principle that militant forms of direct action are legitimate and acceptable forms of political expression.

• **The Buenos Aires strategy:** Another approach is not to engage directly with the political establishment at all, but rather, to try to strip it of all legitimacy. This might be called the Argentina model, or delegitimation approach, and it seems to be more or less what's happening at the time of writing in Greece. It's important to stress that this does not mean abandoning any hope of ameliorating conditions through the apparatus of the state. To the contrary: it serves as a challenge to the political class to demonstrate their relevance, and is often successful in inspiring them to make radical measures to ameliorate conditions they would never have otherwise considered.

Essentially, the strategy is to create alternative institutions, based on horizontal principles, that have nothing to do with the government, and declare the entire political system to be absolutely corrupt, idiotic, and irrelevant to people's actual lives, a clown show that fails even as a form of entertainment, and try to render politicians a pariah class. Hence after the economic collapse in Argentina in 2001, a popular uprising that ousted three different governments in a matter of months settled into a strategy of creating alternative institutions based on the principle of what they themselves called "horizontality": popular assemblies to govern urban neighborhoods, recuperated factories and other workplaces (whose bosses had abandoned them), self-organized unemployed associations engaged in almost constant direct action, even, for a while, an alternative currency system.

Their attitude toward the political class was summed up by the famous slogan *"que se vayan todos,"* roughly translated, "they can all go to hell." Legend has it that by early 2002, it had reached the point where politicians—of any political party—could not even eat out at restaurants without wearing phony mustaches or similar disguises, since if recognized they would be mobbed by angry diners, or pelted with food. The end result was that a Social Democratic government came to power led by a president (Néstor Kirchner) who previously had been the mildest reformist possible, but who recognized that in order to restore any public sense that government *could* be a legitimate institution, he had to take some sort of radical action. He decided to default on a large part of Argentina's international debt. His doing so set off a cascade of events that nearly destroyed international enforcement agencies like the International Monetary Fund, and effectively ended the Third World debt crisis. The ultimate effects were of untold benefit to billions of the world's poor, and led to the strong rebound of the Argentine economy, but none of it would have happened were it not for the campaign to destroy the legitimacy of Argentina's political class. What's more, the strategy adopted ensured that, even when the government did manage to reassert itself, many of the self-governing institutions created during the initial upheaval have been preserved.

Assuming that an actual insurrectionary situation is for the moment unlikely (granted, insurrectionary situations always seem unlikely until the moment they actually happen; but it seems reasonable to imagine that at the very least, economic conditions would have to get considerably worse), we are probably faced with some homegrown combination of these options, or something broadly like them. At least the list might provide a way to start thinking about further possibilities.

It also helps clarify that up till now Occupy Wall Street has effectively been pursuing the last option: a strategy of delegitimation. Considering political attitudes in the contemporary United States, this was probably inevitable. After all, before we even started, we were already halfway there. The overwhelming majority of Americans already saw their political system as corrupt and useless. In fact, the summer when the occupation was first being planned had been marked by an unusually bizarre, childish, and pointless display of political histrionics over the national debt ceiling that had left congressional approval ratings in the single digits (9 percent)—the lowest they had ever been. As most Americans languished in the midst of a crippling recession, millions in desperate situations that the political system had essentially declared itself unwilling or unable to address, congressional Republicans were threatening to cause the U.S. government to default in order to force massive cuts in social services intended to head off a largely imaginary debt crisis that would, in a worst-case scenario, cause the U.S. government to default some years further down the line. President Obama, in turn, had decided the way to appear reasonable in comparison, and thus seem as his advisors liked to put it "the only adult in the room," was not to point out that the entire debate was founded on false economic premises, but to prepare a milder, "compromise" version of the exact same program—as if the best way to expose a lunatic is to pretend that 50 percent of their delusions are actually true. In this context, the only really reasonable thing to do is to point out exactly that the entire debate was meaningless, and that the political order had succeeded only in delegitimizing itself. This is how a ragtag group of anarchists, hippies, unemployed college students, pagan tree sitters, and peace activists suddenly managed to establish themselves, by default, as America's adults in the first place. There are times when staking out a radical position is the only reasonable thing to do.

As I say, I don't want to make specific suggestions about long-term strategy, but I think it is important not to forget that American politics has become a game played between players who have given up on the idea that politics even could be about anything other than collective delusions, realities that are, in effect, created by power. And "power" here usually turns out, in the end, to be a euphemism for organized violence. This is why it's so crucial, whatever we do, to both continue to create spaces where we can genuinely operate through reasonableness and compromise, even at the same time as we lay bare the apparatus of the sheer stupid brute force that lies behind the politicians' claims to be able to "create realities" out of nothing. This must, necessarily, mean facing that brute, stupid power not with any sort of "reasonable" compromise, but with a form of flexible, intelligent counterpower that develops a radical alternative while constantly reminding everyone in no uncertain terms exactly what the basis of that power really is.

FIVE

BREAKING THE SPELL

I n the fall of 2011, most of us felt we were standing in the middle of a global revolution. Everything was happening almost unimaginably rapidly, with a wave of unrest that began in Tunisia suddenly engulfing the world, threatening everywhere. We were seeing sympathy demonstrations in China and almost daily new occupations in places like Nigeria and Pakistan. In retrospect, of course, there was no way things could really continue at such a pace. It was as if just as all the international security structures designed to head off such mass resistance—and which, since the crash of 2008, had been churning out endless studies and working papers on the likelihood of food riots and global unrest—had finally convinced themselves, rather incredulously, that nothing significant was really going to happen, it did; and now that it had they were standing there gaping just as incredulously.

Still, when the inevitable wave of repression came, it left

many of us in temporary confusion. We had expected to see the truncheons come out eventually. What surprised many of us was the reaction of our liberal allies. America, after all, sees itself not as a nation united by any particular ethnic origin, but as a people united by their freedoms; and these were the very people who ordinarily put themselves forth as those freedoms' most stalwart defenders. The fact that they proved happy instead to see civil liberties as so many bargaining chips, to be defended only if strategically convenient, was sobering—even to many anarchists like me who have come to expect almost nothing else from the liberal establishment. The effect was all the more distressing because so many of those left in the lurch had just directly experienced the violence. These were young men and women who'd been first drawn into a euphoric sense of almost unlimited possibility, but who now had to deal with vivid memories of watching their library, so lovingly assembled, trashed and sent off to the incinerators by laughing patrolmen, of seeing their dearest friends beaten with sticks and shackled as the mainstream media dutifully refused to enter the perimeter, unable to do anything to help them, of seeing friends Maced in the face having to face the prospect of lifelong respiratory problems, of having to scramble to find housing for people whose life possessions, however modest, had been destroyed by agents of the state—led to a bubbling up of every conceivable tension and ill-feeling that had been repressed or ignored in the weeks previous when organizing and defending the camps had given us such obvious common purpose. For a month or so, the New York General Assembly and Spokescouncil fell into almost complete dysfunction. There were near fistfights at some meetings; screaming fits; ringing cries of racism; an endless tangle of overlapping crises over tactics, organization, and money; and accusations on everything from police infiltration to narcissistic personality disorder. At moments like this, even professional optimists like myself are tempted to feel cynical. But periodically—with striking regularity, actually—I found myself confronted with reminders of just how much I've already taken for granted.

A few months after the evictions, after one typically fretful hallway conference, I met a solemn, bearded man, perhaps thirty-five years old, conservatively dressed, who remarked, "You know, it doesn't really matter if the May Day actions come off at all—I mean, like anyone I'm hoping they will. But even if it does, even if we never reoccupy, even it all were to end today, as far as I'm concerned, you guys have already changed everything. For me anyway. I think we're looking at the beginning of a transformation of American culture."

"Really? But how many people has it really reached?"

"Well, the thing is for anyone who has, you can't really go back to thinking about things the way you did before. I notice it in my job. Here we might spend all our time complaining about meetings, but just try to go back to the real world again if you'd never experienced a democratic meeting before; you go back to work and suddenly it's, like, wait a minute! This is just completely ridiculous. And you talk to your friends, your sister, your parents, and saying, well, what else is there we've just assumed is the only way you can do something that might seem just as stupid if we didn't just take it for granted? You might be surprised. A *lot* of people are asking that sort of thing."

And I thought: could it be that's all a revolution really is? When that starts to happen? That is, if it really has . . .

———

It's a much vexed question: What is a revolution?

We used to think we knew. Revolutions were seizures of power by some kind of popular forces aiming to transform the very nature of the political, social, and economic system in the country in which the revolution took place, usually according to some visionary dream of a just society. Nowadays, we live in an age when, if rebel armies do come sweeping into a city, or mass uprisings overthrow a dictator, it's unlikely to have any such implications; when profound social transformation does occur—as with, say, the rise of feminism—it's likely to take an entirely different form. It's not that revolutionary dreams aren't out there. But contemporary revolutionaries rarely think they can bring them into being by some modern-day equivalent of storming the Bastille.

At moments like this, it generally pays to go back to the history one already knows and ask, Were revolutions ever really what we thought them to be? For me, the person who has done this the most effectively is the great world historian Immanuel Wallerstein. He argues that for the last quarter millennium or so, revolutions have consisted above all of planetwide transformations of political common sense.

Already by the time of the French Revolution, Wallerstein notes, there was a single world market, and increasingly a single world political system as well, dominated by the huge colonial empires. As a result, the storming of the Bastille in Paris could well end up having effects on Denmark, or even Egypt, just as profound as on France itself—in some cases, even more so. Hence he speaks of the "world revolution of 1789," followed by the "world revolution of 1848," which saw revolutions break out almost simultaneously in fifty countries, from Wallachia to Brazil. In no case did the revolutionaries succeed in taking power, but afterward, institutions inspired by the French Revolution—notably, universal systems of primary education—were put in place pretty much everywhere. Similarly, the Russian Revolution of 1917 was a world revolution ultimately responsible for the New Deal and European welfare states as much as Soviet communism. The last in the series was the world revolution of 1968—which much like 1848 broke out almost everywhere, from China to Mexico, seized power nowhere, but nonetheless changed everything. This was a revolution against state bureaucracies, and for the inseparability of personal and political liberation, whose most lasting legacy will likely be the birth of modern feminism.

Revolutions are thus planetary phenomena. But there is more. What they really do is transform basic assumptions about what politics is ultimately about. In the wake of a revolution, ideas that had been considered veritably lunatic fringe quickly become the accepted currency of debate. Before the French Revolution, the idea that change is good, that government policy is the proper way to manage it, and that governments derive their authority from an entity called "the people" were considered the sorts of things one might hear from crackpots and demagogues, or at best a handful of freethinking intellectuals who spend their time debating in cafés. A generation later, even the stuffiest magistrates, priests, and headmasters had to at least pay lip service to these ideas. Before long, we had reached the situation we are in today: where it's necessary to lay the terms out, as I just did, for anyone to even notice they are there. They've become common sense, the very grounds of political discussion.

Until 1968, most world revolutions really just introduced practical refinements: widening the franchise, introducing uni-

versal primary education, the welfare state. The world revolution of 1968, in contrast, whether it took the form it did in
China—of a revolt by students and young cadres supporting
Mao's call for a Cultural Revolution—or Berkeley and New
York, where it marked an alliance of students, dropouts, and
cultural rebels, or even Paris, where it was an alliance of students and workers, it was in the same initial spirit: a rebellion
against bureaucracy, conformity, of anything that fettered the
human imagination, a project for the revolutionizing not just
of political or economic life, but every aspect of human existence. As a result, in most cases, the rebels didn't even try to
take over the apparatus of state; they saw that apparatus as
itself the problem.

It's fashionable nowadays to view the social movements of
the late 1960s as an embarrassing failure. A case can surely be
made for that view. It's certainly true that in the political sphere,
the immediate beneficiary of any widespread change in political common sense—a prioritizing of ideals of individual liberty,
imagination, and desire, a hatred of bureaucracy, and suspicions over the role of government—was the political right.
Above all, the movements of the 1960s allowed for the mass
revival of free market doctrines that had largely been abandoned since the nineteenth century. It's no coincidence that the
same generation who, as teenagers, made the Cultural Revolution in China was the one who, as forty-year-olds, presided
over the introduction of capitalism. Since the 1980s, "freedom" has come to mean "the market," and "the market" has
come to be seen as identical with capitalism—even, ironically,
in places like China, which had known sophisticated markets
for thousands of years, but rarely anything that could be described as capitalism.

The ironies are endless. While the new free market ideology has framed itself above all as a rejection of bureaucracy, it has, in fact, been responsible for the first administrative system that has operated on a planetary scale, with its endless layering of public and private bureaucracies: the IMF, World Bank, WTO, the trade organizations, financial institutions, transnational corporations, NGOs. This is precisely the system that has imposed free market orthodoxy, and allowed the opening of the world to financial pillage, under the watchful aegis of American arms. It only made sense that the first attempts to re-create a global revolutionary movement, the Global Justice Movement that peaked between 1998 and 2003, was effectively a rebellion against the rule of that very planetary bureaucracy.

In retrospect, though, I think that later historians will conclude that the legacy of the 1960s revolution was deeper than we now imagine, and the triumph of capitalist markets and their various planetary administrators and enforcers, which seemed so epochal and permanent in the wake of the collapse of the Soviet Union in 1991, was, in fact, far shallower.

I'll take an obvious example. One often hears that a decade of antiwar protests in the late 1960s and early 1970s were ultimately failures, since they did not appreciably speed up the U.S. withdrawal from Indochina. But afterward, those controlling U.S. foreign policy were so anxious about being met with similar popular unrest—and even more, with unrest within the military itself, which was genuinely falling apart by the early 1970s—that they refused to commit U.S. forces to any major ground conflict for almost thirty years. It took 9/11, an attack that led to thousands of civilian deaths on U.S. soil, to fully overcome the notorious "Vietnam syndrome"—and even then, those planning the wars placed an almost obsessive effort in making the wars effectively protest-proof. Propaganda was incessant, the media carefully brought on board, experts provided exact calculations on body bag count (how many U.S. casualties it would take to stir mass opposition), and the rules of engagement were carefully written to keep the count below that.

The problem was that since those rules of engagement ensured that thousands of women, children, and old people would end up "collateral damage" in order to minimize deaths and injuries to U.S. soldiers, this meant that in Iraq and Afghanistan intense hatred for the occupying forces would pretty much guarantee that the United States couldn't obtain its military objectives. And remarkably, the war planners seemed to be aware of this. It didn't matter. They considered it far more important to prevent effective opposition at home than to actually win the war. It's as if American forces in Iraq were ultimately defeated by the ghost of Abbie Hoffman.

Clearly, an antiwar movement in the 1960s that is still tying the hands of U.S. military planners in 2012 can hardly be considered a failure. But it raises an intriguing question: what happens when the creation of that sense of failure, of the complete ineffectiveness of political action against the system, becomes the chief objective of those in power?

The thought first occurred to me when participating in the IMF actions in Washington, D.C., in 2002. Coming shortly on the heels of 9/11, we were relatively few and ineffective, the number of police overwhelming; there was no sense that we could actually succeed in shutting down the meetings. Most of us left feeling vaguely depressed. It was only a few days later, when I talked to someone who had friends attending the meetings, that I learned we had in fact shut down the meetings: the police had introduced such stringent security measures, canceling half the events, that most of the actual meetings had been carried out online. In other words, the government had decided it was more important for protesters to walk away feeling like failures than for the IMF meetings to actually take place. If you think about it, they are affording protesters extraordinary importance.

Is it possible that this preemptive attitude toward social movement, the designing of wars and trade summits in such a way that preventing effective opposition is considered more of a priority than the success of the war or summit itself, really reflects a more general principle? What if those currently running the system, most of whom themselves witnessed the unrest of the 1960s firsthand as impressionable youngsters, are—consciously or unconsciously (and I suspect it's more conscious than not)—obsessed by the prospect of revolutionary social movements once again challenging prevailing common sense?

It would explain a lot. In most of the world, the last thirty years has come to be known as the age of neoliberalism—one dominated by a revival of the long since abandoned nineteenth-century creed that held that free markets and human freedom in general were ultimately the same thing. Neoliberalism has always been wracked by a central paradox. It declares that economic imperatives are to take priority over all others. Politics itself is just a matter of creating the conditions for "growing the economy" by allowing the magic of the marketplace to do its work. All other hopes and dreams—of equality, of security— are to be sacrificed for the primary goal of economic productivity. But actually, global economic performance over the last thirty years has been decidedly mediocre. With one or two spectacular exceptions (notably China, which significantly ignored most neoliberal prescriptions), growth rates have been far below what they were in the days of the old-fashioned, state-directed, welfare-state-oriented capitalism of the 1950s, 1960s, and even 1970s.[1] By its own standards, then, the project was already a colossal failure even before the 2008 collapse.

If, on the other hand, we stop taking world leaders at their word and instead think of neoliberalism as a political project, it suddenly looks spectacularly effective. The politicians, CEOs, trade bureaucrats, and so forth who regularly meet at summits like Davos or the G20 may have done a miserable job in creating a world capitalist economy that actually meets the needs of a majority of the world's inhabitants (let alone produces hope, happiness, security, or meaning), but they have succeeded magnificently in convincing the world that capitalism—and not just capitalism, the exact financialized, semifeudal capitalism we happen to have right now—is the only viable economic system. If you think about it this is a remarkable accomplishment.

How did they pull it off? The preemptive attitude toward social movements is clearly a part of it; under no conditions can alternatives, or anyone proposing alternatives, be seen to experience success. This helps explain the almost unimaginable investment in "security systems" of one sort or another: the fact that the United States, which lacks any major rival, spends more on its military and intelligence than it did during the Cold War, along with the almost dazzling accumulation of private security agencies, intelligence agencies, militarized police, guards, and mercenaries. Then there are the propaganda organs, including a massive media industry that did not even exist before the 1960s, celebrating police. Mostly these systems do not so much attack dissidents directly as contribute to a pervasive climate of fear, jingoistic conformity, life insecurity, and simple despair that renders any thought of changing the world seem an idle fantasy. Yet these security systems are also extremely expensive. Some economists estimate that a quarter of the American population is now engaged in "guard labor" of one sort or another—defending property, supervising work, or otherwise keeping their fellow Americans in line.[2] Economically, most of this disciplinary apparatus is pure deadweight.

In fact, most of the economic innovations of the last thirty years make more sense politically than economically. Eliminating guaranteed life employment for precarious contracts doesn't really create a more effective workforce, but it is extraordinarily effective in destroying unions and otherwise depoliticizing labor. The same can be said of endlessly increasing working hours. No one has much time for political activity if they're working sixty-hour weeks. It does often seem that, whenever there is a choice between one option that makes capitalism seem the only possible economic system, and another that would actually make capitalism a more viable economic system, neoliberalism means always choosing the former. The combined result is a relentless campaign against the human imagination. Or, to be more precise: the imagination, desire, individual liberation, all those things that were to be liberated in the last great world revolution, were to be contained strictly in the domain of consumerism, or perhaps in the virtual realities of the Internet. In all other realms they were to be strictly banished. We are talking about the murdering of dreams, the imposition of an apparatus of hopelessness, designed to squelch any sense of an alternative future. Yet as a result of putting virtually all their efforts in the political basket, we are left in the bizarre situation of watching the capitalist system crumbling before our very eyes, at just the moment everyone had finally concluded no other system would be possible.

———

Perhaps this is all we could expect in a world where, as I pointed out in Chapter 2, the ruling class on both sides of the ostensible political divide had come to believe there was no reality outside of what could be created by their own power. Bubble economies are one result of the same political program that has not only made bribery the sovereign principle running our political system, but for those operating within it the very principle of reality itself. It's as if the strategy has consumed everything.

But this means any revolution on the level of common sense would have devastating effects on those presently in power. Our rulers have gambled everything on making such an outburst of imagination inconceivable. Were they to lose that bet, the effects would be (for them) ruinous.

———

Normally, when one challenges the conventional wisdom—that the current economic and political system is the only possible one—the first reaction you are likely to get is a demand for a detailed architectural blueprint of how an alternative system would work, down to the nature of its financial instruments, energy supplies, and policies of sewer maintenance. Next, one is likely to be asked for a detailed program of how this system will be brought into existence. Historically, this is ridiculous. When has social change ever happened according to someone's blueprint? It's not as if a small circle of visionaries in Renaissance Florence conceived of something they called "capitalism," figured out the details of how the stock exchange and factories would someday work, and then put in place a program to bring their visions into reality. In fact, the idea is so absurd we might well ask ourselves how it ever occurred to us to imagine this is how change happens to begin.

My suspicion is that it's really a hangover from Enlightenment ideas that have long since faded out virtually everywhere except America. It was popular in the eighteenth century to imagine that nations were founded by great lawgivers (Lycurgus, Solon . . .) who invented their customs and institutions from whole cloth, much like God was imagined to have created the world, and then (again, like God) stepped away to let the machine essentially run itself. The "spirit of the laws" would thus gradually come to determine the character of the nation. It was a peculiar fantasy, but the authors of the U.S. Constitution believed that was how great nations were founded, and actually attempted to put it into practice. Hence the United States, "a nation of laws and not of men," is perhaps the only one on earth of which this picture is in any sense true. But even in the United States, as we've seen, this is only a very small part of what happened. And later attempts to create new nations and institute political or economic systems from above (the United States' great twentieth-century rival, the USSR, the only other great nation on earth that was primarily an acronym, is the most frequently cited example here) did not work out particularly well.

All this is not to say there's anything wrong with utopian visions. Or even blueprints. They just need to be kept in their place. The theorist Michael Albert has worked out a detailed plan for how a modern economy could run without money on a democratic, participatory basis. I think this is an important achievement—not because I think that exact model could ever be instituted, in exactly the form in which he describes it, but because it makes it impossible to say that such a thing is inconceivable. Still, such models can only be thought experiments. We cannot really conceive the problems that will arise when we start actually trying to build a free society. What now seem likely to be the thorniest problems might not be problems at all; others that never even occurred to us might prove devilishly difficult. There are innumerable X-factors. The most obvious is technology. This is the reason it's so absurd to imagine activists in Renaissance Italy coming up with a model for a stock exchange and factories—what happened was based on all sorts of technologies that they couldn't have anticipated, but which in part only emerged because society began to move in the direction that it did. This might explain, for instance, why so many of the more compelling visions of an anarchist society have been produced by science fiction writers (Ursula K. Le Guin, Starhawk, Kim Stanley Robinson). In fiction, you are at least admitting the technological aspect is guesswork.

———

Myself, I am less interested in deciding what sort of economic system we should have in a free society than in creating the means by which people can make such decisions for themselves. This is why I spent so much of this book talking about democratic decision making. And the very experience of taking part in such new forms of decision making encourages one to look on the world with new eyes.

What might a revolution in common sense actually look like? I don't know, but I can think of any number of pieces of conventional wisdom that surely need challenging if we are to create any sort of viable free society. I've already explored one—the nature of money and debt—in some detail in a previous book. I even suggested a debt jubilee, a general cancellation, in part just to bring home that money is really just a human product, a set of promises, that by its nature can always be renegotiated. Here, I'll list four others:

WORK 1: THE PRODUCTIVIST BARGAIN

A lot of the pernicious assumptions that cripple our sense of political possibility have to with the nature of work.

The most obvious is the assumption that work is necessarily good, that those unwilling to submit to work discipline are inherently undeserving and immoral, and that the solution to any economic crisis or even economic problem is always that people should work more, or work harder, than they already do. This is one of those assumptions that everyone in mainstream political discourse seems obliged to accept as the ground of conversation. But the moment you think about it, it's absurd. First of all, it's a moral position, not an economic one. There is plenty of work being done we'd all probably be better off without, and workaholics are not necessarily better human beings. In fact, I think any levelheaded assessment of the world situation would have to conclude that what's really needed is not more work, but less. And this is true even if we don't take into account ecological concerns—that is, the fact that the current pace of the global work machine is rapidly rendering the planet uninhabitable.

Why is the idea so difficult to challenge? I suspect part of the reason is the history of workers' movements. It is one of the great ironies of the twentieth century that, whenever a politically mobilized working class did win a modicum of political power, it always did so under the leadership of cadres of bu-reaucrats dedicated to just this sort of productivist ethos—one that most actual workers did not share.* One might even call it "the productivist bargain," that if one accepts the old Puri-tan ideal that work is a virtue in itself, you shall be rewarded with consumer paradise. In the early decades of the century, this was the chief distinction between anarchist and socialist unions, which was why the former always tended to demand higher wages, the latter, less hours (the anarchist unions, most famously, are really responsible for the eight-hour workday). The socialists embraced the consumer paradise offered by their bourgeois enemies; yet they wished to manage the productive system themselves; anarchists, in contrast, wanted time in which to live, to pursue forms of value of which the capitalists could not even dream. Yet where did the revolutions happen? It was the anarchist constituencies—those who rejected the productivist bargain—that actually rose up: whether in Spain, Russia, China, or almost anywhere a revolution really took place. Yet in every case they ended up under the administration of socialist bureaucrats who embraced that dream of a con-sumer utopia, even though it was also about the last thing they were ever able to provide. The irony became that the principal social benefit the Soviet Union and similar regimes actually provided—more time, since work discipline becomes a com-pletely different thing when one effectively cannot be fired

---

* As an Indian anarchist pointed out, one can find quotes from everyone from Gandhi to Hitler saying that work is holy, but when real working people refer to a holy day ("holi-day") they are referring to one where you *don't* have to work.

from one's job, and everyone was able to get away with working about half the hours they were supposed to—was precisely the one they couldn't acknowledge; it had to be referred to as "the problem of absenteeism" standing in the way of an impossible future full of shoes and consumer electronics. But here, trade unionists, too, feel obliged to adopt bourgeois terms—in which productivity and labor discipline are absolute values—and act as if the freedom to lounge about on a construction site is not a hard-won right but actually a problem. Granted, it would be much better to simply work four hours a day than do four hours' worth of work in eight, but surely this is better than nothing.

WORK 2: WHAT IS LABOR?

Submitting oneself to labor discipline—supervision, control, even the self-control of the ambitious self-employed—does not make one a better person. In most really important ways it probably makes one worse. To undergo it is a misfortune that at best is sometimes necessary. Yet it's only when we reject the idea that such labor is virtuous in itself that we can start to ask what actually is virtuous about labor. To which the answer is obvious. Labor is virtuous if it helps others. An abandonment of productivism should make it easier to reimagine the very nature of what work is, since, among other things, it will mean that technological development will be redirected less toward creating ever more consumer products and ever more disciplined labor, and more toward eliminating those forms of labor entirely.

What would remain is the kind of work only human beings will ever be able to do: those forms of caring and helping labor that are, I've argued, at the very center of the crisis that brought about Occupy Wall Street to begin with. What would happen if we stopped acting as if the primordial form of work is laboring at a production line, or wheat field, or iron foundry, or even in an office cubicle, and instead started from a mother, a teacher, or caregiver? We might be forced to conclude that the real business of human life is not contributing toward something called "the economy" (a concept that didn't even exist three hundred years ago), but the fact that we are all, and have always been, projects of mutual creation.

At the moment, probably the most pressing need is simply to slow down the engines of productivity. This might seem a strange thing to say—our knee-jerk reaction to every crisis is to assume the solution is for everyone to work even more, but of course, this kind of reaction is really precisely the problem—but if you consider the overall state of the world, the conclusion becomes obvious. We seem to be facing two insoluble problems. On the one hand, we have witnessed an endless series of global debt crises, which have grown only more and more severe since the 1970s, to the point where the overall burden of debt—sovereign, municipal, corporate, personal—is obviously unsustainable. On the other we have an ecological crisis, a galloping process of climate change that is threatening to throw the entire planet into drought, floods, chaos, starvation, and war. The two might seem unrelated. But ultimately they are the same. What is debt, after all, but the promise of future productivity? Saying that global debt levels keep rising is simply another way of saying that, as a collectivity, human beings are promising each other to produce an even greater volume of goods and services in the future than they are creating now. But even current levels are clearly unsustainable. They are precisely what's destroying the planet, at an ever-increasing pace. Even those running the system are reluctantly beginning to conclude that some kind of mass debt cancellation—some kind of jubilee—is inevitable. The real political struggle is going to be over the form that it takes. Well, isn't the obvious thing to address both problems simultaneously? Why not a planetary debt cancellation, as broad as practically possible, followed by a mass reduction in working hours: a four-hour day, perhaps, or a guaranteed five-month vacation? This might not only save the planet but also (since it's not like everyone would just be sitting around in their newfound hours of freedom) begin to change our basic conceptions of what value-creating labor might actually be.

Occupy was surely right not to make demands, but if I were to have to formulate one, that would be it. After all, this would be an attack on the dominant ideology at its very strongest points. The morality of debt, and the morality of work, are the most powerful ideological weapons in the hands of those running the current system. That's why they cling to them even as they are effectively destroying everything. It's also why it would make the perfect revolutionary demand.

WORK 3: BUREAUCRACY

One genuinely disastrous failure of the mainstream left has been its inability to produce a meaningful critique of bureaucracy. I think this is the most obvious explanation of the failure of the mainstream left, pretty much everywhere, to take advantage of the catastrophic failure of capitalism in 2008. In Europe, the parties that successfully managed to take advantage of popular outrage were, in almost all cases, on the right. This is because the moderate, Social Democratic left had long since embraced both the market and bureaucracy; the right (and particularly the far right) not only found it easier to abandon blind faith in market solutions, but already had a critique of bureaucracy as well. It is a crude, outmoded, and in many ways irrelevant critique. But at least it exists. The mainstream left, in rejecting the hippies and communes of the 1960s, has effectively left itself with no critique at all.

Yet bureaucracy fills every aspect of our lives in ways it never has before. Bizarrely, we are almost completely unable to see or talk about it. Partly because we have come to see bureaucracy as simply an aspect of government—ignoring the often vastly more powerful private bureaucracies, or, even more crucially, the way that public and private (corporate, financial, even educational) bureaucracies now are so completely entangled that it's impossible to really distinguish them.

I once read that the average American spends about half a year, over the course of their lives, waiting for a traffic light to change. I don't know if anyone has ever calculated how much time he or she spends filling out forms—I doubt they have—but I can't imagine it would be substantially less. I am quite sure that no previous population in history has ever had to spend so much of their lives on paperwork. And while the government does seem to specialize in particularly excruciating forms, as anyone who spends much time on the Internet knows, what paperwork really surrounds is anything involving the giving and receiving of money. This is true from the top of the system (the vast administrative system put into place to regulate global trade in the name of the "free market") to the most intimate details of everyday life, where technologies that were originally supposed to save labor have turned us all into amateur accountants, legal clerks, and travel agents.

Yet somehow, unlike in the 1960s, when the problem was much less, this unprecedented cascade of documents is no longer seen as a political issue. Again, we have to make the world around us visible again. Especially since one of the instinctive suspicions that nonpolitical people have of the left is that it will likely produce even more bureaucratization. To the contrary. It would be almost impossible to have more bureaucratization than we do already. Any revolutionary transformation—even if it doesn't eliminate the state entirely—will almost certainly mean far less.

WORK 4: RECLAIMING COMMUNISM

Here we have the most difficult challenge of all, but as long as we're at it, why not go for broke?

Something indeed strange began to happen in the 1980s. This was perhaps the first period in the history of capitalism when capitalists actually began calling themselves "capitalists." For most of the previous two centuries of its existence, the word had been basically a term of abuse. I remember well how *The New York Times,* which at the time became the real ideological driving force for the popularization of what was to become conventional neoliberal wisdom, led the way, with an endless series of headlines crowing over how some communist regime, or socialist party, or cooperative enterprise, or other ostensibly left-wing institution, had been forced, by sheer expedience, to embrace one or another element of "capitalism." It was tied to the endlessly repeated mantra of "communism just doesn't work"—but it also represented a kind of ideological back-flip, one first pioneered by right-wing lunatic fringe figures like Ayn Rand, where "capitalism" and "socialism" were essentially made to change places. Where once capitalism had been the tawdry reality, and socialism the unrealized ideal, now it was the other way around. It was all the more extreme in the case of "communism," which had always been used, even for those regimes that called themselves "communist," for a vague utopian future usually only to be realized after the withering away of the state, and, certainly, that bore little resemblance to the "socialist" system that existed at the time. After 1989, the meaning of "communism" seemed to shift to "whatever system of organization prevailed under 'communist' regimes." This, in turn, was followed by a genuinely peculiar rhetorical shift, whereby such regimes—once written off as ruthlessly efficient in the maintenance of armies and secret police, but woefully inept at the production of consumer pleasures—were treated as themselves utopian, that is, as so completely defying the basic realities of human nature (as revealed by economics) that they simply "didn't work" at all, that they were, in effect, impossible—a truly remarkable conclusion when speaking, say, of the USSR, which for seventy years controlled a large share of the earth's surface, defeated Hitler, and launched the first satellite, and then human, into outer space. It was as if the collapse of the Soviet Union was taken to prove that it could never have existed in the first place!

The ideological deployment of the term on the popular level is fascinating, and no one really talks about it. I keenly remember, as an adolescent working in restaurant kitchens and similar places, how any suggestion by the staff on how things might be organized in a more reasonable, or even efficient, manner was immediately met with one of two responses: "this isn't a democracy," or, "this isn't communism." In other words, from the perspective of employers, the two words really were interchangeable. Communism meant workplace democracy and that's exactly why they found it objectionable. This was the 1970s and 1980s; the idea that communism (or democracy) was inefficient let alone intrinsically unworkable did not really enter in. By the current decade, we've reached the point where I have witnessed middle-class Londoners—ones who considered themselves distinctly left of center—appeal to the idea automatically even when dealing with their children, like the one who responded to a daughter's suggestion of more democratic allocation of dog-walking responsibilities by saying, "No, that would be communism, and we all know that communism doesn't work."

The irony is that if one takes a more realistic definition of the term "communism," exactly the opposite has been proved to be true. It could well be argued that we're in the reverse of the situation so widely touted in the 1980s. Capitalism has been forced, in a thousand ways in a thousand places, to fall back on communism, precisely because it's the only thing that works.

I've made this argument repeatedly before and it's a simple one. All it requires is to stop imagining "communism" as the absence of private property arrangements, and go back to the original definition: "from each according to their abilities, to each according to their needs."* If any social arrangement

---

* It seems to have been first set out in writing, in that form, by Louis Blanc in 1840 but an earlier version is also attributed to the French communist writer Morelly in his *Code of Nature* as far back as 1755.

grounded and operating on such a principle can be described as "communism," all of our most fundamental understandings of social reality completely change. It becomes apparent that communism—at least in its most attenuated form—is the basis of all amicable social relations, since, sociality of any sort always assumes a certain baseline communism, an understanding that, if the need is great enough (e.g., to save a drowning person) or the request small enough (e.g., a light, directions), these are the standards that will be applied. We are all communists with those we love and trust the most; yet no one behaves communistically in all circumstances with everyone, or, presumably, ever has or will. Above all, work tends to be organized on communistic grounds, since in practical situations of cooperation, and especially when the need is immediate and pressing, the only way to solve a problem is to identify who has what abilities to get them what they need. If two people are fixing a pipe, it doesn't matter if they're working for the Heritage Foundation or Goldman Sachs, if one says "Hand me the wrench," the other doesn't normally say, "And what do I get for that?" Hence, there's no point in imagining some ideal future "communism," and arguing whether it would be possible. All societies are communistic at base, and capitalism is best viewed as a bad way of organizing communism. (It is bad among other things because it tends to encourage extremely authoritarian forms of communism on the workplace level. One key political question is: what better way of organizing communism can we find that will encourage more democratic

---

Anyway, it was popular in radical circles well before Karl Marx took it up in his *Critique of the Gotha Program*.

ones? Or even better, one that eliminates our contemporary institution of "workplaces" entirely.)

Just putting things this way seems startling, but it's really very commonsensical, and pushes away the endless accretions the concept of communism has taken on, both from those who claimed to speak in its name, and those who claimed to revile it. It would mean there can never be such a thing as a "communist" system, in the sense that *everything* is organized on communistic terms. It would also mean that in the most important sense we are already living in one.

————

The reader can perhaps get a sense now of the overall direction I have in mind. We are already practicing communism much of the time. We are already anarchists, or at least we act like anarchists, every time we come to understandings with one another that would not require physical threats as a means of enforcement. It's not a question of building an entirely new society whole cloth. It's a question of building on what we are already doing, expanding the zones of freedom, until freedom becomes the ultimate organizing principle. I actually don't think the technical aspects of coming up with how to produce and distribute manufactured objects is likely to be the great problem, though we are constantly told to believe it's the only problem. There are many things in short supply in the world. One thing of which we have a well-nigh unlimited supply is intelligent, creative people able to come up with solutions to problems like that. The problem is not a lack of imagination. The problem is the stifling systems of debt and violence, created to ensure that those powers of imagination are not used—

or not used to create anything beyond financial derivatives, new weapons systems, or new Internet platforms for the filling out of forms. This is, of course, exactly what brought so many to places like Zuccotti Park.

Even what now seem like major screaming ideological divides are likely to sort themselves easily enough in practice. I used to frequent Internet newsgroups in the 1990s, which at the time were full of creatures that called themselves "anarcho-capitalists." (They seem to exist almost entirely on the Internet. To this day I'm not sure I've ever met one in real life.) Most spent a good deal of their time condemning left anarchists as proponents of violence. "How can you be for a free society and be against wage labor? If I want to hire someone to pick my tomatoes, how are you going to stop me except through force?" Logically then any attempt to abolish the wage system can only be enforced by some new version of the KGB. One hears such arguments frequently.* What one never hears, significantly, is anyone saying "If I want to hire myself out to pick someone else's tomatoes, how are you going to stop me except through force?" Everyone seems to imagine that in a future stateless society, they will somehow end up members of the employing class. Nobody seems to think *they'll* be the tomato pickers. But where, exactly, do they imagine these tomato pickers are going to come from? Here one might employ a little thought experiment: let's call it the parable of the divided island. Two groups of idealists each claim half of an island. They agree to draw the border in such a way that there are roughly equal resources on each side. One group proceeds to create an economic system

---

* They actually recur in the Matthew Continetti piece cited at the beginning of Chapter 3.

where certain members have property, others have none, and those who have none have no social guarantees: they will be left to starve to death unless they seek employment on any terms the wealthy are willing to offer. The other group creates a system where everyone is guaranteed at least the basic means of existence and welcomes all comers. What possible reason would those slated to be the night watchmen, nurses, and bauxite miners on the anarcho-capitalist side of the island have to stay there? The capitalists would be bereft of their labor force in a matter of weeks. As a result, they'd be forced to patrol their own grounds, empty their own bedpans, and operate their own heavy machinery—that is, unless they quickly began offering their workers such an extravagantly good deal that they might as well be living in a socialist utopia after all.

For this and any number of other reasons, I'm sure that in practice any attempt to create a market economy without armies, police, and prisons to back it up will end up looking nothing like capitalism very quickly. In fact I strongly suspect it will soon look very little like what we are used to thinking of as a market. Obviously I could be wrong. It's possible someone will attempt this, and the results will be very different than I imagined. In which case, fine, I'll be wrong. Mainly I'm interested in creating the conditions where we can find out.

———

I can't really say what a free society would be like. Still, since I have said that one thing we really need now is an unleashing of political desire, I guess I can end by describing some things that I'd myself, personally, like to see.

I would like to see something like the principle behind consensus—in which respect for radical, incommensurable difference becomes the basis for commonality—generalized to social life itself. What would that actually mean?

Well, first of all, I don't think it would mean everyone spending all their time sitting in circles in formal meetings all day long. I think most of us would concur that such a prospect would drive most of us at least as insane as the present system does. Obviously, there are ways to make meetings fun and entertaining. The key thing is as I insisted in the last chapter, it's not so much the form, as the spirit of the thing. This is why I kept emphasizing that anything could be considered an anarchist form of organization that does not involve ultimate recourse to bureaucratic structures of violence. It is often asked how direct democracy can "scale up" from local face-to-face meetings to a whole city, region, or nation. Clearly, they won't take the same form. But there are all sorts of possibilities. Very few options that have been tried in the past are no longer available,* and new technological possibilities are invented all the time. So far most of the experimentation has been in recallable delegates, but I personally think there's a lot of unexplored potential in the revival of lottery systems like those I mentioned in Chapter 3: something vaguely like jury duty, except noncompulsory, with some way of screening obsessives, cranks, and hollow-earthers, but nonetheless allowing an equal chance of participation in great decisions to all who actually do wish to participate. There would have to be mechanisms put in

---

* A few are unavailable. In ancient Athens, one way of ensuring that technical specialists, whose jobs could not be rotated, did not end up acquiring institutional power over their peers was to make sure they weren't peers: most civil servants, even police, were slaves. But most expedients are still open to us.

place to prevent abuses. But it's hard to imagine those abuses could actually be worse than the mode of selection we use now.

Economically, what I would really like to see is some kind of guarantee of life security that would allow people to pursue those kinds of value they actually consider worth pursuing—individually, or with others. As I've observed, that's the main reason people pursue money anyway. To be able to pursue something else: something they consider noble, or beautiful, profound, or simply good. What might they pursue in a free society? Presumably, many things we could barely now imagine, though one might expect familiar values like arts or spirituality or sports or landscape gardening or fantasy games or scientific research or intellectual or hedonistic pleasures would figure in, in every sort of unanticipated combination.

The challenge will obviously be how to allocate resources between pursuits that are utterly incomparable, forms of value that simply cannot be translated into one another. Which in turn leads to another question I'm sometimes asked: what does "equality" really mean?

I get this sort of question a lot. Usually from very rich people. "So what are you calling for? Complete equality? How could that be possible? Would you really want to live in a society where everyone would have exactly the same thing?"—and, once again, with the tacit suggestion that any such project would, necessarily, mean the KGB again. Such are the concerns of the 1 percent. The answer is: "I would like to live in a world where asking that question would be nonsensical."

Instead of a parable here, perhaps a historical example. In recent years, archaeologists have discovered something that has thrown all previous understandings of human history askew. In both Mesopotamia and the Indus Valley, the first thousand years of urban civilization were rigorously egalitarian. Almost obsessively so. There is no evidence of social inequality at all: no remains of palaces, no sumptuous burials; the only monumental structures were such as could be shared by everyone (e.g., gigantic public baths). Often, every house in an urban neighborhood was of precisely the same size. It's hard to escape the impression that this obsession with uniformity was exactly the problem. As my friend, the brilliant British archaeologist David Wengrow always likes to point out, the birth of urban civilization came in the immediate wake of what was possibly an even more important innovation: the birth of mass production, the first time in history it was possible to create a thousand containers of oil or grain of exactly the same size, each stamped with an identical seal impression. Apparently, everyone quickly became aware of the implications, and they were terrified. After all, it's only once you have such uniform products that you can also begin comparing exactly how much more one person has than another. It's only such technologies of equality that make inequality, as we know it today, possible. The inhabitants of the first cities managed to hold off the inevitable for a thousand years, which is a remarkable testimony to sheer determination, but what happened eventually had to happen, and we have been dealing with the legacy ever since.

It's not likely we will ever be able to undo a six-thousand-year-old innovation. Neither is it clear why we ever should. Large impersonal structures, like uniform products, will always exist. The question is not how to undo such things but how to put them to work in the service of their opposite: a world where freedom becomes the ability to pursue completely incommensurable ends. Our current consumer society claims to hold that out as its ultimate ideal, but, in fact, what it holds out is a hollow simulacrum.

It is often remarked that you can conceive equality in two ways: either by saying two things are (in any important respect anyway) precisely the same, or else by saying they are so different, there's simply no way to compare them at all. It's the latter logic that allows us to say that, since we are all unique individuals, it's impossible to say any one of us is intrinsically better than any other, any more, for instance, than it would be possible to say there are superior and inferior snowflakes. If one is going to base an egalitarian politics on that understanding, the logic would have to be: since there's no basis for ranking such unique individuals on their merits, everyone deserves the same amount of those things that *can* be measured: an equal income, an equal amount of money, or an equal share of wealth.

Still, if you think about it this is odd. It assumes that we are all completely different in what we are, but identical in what we want. What if we were to turn this around? In a funny way, the current feudalized version of capitalism, where money and power have become effectively the same thing, makes it easier for us to do so. The 1 percent who rule the world may have turned the pursuit of both into a kind of pathological game where money and power are ends in themselves, but for the rest of us, having money, having an income, being free from debt, has come to mean having the power to pursue something other than money. Certainly, we all want to ensure our loved ones are safe, and taken care of. We all want to live in healthy and beautiful communities. But beyond that, the things we wish to pursue are likely to be wildly different. What if freedom were the ability to make up our minds about what it was we wished to pursue, with whom we wished to pursue it, and what sort of commitments we wish to make to them in the process? Equality, then, would simply be a matter of guaranteeing equal access to those resources needed in the pursuit of an endless variety of forms of value. Democracy in that case would simply be our capacity to come together as reasonable human beings and work out the resulting common problems—since problems there will always be—a capacity that can only truly be realized once the bureaucracies of coercion that hold existing structures of power together collapse or fade away.

All this might still seem very distant. At the moment, the planet might seem poised more for a series of unprecedented catastrophes than for the kind of broad moral and political transformation that would open the way to such a world. But if we are going to have any chance of heading off those catastrophes we're going to have to change our accustomed ways of thinking. And as the events of 2011 reveal, the age of revolutions is by no means over. The human imagination stubbornly refuses to die. And the moment any significant number of people simultaneously shake off the shackles that have been placed on that collective imagination, even our most deeply inculcated assumptions about what is and is not politically possible have been known to crumble overnight.

ACKNOWLEDGMENTS

I'd like to give thanks to everyone in the movement, who taught me everything I know.

NOTES

INTRODUCTION

1. Charles Pierce, "Why Bosses Always Win if the Game Is Always Rigged," Esquire.com, October 18, 2012.

CHAPTER 1: THE BEGINNING IS NEAR

1. The information has appeared all over the Internet but it originally appeared in Christopher Helman, "What the Top U.S. Companies Pay in Taxes," *Forbes*, April 2, 2010.
2. Joseph E. Stiglitz, "Of the 1%, by the 1%, for the 1%," *Vanity Fair*, May 2011.

CHAPTER 2: WHY DID IT WORK?

1. Ginia Bellafante, "Gunning for Wall Street, With Faulty Aim," *The New York Times,* September 23, 2011.
2. China Study Group, "Message from Chinese Activists and Academics in Support of Occupy Wall Street," chinastudygroup.net, October 2, 2011.

3. Amanda Fairbanks, "Seeking Arrangement: College Students Seeking 'Sugar Daddies' to Pay Off Loan Debt," huffingtonpost.com, July 29, 2011. While we don't have figures for the United States, a recent British survey revealed that a staggering 52 percent of female undergraduates had engaged in some sort of sex work to help fund their education, with just under a third having resorted to outright prostitution.

4. David Graeber, "Occupy Wall Street Rediscovers the Radical Imagination," *The Guardian*, September 25, 2011.

5. "Tea Party supporters are likely to be older, white and male. Forty percent are age 55 and over, compared with 32 percent of all poll respondents; just 22 percent are under the age of 35, 79 percent are white, and 61 percent are men. Many are also Christian fundamentalists, with 44 percent identifying themselves as 'born-again,' compared with 33 percent of all respondents." Heidi Przybyla, "Tea Party Advocates Who Scorn Socialism Want a Government Job," Bloomberg, March 26, 2010, citing a poll by Selzer & Company taken in March 2010.

6. Malcolm Harris, "Bad Education," *n+1* magazine, April 25, 2001.

7. The debate was kicked off by a post on August 19 on the Freakonomics blog: Justin Wolfers, "Forgive Student Loan Debt? Worst Idea Ever," www.freakonomics.com.

8. Some excellent case histories can be found in Anya Kamentz, *Generation Debt: Why Now Is a Terrible Time to Be Young* (New York: Riverhead Books, 2006). Interestingly, this phenomenon was also very much in the news right around the time the occupation began, for instance in an article in *The New York Times*: "College Graduation Rates Are Stagnant Even as Enrollment Rises, a Study Finds" (Tamar Lewin, September 27, 2011, p. A15). A sample paragraph: "The numbers are stark: In Texas, for example, of every 100 students who enrolled in a public college, 79 started at a community college, and only 2 of them earned a two-year degree on time; even after four years, only 7 of them graduated. Of the 21 of those 100 who enrolled at a four-year college, 5 graduated on time; after eight years, only 13 had earned a degree." According to a Pew study, about two-thirds of dropouts reported they did so because of the

impossibility of both financing their education and helping support a family. (Pew Research Center, "Is College Worth It?" May 16, 2011)

9. A dramatic case is Stockton, California, which declared bankruptcy in early 2012. The city announced it intended to find the revenue to pay its creditors through massively increasing "code enforcement": essentially, through parking tickets, and fines for unkempt lawns or not removing graffiti quickly enough; such penalties will inevitably fall disproportionally on the working poor. See "Stockton Largest U.S. City Going Bankrupt," *Daily News,* June 26, 2012.

10. "Parsing the Data and Ideology of the We Are 99% Tumblr," http://rortybomb.wordpress.com/2011/10/09/parsing-the-data-and-ideology-of-the-we-are-99-tumblr/.

11. See, for example, http://lhote.blogspot.com/2011/10/solidarity-first-then-fear-for-this.html, http://attempter.wordpress.com/2011/10/12/underlying-ideology-of-the-99/, and the accompanying comment section.

12. Linda Lowen, "Women Union Members: The Changing Face of Union Membership," womensissues.about.com, updated December 17, 2008.

13. Giovanni Arrighi, *The Long Twentieth Century: Money, Power, and the Origins of Our Times* (London: Verso, 1994).

14. Michael Hudson *Super Imperialism: The Economic Strategy of American Empire* (London: Pluto, 2006), p. 288.

15. Pam Martens, "Financial Giants Put New York City Cops on Their Payroll," October 10, 2011, Counterpunch. Technically during those hours they are working as private security, but they do so in their uniforms, with guns and badges and full power of arrest.

16. Andrew Ross Sorkin, "On Wall Street, a Protest Matures," *New York Times,* Dealbook, October 3, 2011.

17. Ron Suskind, "Faith, Certainty and the Presidency of George W. Bush," *New York Times Magazine,* October 17, 2004.

18. George Gilder, *Wealth and Poverty* (New York: Basic Books, 1981), and Pat Robertson quote both cited in Melinda Cooper, "The Unborn Born Again: Neo-Imperialism, the Evangelical Right and the Culture of Life," *Postmodern Culture,* 17 (1), Fall 2006; Robertson 1992:153.

19. Rebecca Solnit, "Why the Media Loves the Violence of Protestors and Not of Banks," Tomdispatch.com, February 21, 2012. The KTVU story can be found at: http://www.ktvu.com/news/news/emails -exchanged-between-oakland-opd-reveal-tensio/nGMkF/. On the issue of sexual assault, inflated figures appeared, but these were based largely on tabulating all reports of sexual assault that occurred anywhere near occupations, whether or not those accused had ever set foot in the camps.

20. Those interested might consult Norman Finkelstein's recent *What Gandhi Says: About Nonviolence, Resistance and Courage* (New York: OR Books, 2012), which contains numerous quotes making clear Gandhi felt the worst crime was passivity. He also, most famously, wrote that in the face of manifest injustice "if the only choice is between violence and cowardice, I would recommend violence."

CHAPTER 3: "THE MOB BEGIN TO THINK AND TO REASON": THE COVERT HISTORY OF DEMOCRACY

1. Matthew Continetti, "Anarchy in the U.S.A.: The Roots of American Disorder," *Weekly Standard*, November 28, 2011.

2. John Adams, *The Works of John Adams* (Boston: Little, Brown, 1854), Volume 6, p. 481.

3. R. C. Winthrop, *The Life and Letters of John Winthrop* (Boston: Little, Brown, 1869).

4. James Madison, "Federalist #10," in *The Federalist Papers,* p. 103. Note that while Madison calls this "pure democracy," and Adams, "simple democracy," rule by popular assembly is the only form of government to which they are willing to give the name.

5. Federalist Papers, No. 10, p. 119.

6. For a good description of how parliamentary elections worked under Henry VII, see P. R. Cavill, *The English Parliaments of Henry VII, 1485–1504* (Oxford: Oxford University Press, 2009), pp.117–31. Generally the electorate was a local council of worthies; in London, for instance, such a group might consist of 150 out of 3,000 local inhabitants.

7. Bernard Manin, *The Principles of Representative Government* (Cambridge: The Cambridge University Press, 1992), p. 38. In ancient Greece, for instance, democracies tended to choose holders of executive positions by lot, from among a pool of volunteers, while election was considered the oligarchic approach.

8. See John Markoff, "Where and When Was Democracy Invented?," *Comparative Studies in Society and History* 41, no.4 (1991): 663–65.

9. Gouverneur Morris to [John] Penn, May 20, 1774, in Jared Sparks, *The Life of Gouverneur Morris: With Selections from His Correspondence and Miscellaneous Papers: Detailing Events in the American Revolution, the French Revolution, and in the Political History of the United States* (Boston: Grey & Bowen, 1830), p. 25.

10. Both quoted from Morris in E. James Ferguson, *The Power of the Purse: A History of American Public Finance, 1776–1790* (Chapel Hill: University of North Carolina Press, 1961), p. 68.

11. Adams, *The Works,* Volume 6, pp. 8–9.

12. Madison, *Federalist Papers,* No. 10, pp. 54–55.

13. Jennifer Tolbert Roberts, *Athens on Trial* (Princeton: Princeton University Press, 1994), p. 183.

14. Benjamin Rush, *Medical Inquiries and Observations*, vol. 1 (Philadelphia: J. Conrad, 1805), pp. 292–93.

15. Francis Dupuis-Déri, "History of the Word 'Democracy' in Canada and Québec: A Political Analysis of Rhetorical Strategies," *World Political Science Review*, 6, no. 1 (2010): 3–4.

16. John Markoff, "Where and When Was Democracy Invented?," *Comparative Studies in Society and History,* no. 41 (1999): 673.

17. As reconstructed by Marcus Rediker in *Villains of All Nations: Atlantic Pirates in the Golden Age* (Boston: Beacon Press, 2004).

18. Ibid., p. 53.

19. Colin Calloway, *New Worlds for All* (Baltimore: Johns Hopkins University Press, 1997). (cf. Axtell 1985)

20. Cotton Mather, *Things for a Distress'd People to Think Upon* (Boston, 1696).

21. Ron Sakolsky and James Koehnline, *Gone to Croatan: Origins of North American Dropout Culture* (Oakland: AK Press, 1993).

22. Mediker, *Many-Headed Hydra* (Boston: Beacon Press, 2001).

23. Angus Graham, *The Inner Chapters* (Indianapolis: Hackett Publishing Co., 2001).

24. James Scott, *The Art of Not Being Governed: An Anarchist History of Upland Southeast Asia* (New Haven: Yale University Press, 2010).

25. Many of the historical reasons for my thinking on this are outlined in *Debt: The First 5,000 Years* (Brooklyn: Melville House, 2011), particularly chaps. 10–12.

26. Quoted in Francesca Polletta, *Freedom Is an Endless Meeting: Democracy in American Social Movements* (Chicago: University of Chicago Press, 2004), p. 39.

27. I am offering only a very brief summary of what happened because I have written about it at greater length elsewhere. See, for instance, *Direct Action: An Ethnography* (Oakland: AK Press, 2009), pp. 228–37.

28. As Aristotle puts it: "Here the very constitution of the soul has shown us the way; in it one part naturally rules, and the other is subject, and the virtue of the ruler we maintain to be different from that of the subject; the one being the virtue of the rational, and the other of the irrational part. Now, it is obvious that the same principle applies generally, and therefore almost all things rule and are ruled according to nature. But the kind of rule differs; the freeman rules over the slave after another manner from that in which the male rules over the female, or the man over the child; although the parts of the soul are present in any of them, they are present in different degrees. For the slave has no deliberative faculty at all; the woman has, but it is without authority, and the child has, but it is immature." *Politics* 1.30. I'm grateful to Thomas Gibson for pointing out how odd this view of human nature is compared to almost any other agrarian society.

29. I owe this reflection to a brilliant essay by the French political philosopher Bernard Manin.

30. Deborah K. Heikes, *Rationality and Feminist Philosophy* (London: Continuum, 2010), p. 146.

31. Samuel Blixen and Carlos Fazio, "Interview with Marcos About Neoliberalism, the National State and Democracy," Struggle archive, Autumn 1995, http://www.struggle.ws/mexico/ezln/inter_marcos_aut95.html.

32. The evidence has recently been surveyed in a working paper by econ-omist Peter Leeson, who concluded that "while the state of develop-ment remains low, on nearly all of 18 key indicators that allow pre- and post-stateless welfare comparisons, Somalis are better off under anarchy than they were under government." See Leeson, "Bet-ter Off Stateless: Somalia Before and After Government Collapse," *Journal of Comparative Economics,* vol. 35, no. 4, 2007. You can find the full essay at www.peterleeson.com/Better_Off_Stateless.pdf.

33. Rebecca Solnit, for instance, has written a brilliant book, *A Paradise Built in Hell: The Extraordinary Communities That Arise in Disas-ter* (New York, Viking Books, 2009), about what actually happens in natural disasters: people almost invariably invent forms of spontane-ous cooperation and, often, democratic decision making that dra-matically contrasts with the way they are used to behaving in their ordinary lives.

CHAPTER 5: BREAKING THE SPELL

1. David Harvey, *A Brief History of Neoliberalism* (London: Oxford University Press, 2007).

2. Arjun Jayadev and Samuel Bowles, "Guard Labor," *Journal of De-velopment Economics* 79 (2006): 328–48. Some of the figures here could easily be contested—the authors include in the count not just members of the security forces but the "reserve army" of unem-ployed and prisoners, the logic being that insofar as they contribute to the economy at all, it's by driving down wages and through other "disciplinary functions." Still, even if you eliminate the contestable categories the numbers are striking, and even more, the fact that the numbers vary dramatically between countries: with Greece, the United States, United Kingdom, and Spain having roughly 20–24 per-cent of workers doing some sort of guard labor, and Scandinavian countries a mere 1 in 10. The key factor seems to be social inequality: the more wealth is in the hands of the 1 percent, the larger a percent-age of the 99 percent they will employ in one way or another to pro-tect it.

INDEX

NOTE: Initials OWS stand for Occupy Wall Street.

Gandhian tactics, 60–62, 254
creativity and improvisation in,
255–56
of KRSS, 234–35
9/11's impact on, 142–46
on passivity and violence, 145–46,
307n20
See also nonviolent tactics
General Assemblies (of OWS), 240
Adbusters announcements of, 21,
32–38, 43
at Bowling Green (August 2),
23–37
collapse of, 136–38, 272–73
facilitation of, 42, 49–50
hand signals in, 45, 46
at Irish Hunger Memorial, 41–42
People's Microphone of, 50–51
process in, 41, 42, 52–53
on September 17 (at Zuccotti
Park), 43, 46–54
shunning of intentional disruptions
in, 219
Spanish language use in, 58
Spokescouncils of, 232
at Tompkins Square Park, 42,
233–34
working groups of, 33–34, 56–57,
227–32, 240–41
at Zuccotti Park, 43, 46–54, 56, 136
General Assembly movement, 30
General Motors (GM), 76, 78
Georgia (nation), 11
Gilder, George, 119, 120–21
Gitlow v. New York, 236n
Gladstone, William, 172
Glass-Steagall Act of 1933, 21, 37
global capitalism, 79n
financial institutions of, 277
financialized capitalism of, 101–8
market fundamentalism of, 90n,
107–8, 110–11, 276–77, 279
neoliberalism of, 279–80
U.S. power and, 102–8, 119
See also anti-globalization
movement
Global Justice Movement, 6–7,
239–40, 277
anarchist principles of, 192–95

creativity and improvisation in,
255–56
debates on tactics in, 209–10
on direct democracy and
contaminationism, 22–23,
89–90
egalitarian process of, 10–11,
136–37
media coverage of, 150–51
repression of, 131–35
Washington IMF action of 2002 of,
278–79
See also Seattle WTO protests
Goldman, Emma, 191
Gore, Al, 99
Gracchi brothers, 162–63
Graeber, David, 85, 151–52
Graves, Robert, 201–2
Great Recession, xxi–xxii, 95, 100,
269
auto industry collapse of, 75–76
bank bailouts of, 67, 69, 79–80,
96–97
debt reduction in, 82–83
mortgage crisis of, 84, 97
student loans in, 71–73
See also anti-austerity movement
Greece, 172–73
ancient communal self-governance
in, 155–56, 172, 197–98, 298n,
309n7
ancient voting practices, 159,
185–86
anti-austerity movement in, 17, 21,
44, 52, 109, 129, 237, 266
austerity budget, 130
delegitimation strategy in, 266–67
guard labor in, 311n2
slavery in, 298n
Syntagma Square occupations in,
21, 52, 129, 237
Grinde, Donald, 174–75, 181
Ground Zero, 20–21, 142–43
The Guardian, 62, 68–69
guard labor, 281, 311n2
Guevara, Che, 70

Hamilton, Alexander, xv, 164n
Harris, Malcolm, 71

ABOUT THE AUTHOR

DAVID GRAEBER teaches anthropology at Goldsmiths, University of London. He is the author of several books, including *Debt: The First 5,000 Years*. He has written for *Harper's, The Nation*, and other magazines and journals.